GRAMMAR
EXPLORER 2A

Paul Carne

Series Editors: Rob Jenkins and Staci Johnson

NATIONAL GEOGRAPHIC LEARNING | CENGAGE Learning

Australia • Brazil • Japan • Korea • Mexico • Singapore • Spain • United Kingdom • United States

Grammar Explorer 2A

Paul Carne

Publisher: Sherrise Roehr

Executive Editor: Laura Le Dréan

Managing Editor: Eve Einselen Yu

Senior Development Editors: Mary Whittemore, Eve Einselen Yu

Development Editor: Maureen Sotoohi

Associate Development Editor: Alayna Cohen

Assistant Editor: Vanessa Richards

Senior Technology Product Manager: Scott Rule

Director of Global Marketing: Ian Martin

Marketing Manager: Lindsey Miller

Sr. Director, ELT & World Languages: Michael Burggren

Production Manager: Daisy Sosa

Content Project Manager: Andrea Bobotas

Print Buyer: Mary Beth Hennebury

Cover Designer: 3CD, Chicago

Cover Image: BRIAN J. SKERRY/National Geographic Creative

Compositor: Cenveo Publisher Services

© 2015 National Geographic Learning, a part of Cengage Learning

ALL RIGHTS RESERVED. No part of this work covered by the copyright herein may be reproduced, transmitted, stored, or used in any form or by any means graphic, electronic, or mechanical, including but not limited to photocopying, recording, scanning, digitizing, taping, Web distribution, information networks, or information storage and retrieval systems, except as permitted under Section 107 or 108 of the 1976 United States Copyright Act, or applicable copyright law of another jurisdiction, without the prior written permission of the publisher.

For product information and technology assistance, contact us at
**Cengage Learning Customer & Sales Support,
1-800-354-9706**

For permission to use material from this text or product,
submit all requests online at **www.cengage.com/permissions.**
Further permissions questions can be e-mailed to
permissionrequest@cengage.com.

Student Book 2A: 978-1-111-35133-5

National Geographic Learning
20 Channel Center Street
Boston, MA 02210
USA

Cengage Learning is a leading provider of customized learning solutions with office locations around the globe, including Singapore, the United Kingdom, Australia, Mexico, Brazil and Japan.

Cengage Learning products are represented in Canada by Nelson Education, Ltd.

Visit National Geographic Learning online at **ngl.cengage.com**

Visit our corporate website at **www.cengage.com**

Printed in the United States of America
Print Number: 01   Print Year: 2014

CONTENTS

UNIT 1   Customs and Traditions   2

The Present

UNIT 2   Survival   24

The Past

UNIT 3 Health and Fitness   58

Nouns

Fall 1

UNIT 4 Going Places   86

Pronouns, Prepositions, and Articles

UNIT 5   A Changing World   120
The Present Perfect

UNIT 6   Appearances and Behavior   156
Adjectives and Adverbs

The authors and publisher would like to thank the following reviewers and contributors:

Gokhan Alkanat, Auburn University at Montgomery, Alabama; **Dorothy S. Avondstondt**, Miami Dade College, Florida; **Heather Barikmo**, The English Language Center at LaGuardia Community College, New York; **Kimberly Becker**, Nashville State Community College, Tennessee; **Lukas Bidelspack**, Corvallis, Oregon; **Grace Bishop**, Houston Community College, Texas; **Mariusz Jacek Bojarczuk**, Bunker Hill Community College, Massachusetts; **Nancy Boyer**, Golden West College, California; **Patricia Brenner**, University of Washington, Washington; **Jessica Buchsbaum**, City College of San Francisco, California; **Gabriella Cambiasso**, Harold Washington College, Illinois; **Tony Carnerie**, English Language Institute, University of California San Diego Extension, California; **Whitney Clarq-Reis**, Framingham State University; **Julia A. Correia**, Henderson State University, Arkansas; **Katie Crowder**, UNT Department of Linguistics and Technical Communication, Texas; **Lin Cui**, William Rainey Harper College, Illinois; **Nora Dawkins**, Miami Dade College, Florida; **Rachel DeSanto**, English for Academic Purposes, Hillsborough Community College, Florida; **Aurea Diab**, Dillard University, Louisiana; **Marta Dmytrenko-Ahrabian**, English Language Institute, Wayne State University, Michigan; **Susan Dorrington**, Education and Language Acquisition Department, LaGuardia Community College, New York; **Ian Dreilinger**, Center for Multilingual Multicultural Studies, University of Central Florida, Florida; **Jennifer Dujat**, Education and Language Acquisition Department, LaGuardia Community College, New York; **Dr. Jane Duke**, Language & Literature Department, State College of Florida, Florida; **Anna Eddy**, University of Michigan-Flint, Michigan; **Jenifer Edens**, University of Houston, Texas; **Karen Einstein**, Santa Rosa Junior College, California; **Cynthia Etter**, International & English Language Programs, University of Washington, Washington; **Parvanak Fassihi**, SHOWA Boston Institute for Language and Culture, Massachusetts; **Katherine Fouche**, The University of Texas at Austin, Texas; **Richard Furlong**, Education and Language Acquisition Department, LaGuardia Community College, New York; **Glenn S. Gardner**, Glendale College, California; **Sally Gearhart**, Santa Rosa Junior College, California; **Alexis Giannopolulos**, SHOWA Boston Institute for Language and Culture, Massachusetts; **Nora Gold**, Baruch College, The City University of New York, New York; **Ekaterina V. Goussakova**, Seminole State College of Florida; **Lynn Grantz**, Valparaiso University, Indiana; **Tom Griffith**, SHOWA Boston Institute for Language and Culture, Massachusetts; **Christine Guro**, Hawaii English Language Program, University of Hawaii at Manoa, Hawaii; **Jessie Hayden**, Georgia Perimeter College, Georgia; **Barbara Inerfeld**, Program in American Language Studies, Rutgers University, New Jersey; **Gail Kellersberger**, University of Houston-Downtown, Texas; **David Kelley**, SHOWA Boston Institute for Language and Culture, Massachusetts; **Kathleen Kelly**, ESL Department, Passaic County Community College, New Jersey; **Dr. Hyun-Joo Kim**, Education and Language Acquisition Department, LaGuardia Community College, New York; **Linda Koffman**, College of Marin, California; **Lisa Kovacs-Morgan**, English Language Institute, University of California San Diego Extension, California; **Jerrad Langlois**, TESL Program and Office of International Programs, Northeastern Illinois University; **Janet Langon**, Glendale College, California; **Olivia Limbu**, The English Language Center at LaGuardia Community College, New York; **Devora Manier**, Nashville State Community College, Tennessee; **Susan McAlister**, Language and Culture Center, Department of English, University of Houston, Texas; **John McCarthy**, SHOWA Boston Institute for Language and Culture, Massachusetts; **Dr. Myra Medina**, Miami Dade College, Florida; **Dr. Suzanne Medina**, California State University, Dominguez Hills, California; **Nancy Megarity**, ESL & Developmental Writing, Collin College, Texas; **Joseph Montagna**, SHOWA Boston Institute for Language and Culture, Massachusetts; **Richard Moore**, University of Washington, Washington; **Monika Mulder**, Portland State University, Oregon; **Patricia Nation**, Miami Dade College, Florida; **Susan Niemeyer**, Los Angeles City College, California; **Charl Norloff**, International English Center, University of Colorado Boulder, Colorado; **Gabriella Nuttall**, Sacramento City College, California; **Dr. Karla Odenwald**, CELOP at Boston University, Massachusetts; **Ali Olson-Pacheco**, English Language Institute, University of California San Diego Extension, California; **Fernanda Ortiz**, Center for English as a Second Language, University of Arizona, Arizona; **Chuck Passentino**, Grossmont College, California; **Stephen Peridore**, College of Southern Nevada, Nevada; **Frank Quebbemann**, Miami Dade College, Florida; **Dr. Anouchka Rachelson**, Miami Dade College, Florida; **Dr. Agnieszka Rakowicz**, Education and Language Acquisition Department, LaGuardia Community College, New York; **Wendy Ramer**, Broward College, Florida; **Esther Robbins**, Prince George's Community College, Maryland; **Helen Roland**, Miami Dade College, Florida; **Debbie Sandstrom**, Tutorium in Intensive English, University of Illinois at Chicago, Illinois; **Maria Schirta**, Hudson County Community College, New Jersey; **Dr. Jennifer Scully**, Education and Language Acquisition Department, LaGuardia Community College, New York; **Jeremy Stubbs**, Tacoma, Washington; **Adrianne Thompson**, Miami Dade College, Florida; **Evelyn Trottier**, Basic and Transitional Studies Program, Seattle Central Community College, Washington; **Karen Vallejo**, University of California, Irvine, California; **Emily Young**, Auburn University at Montgomery, Alabama.

From the Author: It has been an honor to work with National Geographic material in the preparation of this book. My thanks are due to my excellent development editors Maureen Sotoohi and Eve Einselen Yu, to Laura LeDréan, Tom Jefferies, Mary Whittemore, and the entire team at National Geographic Learning. The project has benefited from the expertise and enthusiasm of many experienced reviewers, and their contribution is also greatly appreciated. Finally, it has been an absolute privilege to work alongside my fellow authors, Daphne Mackey, Amy Cooper, and Sammi Eckstut. Hats off to you all!

Dedication: To Vicky, my wife and best friend, for her timeless love and support; to my wonderful sons, Thomas and Robin, for keeping me going; and last but not least, to my beloved border terrier, Bodhi, for his patience (sometimes!) and unflagging optimism throughout.

National Geographic **images** introduce the unit theme—real world topics that students want to read, write, and talk about.

UNIT **8** Consumer Society

Comparatives and Superlatives

▲ Cars in a scrap yard in Canada.

Lesson **1**	Lesson **2**	Lesson **3**	Review the Grammar
page 206	page 213	page 220	page 227
Comparative Adjectives and Adverbs	Comparisons with (*Not*) *As ... As* and *Less*	Superlative Adjectives and Adverbs	Connect the Grammar to Writing
			page 230

205

Units are organized in **manageable lessons**, which ensures students **explore, learn, practice,** and **apply** the grammar.

LESSON 1   Comparative Adjectives and Adverbs

EXPLORE

🎧 CD2-28 **1 READ** the article about consumer societies. Notice the words in **bold**.

What is a Consumer Society?

A *consumer* is a person who buys things, and a *consumer society* is a society that encourages people to buy and use goods.[1] Some people think that a consumer society provides people with **better** lives. People in consumer societies tend to live **more comfortably**. They eat a **wider** variety of food. They go to restaurants **more often**. They also buy a lot of products, maybe more than they need.

Products such as TVs, cell phones, and computers used to be luxuries.[2] Today people can buy these things **more easily than** ever before. The market for these goods is growing **faster** all the time. Consumer societies encourage people to buy **bigger** and **better** products. For example, **"smarter"** phones come out every year. In a consumer society, people are often buying **newer** and **more advanced** products. This creates a lot of waste. Nowadays, many people are thinking **more seriously** about the effects of consumer societies on the environment, and they are trying to become **more responsible** consumers.

[1] **goods:** items that can be bought or sold
[2] **luxury:** something that is expensive but not necessary

206

Each lesson begins with the *Explore* section, featuring a captivating National Geographic article that introduces the target grammar and builds students' knowledge in a variety of academic disciplines.

Comparisons with (Not) As ... As and Less   LESSON 2

EXPLORE

🎧 CD2-30 **1 READ** the excerpt from a discussion between the professor of a business class and a guest speaker. Notice the words in **bold**.

Online Reviews: ★ or ★★★★?

Professor: So, Dennis, what changes have you seen in marketing recently?

Dennis: Well, as you know, customers love to post online reviews of products these days. These reviews are now just **as important as** traditional advertising. Maybe even more important. TV advertising is **as useful as** it was before, of course. On the other hand, newspaper ads[1] are much **less**

Professor: Hmm. Tha who aren't

Dennis: Really? I'm online revie write revie there migh shoppers a **as** they use ads. If a cu **enthusiast**

[1] **ad:** short for advertisement
[2] **endorse:** to say that you support
[3] **enthusiastically:** to do somethin

▼ A billboard, a traditional form of advertising

ATLA
A name for
CHEVRON

LESSON 3   Superlative Adjectives and Adverbs

EXPLORE

🎧 CD2-31 **1 READ** the article about a problem on Mount Everest. Notice the words in **bold**.

Mount Everest:
The Highest Garbage Dump in the World?

Most people know that Mount Everest is **the highest** mountain in the world. However, there is another fact that many people don't know: it has become one of **the dirtiest** mountains in the world.

Mount Everest is one of **the toughest** and **most exciting** mountains to climb on Earth. It is not **the coldest** or **the windiest** place on Earth, but it comes close! These challenges make it one of **the most attractive** mountains for serious climbers. Since 1952, over 3500 climbers have reached the top. Unfortunately, most of them have left equipment and trash on the mountain.

In fact, trash is now one of **the biggest** threats to the environment on Mount Everest. Local organizations have brought tons of trash down from the mountain. One of **the most interesting** projects handed over more than a ton of tin cans, glass bottles, and old climbing tools to artists in Nepal. The artists used the trash to create works of art. Then, they sold the art to raise money for local charities.[1] **The least expensive** work of art cost $17, and **the most expensive** one cost $2400.

[1] **charity:** an organization that raises money to help people

▶ The consumer society produces a lot of waste, even in the Himalayas. Here, a climber collects trash on Mount Everest.

220 COMPARATIVES AND SUPERLATIVES

In the *Explore* section, students discover how the grammar structures are used in the readings and in real academic textbooks.

The *Learn* section features clear grammar charts and explanations followed by controlled practice of the grammar forms.

INSIDE A UNIT

PRACTICE

9 Use the words in parentheses to complete the conversation with comparative adjectives or adverbs. Add *than* where necessary. In some cases, more than one answer is possible.

Matt: My phone is working (1) _worse than_ (badly) ever! And it's
(2) _____ (old) all the other phones I see, too.
I want a (3) _____ (modern) phone.

Lara: Take a look at my phone. It was (4) _____ (cheap) my
last phone, and I'm much (5) _____ (happy) with it. When I'm
traveling, I listen to music (6) _____ (often) I do when I'm at
home, so I wanted a phone with a (7) _____ (big) memory card.

Matt: Wow, it's much (8) _____ (nice) mine! The screen is a lot
(9) _____ (large), too. I want one like that!

Lara: Yeah, you need a big screen, because you watch videos on your phone
(10) _____ (frequently) I do.

10 Look at the charts comparing three laptop co...
the comparative form of the adjectives and a...

Product Details	T400
Screen size	15 inches
Weight	5.5 pounds
Amount of time on the market	18 months
Cost	$565

Customer Ratings	T400
Starts quickly	★ ★ ★
Runs reliably	★ ★ ★ ★ ★
Operates quietly	★ ★ ★ ★
Displays pictures well	★ ★ ★

1. (large / small) The screen of the T400 is _la___
smaller than the XJ7's.

2. (light / heavy) The XJ7 is _____
the T400.

3. (new / old) The A-50 is _____
the XJ7.

4. (cheap / expensive) The T400 is _____

5. (quickly / slowly) The T400 starts _____
_____ the A-50.

> In the ***Practice*** section, students practice the grammar using all four skills through communicative activities that prepare them for academic work.

PRACTICE

8 Complete the sentences with the superlative form of the adjectives and adverbs in parentheses. Use *least* if *not* is included in the parentheses.

1. Kelly: I think people are too concerned about having (1) _the most modern_
(modern) cell phones. Cell phones contain some of (2) _____
(rare) minerals on Earth, but many people just throw their old cell phones away
when they buy a new one. This is (3) _____
(one of the / bad / thing) you can do! But if you recycle your old cell phones,
it's (4) _____ (one of the / good / thing) you can do.

2. Amir: My cell phone is (5) _____ (important / thing) I own. It's
(6) _____ (convenient / place) I have to keep information.

3. Brad: My new cell phone is a piece of junk! It was (7) _____
(not expensive) phone in the store. What a mistake! Also, the salesperson in that
store was one of (8) _____ (not helpful /
salesperson) I've ever spoken to.

9 **EDIT.** Read the article about trash in the desert. Find and correct eight more errors with superlatives.

Cameron's Camels

The Arabian Desert in the Middle East is one of the ~~most hot~~ _hottest_ environments on Earth, and it has
the less amount of rainfall. But to the camel, it is home. The camel is one of the most strong animals
in the world. Camels can go for many days with only a little food and water. When they do find water,
they probably drink the most quick of any land animal. Adult camels can drink about 25 to 30 gallons
(95–114 liters) in ten minutes. Unfortunately, finding water is not the seriousest problem camels face.
Most dangerous threat to camels comes from humans. Tourists in the desert leave trash behind. Camels
think the trash is food and eat it. This is very dangerous for the camels, because it can kill them.

One of the most polluted part of the desert is outside the city of Abu Dhabi. Each year, many ...

10 **APPLY.**

A Work with a partner. Use the words in parentheses to write superlatives. Then choose the correct answer to complete each fact on the quiz.

General Knowledge Quiz

1. _____ is _the highest mountain_ (high / mountain) on Earth.
   a. Mount Kilimanjaro   b. Mount Everest   c. K2
2. _____ is _____ (fast / animal) in the world.
   a. the camel   b. the zebra   c. the cheetah
3. _____ is _____ (long / river) in the world.
   a. The Nile River   b. The Amazon River   c. The Yangtze River
4. _____ is _____ (wide / ocean) on Earth.
   a. The Pacific Ocean   b. The Atlantic Ocean   c. The Indian Ocean
5. _____ is _____ (small / continent).
   a. Africa   b. Antarctica   c. Australia
6. _____ is _____ (large / animal) on Earth.
   a. the elephant   b. the blue whale   c. the giraffe
7. _____ is _____ (cold / place) on Earth.
   a. Antarctica   b. Alaska   c. Canada
8. _____ is _____ (close / planet) to the sun.
   a. Mars   b. Venus   c. Mercury

B Check your answers at the bottom of this page. How many of your answers were correct?

C With your partner, write six more general knowledge facts like the ones from the quiz in exercise **A**. Use superlative adjectives and adverbs.

1. The Nile River is the longest river in the world.

D Use the facts from exercise **C** and quiz your classmates.

A: *This is the largest country in South America.*
B: *Is it Argentina?*
A: *No.*
C: *Is it Brazil?*
A: *Yes, it is!*

> Students use their new language and critical thinking skills in the ***Apply*** section.

Answers: 1. b Mount Everest. 2. c the cheetah. 3. a The Nile River. 4. a the Pacific Ocean. 5. c Australia. 6. b the blue whale. 7. a Antarctica. 8. c Mercury

226 COMPARATIVES AND SUPERLATIVES

UNIT 8 Review the Grammar

Charts
8.1, 8.3–8.7

1 READ & WRITE.

A Read the information about the Greendex survey, and look at the chart. Then complete each sentence according to the information in the chart. Use the comparative or superlative form of the adjective or adverb in parentheses. For some sentences, more than one answer is possible.

Greendex↗

The Greendex is a survey of 1000 consumers in several countries. It asks consumers how they spend their money. Each consumer receives a score. High scores indicate "green," or environmentally friendly, attitudes. Low scores indicate environmentally unfriendly attitudes.

Greendex: Rankings

	Overall	Housing	Transportation	Food	Goods
Americans	44.7	31.5	54.9	57.0	44.2
Brazilians	55.5	48.9	67.1	57.5	53.8
British	49.4	35.9	62.7	62.2	47.1
Canadians	47.9	35.1	57.8	60.9	45.7
Chinese	57.8	48.2	69.0	63.7	56.8
Germans	51.5	40.3	61.9	61.9	47.1
Indians	58.9	51.4	67.3	71.1	57.3
Japanese	48.5	35.3	65.9	54.7	52.7
Mexicans	53.9	48.0	62.2	53.6	54.5
Russians	53.1	44.1	66.4	60.4	47.9

Transportation

1. The Chinese make ___the greenest___ (green) choices.

2. Americans are _____ (green) consumers.

3. British consumers make _____ (green) choices than Canadian consumers.

4. Mexican consumers are _____ (green) Japanese consumers.

Food

5. The British are _____ (concerned) the Chinese.

6. Indians are _____ (concerned) consumers.

7. Russians are _____ (concerned) Brazilians.

8. American

Goods

9. Canadians don't buy goods _____ (responsibly) Mexicans do.

10. Indians buy goods _____ (responsibly).

11. Germans buy goods _____ (responsibly) Brazilians.

12. Americans buy goods _____ (responsibly).

B In your notebook, write four or five sentences based on the housing data from the Greendex chart in exercise **A** on page 227. Use comparative and superlative adjectives and adverbs. Use the sentences from exercise **A** to help you.

Mexicans make greener housing choices than Canadians.
Indian consumers are more concerned about green housing than German consumers are.

Charts
8.1–8.7

2 EDIT. Read the article about the results of the Greendex survey. Find and correct eight more errors with comparatives and superlatives.

The Greendex Survey: Some Overall Conclusions

- According to a recent Greendex survey, people in India were the ~~most green~~ *greenest* consumers in the world. They scored lower in transportation than the Chinese were, but they scored the highest than the Chinese in three other categories.

- Mexicans were more concerned about green transportation as green food or goods. For them, the low score of all was in the housing category.

- Germans scored highly in the transportation category than they did in the food category. However, they were least concerned about housing than goods.

- The Japanese were one of the least concerned nationality overall. They had one of the most bad scores in the housing category.

- Americans had the lowest overall score of all the nationalities in the survey. Food was the only category in which Americans did not score lower then the other nationalities.

Charts
8.1–8.4, 8.6

3 LISTEN & SPEAK.

A Listen to a professor discussing the Greendex survey with her students. Then complete the students' opinions about the survey.

Martin:

1. Most people think that their country is _____ the results show.

2. Many people think they buy goods _____ they really do.

3. We like to think we're trying _____ we can to be green.

Karin:

4. Life in the United States is much _____ without a car.

5. Cars that use less gas are becoming _____ in the United States.

6. Attitudes about the environment aren't changing _____ people think.

Andrew:

7. Most people want to make life _____ for themselves and their families.

8. Everyone wants an _____ life.

B Look at the sentences from exercise **A**. Then listen again. Do you agree or disagree with the students' ideas and opinions? Why, or why not? Write notes on your own ideas and opinions in your notebook.

C Work with a partner. Share your ideas and opinions from exercise **B**. Use comparatives and superlatives.

I agree with Martin's opinion about goods. People don't shop as carefully as they think they do.

Charts
8.1–8.7

4 WRITE & SPEAK.

A Look at the items in the box. Then rank the items from 1 to 8, with (1 = the least important and 8 = the most important).

___ a. a big car	___ d. a smart phone	___ g. plastic bags
___ b. stylish clothing	___ e. meals in restaurants	___ h. a gold watch
___ c. a computer	___ f. a TV	

B In your notebook, write six sentences about the items from exercise **A**. Use comparatives and superlatives and your own ideas and opinions.

I think a computer is less important than a smart phone.

C Work with a partner. Share your rankings from exercise **A** and your opinions from exercise **B**.

228 COMPARATIVES AND SUPERLATIVES

UNIT 8 REVIEW THE GRAMMAR **229**

Review the Grammar gives students the opportunity to consolidate the grammar in their reading, writing, listening, and speaking.

Connect the Grammar to Writing

1 READ & NOTICE THE GRAMMAR.

A Before you buy something, do you compare it with similar products? Discuss your shopping habits with a partner. Then read the text.

The Best Sleeping Bag

I needed to buy a new sleeping bag for a winter camping trip. So, I went to a camping store and compared three different brands[1] of sleeping bags: Ultra Comfort, Snowy Down, and Northern Trek. I wanted to look at each sleeping bag very carefully. For winter camping, the Snowy Down had the highest rating. But in some ways, the other two sleeping bags were better. Of the three sleeping bags, the Snowy Down was the warmest, but it was also the most expensive. The Northern Trek cost less than the Snowy Down, but it was just as expensive as the Ultra Comfort. The Ultra Comfort was warmer than the Northern Trek. Finally, the Ultra Comfort was lighter than the other sleeping bags, so it was easier to carry.

I decided not to get the Northern Trek for camping outside. It wasn't as warm as the other sleeping bags. But we were having a mild winter, so I didn't need the warmest kind of sleeping bag. So I looked more closely at the lightest sleeping bag, the Ultra Comfort. That's the one I chose.

[1] **brand:** the commercial name for a product

> **GRAMMAR FOCUS**
>
> In exercise **A**, the writer uses comparatives and superlatives to discuss three sleeping bags.
>
> *The Ultra Comfort was **warmer than** the Northern Trek.*
>
> *. . . it was just **as expensive as** the Ultra Comfort.*
>
> *Of the three sleeping bags, the Snowy Down was **the warmest** and **most expensive**.*

B Read the text in exercise **A** again. Underline the compa... Then work with a partner and compare your answers.

C Work with a partner. Complete the chart with informati...

Product Details	Ultra Comfort	Snow...
Cost	as expensive as the Northern Trek	
Warmth		the war...
Weight		

230 COMPARATIVES AND SUPERLATIVES

Connect the Grammar to Writing provides students with a clear model and a guided writing task where they first notice and then use the target grammar in one of a variety of writing genres.

Write a Product Review

2 BEFORE YOU WRITE. Think of a product that you plan to buy. Compare three different brands of this product. Complete the chart with information about each brand. Use the chart from exercise **1C** as a model.

Product Details	Product #1	Product #2	Product #3
Cost			

3 WRITE a review comparing the three different brands of the product you chose. Write two paragraphs. Use the information from your chart in exercise **2** and the article in exercise **1A** to help you.

> **WRITING FOCUS**   Correcting Run-on Sentences
>
> A run-on sentence is an error that happens when two independent clauses are connected without a connecting word or correct punctuation.
>
> ✗ *I enjoyed my winter camping trip next year, I'll invite a few friends to join me.*
>
> To correct a run-on sentence, you can divide the run-on sentence into separate sentences.
>
> ✓ *I enjoyed my winter camping **trip. Next** year, I'll invite a few friends to join me.*
>
> You can also use a comma and a conjunction (*and, but, or*) between the two independent clauses.
>
> ✓ *I enjoyed my winter camping **trip, but** next year I'll invite a few friends to join me.*

4 SELF ASSESS. Read your review and underline the comparatives and superlatives. Then use the checklist to assess your work.

- ☐ I used comparative adjectives and adverbs correctly. [8.1, 8.2, 8.3]
- ☐ I used comparisons with *less* and (*not*) *as . . . as* correctly. [8.4, 8.5]
- ☐ I used superlative adjectives and adverbs correctly. [8.6, 8.7]
- ☐ I checked for and corrected run-on sentences. [WRITING FOCUS]

UNIT 8   CONNECT THE GRAMMAR TO WRITING   **231**

Customs and Traditions

The Present

► A bride wears paint on her face to prevent bad luck during a traditional wedding ceremony in the village of Donje Ljubinje, Kosovo.

EXPLORE

1 READ the article about weddings among the Afar people of Djibouti. Notice the words in **bold**.

An Afar Wedding

Djibouti

What is an Afar wedding ceremony like?

The actual wedding ceremony is only for men. The bride[1] **does not go** to this ceremony. Instead, her father **represents**[2] her. The women **celebrate**[3] in a different place. They **sit** and **talk** about the bride's life. The women's ceremony often **includes** a lot of dancing.

What happens next?

After these separate ceremonies, the bride and groom[4] **meet** with their families and friends. Sometimes this party **lasts** all night. The next day, the bride and groom **invite** their families to their new home. They **eat** a traditional[5] meal. A typical meal is goat with rice.

What do the bride and groom wear?

Often they both **dress** in traditional clothes, but the bride sometimes **wears** a western-style dress. Some brides **wear** a lot of gold jewelry.

Who pays for the wedding?

In the Afar culture, the man **pays** for the wedding. He also **provides** a home for his new wife, but they **do not live** there together until three days after the wedding.

[1] **bride:** a woman on her wedding day
[2] **represent:** to act in the place of someone
[3] **celebrate:** to have a party or a meal to mark a special occasion
[4] **groom:** a man on his wedding day
[5] **traditional:** based on things that people have done in a certain way for a long time

▶ This Afar bride wears gold jewelry for her wedding.

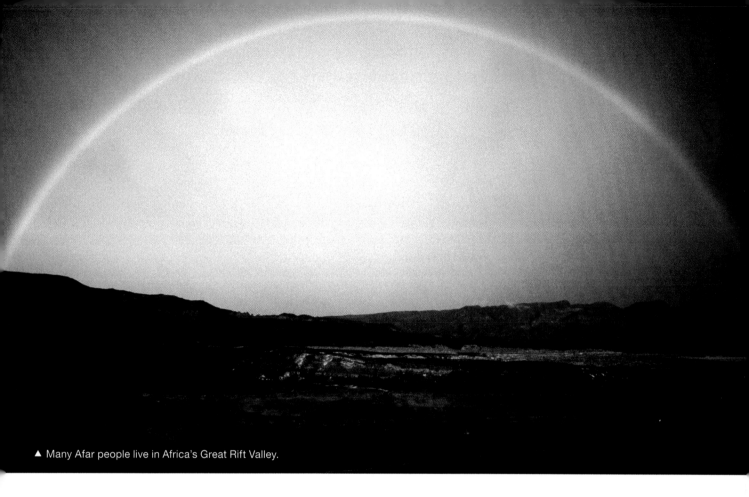

▲ Many Afar people live in Africa's Great Rift Valley.

2 CHECK. Read the statements. Circle **T** for *true* or **F** for *false*.

1. The bride and groom go to the wedding ceremony together.   **T**   (**F**)

2. Women dance to celebrate the wedding.   **T**   **F**

3. Sometimes the bride does not wear traditional clothing.   **T**   **F**

4. The family eats a traditional meal.   **T**   **F**

5. The bride's father pays for the wedding.   **T**   **F**

3 DISCOVER. Complete the exercises to learn about the grammar in this lesson.

A Look at these sentences from the article in exercise **1**. The subject of each sentence is underlined. Write **S** if the subject is singular. Write **P** if the subject is plural.

1. <u>S</u> The bride **does not go** to this ceremony.

2. _____ Instead, her father **represents** her.

3. _____ The women **celebrate** in a different place.

4. _____ They **sit** and **talk** about the bride's life.

5. _____ The women's ceremony often **includes** a lot of dancing.

B Notice the verbs in **bold** in the sentences in exercise **A**. How are the verbs in the sentences with a singular subject different from the verbs in the sentences with a plural subject? Discuss your answer with your classmates and teacher.

LEARN

1.1 Simple Present: Affirmative and Negative Statements

Affirmative		
Subject	Verb	
I/You/We/They	**eat**	a lot.
He/She/It	**eats**	a lot.

Negative			
Subject	*Do Not/Does Not*	Base Form	
I/You/We/They	do not don't	**eat**	a lot.
He/She/It	does not doesn't	**eat**	a lot.

1. Use the simple present to talk about:
   a. habits and repeated actions
   b. facts and general truths
   c. how often something happens

   a. We **eat** dinner at 7:30.
   b. The mail **doesn't come** on Sundays.
   c. Jim **visits** his uncle twice a year.

2. **Be careful!** Don't forget to add -s, -es, or -ies to verbs when the subject is *he, she, it,* or a singular noun.

   ✓ Rosa **teaches** math.
   ✗ Rosa <u>teach</u> math.

See page **A1** for simple present spelling rules.

See page **A1** for simple present spelling rules.

REAL ENGLISH

Contractions are usually used in conversation and informal writing.

*He **doesn't** watch TV.*
*We **don't** like pizza.*

4 Complete each sentence with the correct form of the verb in parentheses.

1. At an Afar wedding the families _____*eat*_____ (eat) a traditional meal.

2. An Afar bride _____ (not attend) the actual wedding ceremony.

3. The women _____ (dance) during their celebration.

4. The bride and groom _____ (invite) their friends and family to a party.

5. The bride's parents _____ (not pay) for the wedding.

6. The wedding _____ (not end) on the first day.

7. A groom _____ (provide) a new home for his bride.

8. They _____ (not live) together immediately.

5 **SPEAK.** Work with a partner. Take turns making affirmative or negative statements. Use the subjects and verbs from the chart below.

The groom pays for the wedding. The bride doesn't go to the wedding ceremony.

Subjects	Verbs
the bride	dance
the wedding guests	eat
the groom	go
the bride's father	live
they	pay
she	sing
he	wear

1.2 Simple Present: Questions and Answers

Yes/No Questions			Short Answers
Do/Does	Subject	Base Form	
Do	I/you/we/they	sing?	Yes, I **do**. / No, I **don't**.
Does	he/she/it		Yes, he **does**. / No, **he doesn't**.

Wh- Questions				Short Answers
Wh- Word	Do/Does	Subject	Base Form	
What		I		Popular songs.
When	do	you	sing?	Every Saturday night.
Why		they		They love music.
Who		she		Her father.
How often	does	she	visit?	Twice a year.
How		he	celebrate?	He has a party.

Who or What as Subject			Short Answers
Wh- Word	Verb		
Who	teaches	this class?	Professor Ortega.
What	makes	you happy?	My family.

1. *Yes/No* questions ask for answers of *yes* or *no*.	A: **Do you speak Russian?** B: Yes, I do. / No, I don't.
2. *Wh-* questions ask for specific information. The answer is a person, place, thing, or other piece of information.	A: **Where** does Jeff live? B: In Sydney.
3. *Who* or *What* can be the subject in a *Wh-* question. When *Who* or *What* is the subject, the verb is always in the third person singular form (*-s/-es* form).	A: **Who** teaches math? (*Who* = subject) B: Arlene.
4. **Be careful!** When *Who* or *What* is the subject, do not use *do* or *does* with the main verb.	✓ **Who** teaches this class? ✗ **Who** <u>does</u> teach this class?

6 Complete each question. Use the words in parentheses and the simple present.

1. _____ Do all brides wear _____ (all brides / wear) white dresses?

2. _____ (what / people / give) the bride and groom?

3. _____ (the bride's mother / cut) the wedding cake?

4. _____ (the bride and groom / have) a party after the ceremony?

5. _____ (who / the bride / dance) with first?

6. _____ (what / the bride and groom / do) after the wedding?

7. _____ (what / the guests / do) at the wedding?

8. _____ (who / pay) for the wedding?

7 **SPEAK.** Work with a partner. Take turns asking and answering the questions from exercise **6**. In your answers, talk about weddings in your own culture or country.

A: *Do all brides wear white dresses?*

B: *No, they don't. Some brides wear red dresses.*

1.3 Frequency Adverbs with the Simple Present

1. Frequency adverbs are often used with the simple present. They tell how often something happens.	I **usually** <u>enjoy</u> parties. I don't **always** <u>remember</u> his birthday. Do you **sometimes** <u>eat</u> at restaurants?
2. Frequency adverbs usually come after the verb *be*. They usually come before other verbs.	I <u>am</u> **sometimes** early for class. Jenny <u>isn't</u> **often** late. Wedding guests <u>are</u> **usually** happy.
3. *Sometimes, usually, frequently,* or *often* can come at the beginning or end of a statement.	Brides wear red dresses **sometimes**. **Usually** Western brides wear white.
4. *Ever* is common in questions about frequency. It means *at any time*. It is not usually used in affirmative statements.	A: Do you **ever** eat at restaurants? B: No, I **never** do. / Yes, I **often** do.

8 Rewrite each statement or question using the adverb in parentheses. Place the adverb in a correct position.

1. (usually) I am with friends on my birthday.

   <u>I am usually with friends on my birthday.</u>

2. (hardly ever) Marco is on time for parties.

   _____

3. (never) My parents forget my birthday.

   _____

4. (always) Children aren't happy at birthday parties.

   _____

5. (often) Does your sister send you photos?

   _____

6. (sometimes) Jackie buys unusual presents for her family.

   _____

7. (rarely) In the United States, brides wear red dresses.

_____

8. (frequently) I go back to my hometown.

_____

9. (seldom) Carlos talks to his brother on the phone.

_____

10. (ever) Do you visit your cousin in Spain?

_____

PRACTICE

CD1-03

9 Complete the conversation. Use the words in parentheses and the
simple present. Then listen and check your answers.

Valerie: Tell me, Kofi . . . How (1) _do people usually celebrate_
(people / usually / celebrate) birthdays in Ghana?

Kofi: Well, I am Asante, and the Asante people (2) _____
(not celebrate) our birthdays on the date we were born. Instead, we celebrate on the
day of the week we were born. It is a special day, called *krada*. For example, I was born
on a Friday, so I (3) _____ (always / wait) until the
first Friday after my birthday to celebrate.

Valerie: Oh, that's interesting. When (4) _____
(*krada* / start)?

Kofi: In the morning. For the Asante, a new day (5) _____
(never / begin) at midnight. The day (6) _____ (always / start)
at sunrise.

Valerie: What (7) _____ (you / usually / do) to
celebrate *krada*?

Kofi: Well, for children, parents (8) _____ (often /
prepare) a special breakfast for *krada*. They (9) _____
(usually / make) a dish called *oto* from sweet potatoes and eggs.
They (10) _____ (always / fry) the *oto* in
palm oil. Later in the day, the child has a party. At the party, children
(11) _____ (usually / eat) meat
with rice and a sweet dish called *kelewele*.

10 **SPEAK.** How do people usually celebrate their birthdays in your culture? In your family?
Share your answers with a partner.

A: *In my country, we usually cook a big meal for our friends.*   B: *Really? That's a lot of work!*

11 Complete the exercises.

A Read the statements. Then add a frequency adverb from the box to make true statements about yourself and your family. You can use some frequency adverbs more than once.

always	ever	hardly ever	never	often	rarely	seldom	sometimes	usually

        usually

1. We don't ⌄give each other expensive presents.

2. I send my parents a card on their wedding anniversary.

3. We get together as a family.

4. I am late for family parties.

5. My family has big celebrations.

6. My parents are happy to see me.

7. People in my family aren't quiet during meals.

8. We spend weekends together.

B Work with a partner. Share your statements from exercise **A**. Ask and answer questions abou your statements.

A: *We don't usually give each other expensive presents.*

B: *Do you ever give each other expensive presents?*

A: *Not often. We usually buy something small or go out for dinner.*

12 **EDIT.** Read the conversation. Find and correct seven more errors with the simple present an frequency adverbs.

                           does your family get

Kenji: How often ⌄~~your family does get~~ together?

Raoul: We get together about two or three times a year, but it's not always easy. My brother lives on the West Coast, and my sister often is away on business trips.

Kenji: So, where you meet when you get together?

Raoul: Well, we go usually to my parents' house. We tries to get home to celebrate their wedding anniversary every year. Sometimes, my brother and I visit each other on our birthdays. Once every two or three years we take a vacation together. I'd like to do it every year, but it cost a lot of money.

Kenji: Have you a good time with your brother and sister?

Raoul: Oh, yes, most of the time. We have sometimes a few arguments, just like any family.

13 LISTEN, WRITE & SPEAK.

A Look at the photos and read the captions. Then work with a partner and answer the questions.

1. Where are the people in each picture?
2. What is the name of each activity?
3. Would you like to do these activities? Why, or why not?

▲ Bungee jumping is a popular vacation activity. Here a woman bungee jumps from a cliff in Ukraine.

▲ A boy jumps from a high tower on Pentecost, Vanuatu. This is called *land diving*. He uses vines as a rope.

 CD1-04

B Put the words in the correct order to make questions. Then listen to the radio show and take notes to help you answer each question.

1. the tower / climb / the boys / do / why _____

_____ Notes: _____

2. the boys / how / jump / do / off the tower _____

_____ Notes: _____

3. digs / the ground / who / below the tower _____

_____ Notes: _____

4. do / the boys / get killed / rarely / why _____

_____ Notes: _____

 CD1-04

C Listen to the interview again. In your notebook, write the answers to the questions from exercise **B**. Then work with a partner and compare your answers.

14 APPLY. Work in a small group. How do people in your country celebrate the change from childhood to adulthood? Is there a special ceremony? Discuss your answers.

A: *In my country, your 20th birthday is special. It means you're an adult. We celebrate with a big ceremony.*

B: *Really? Do you wear special clothes?*

A: *Yes. Women usually wear traditional clothes. Men usually wear suits and ties.*

EXPLORE

CD1-05

1 READ the article about Diwali. Notice the words in **bold**.

Diwali

What are these women doing?

These women in India **are getting** ready for *Diwali*. Diwali is an important holiday for Hindus. It is also called the Festival of Lights. Diwali **happens** in late October or early November every year.

What do Hindus do during Diwali?

People **like** to have new clothes for Diwali. The women in the photo **are wearing** new *saris*.[1] They **are lighting** sparklers and **placing** them around their home. They **want** their family to have a successful future. The women **hope** that the sparklers attract Lakshmi, the Hindu goddess of wealth and success. The star-shaped design on the floor is a *rangoli*. It also **helps** to attract the goddess.

Hindus **believe** that Lakshmi **visits** people's homes during Diwali. In the Hindu religion, a visit from Lakshmi is a very good thing. It **means** a happy future for the family.

[1] **sari:** a traditional form of dress for women in India and other south Asian countries

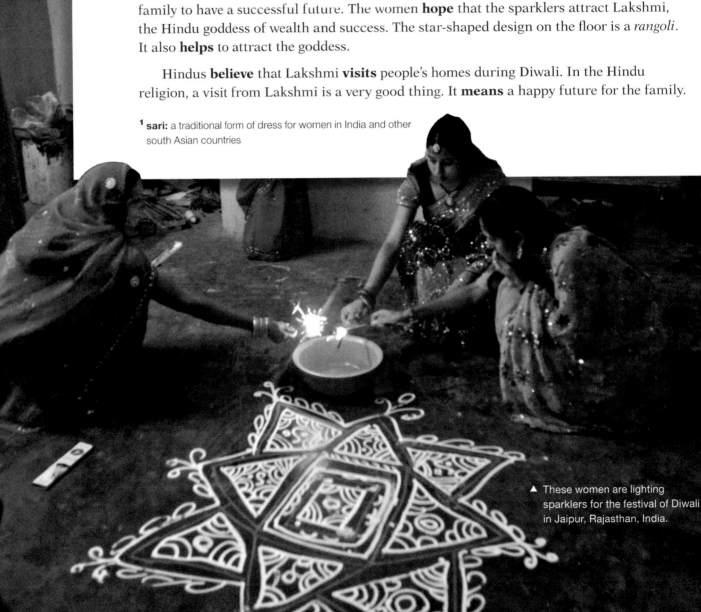

▲ These women are lighting sparklers for the festival of Diwali in Jaipur, Rajasthan, India.

2 CHECK. Read the questions. Then write short answers.

1. What is another name for Diwali? _the Festival of Lights_

2. When does Diwali take place? _____

3. What are the women in the photograph wearing? _____

4. Where is the *rangoli*? _____

5. Who is Lakshmi? _____

6. What does a visit from Lakshmi mean? _____

3 DISCOVER. Complete the exercises to learn about the grammar in this lesson.

A Look at these sentences from the article in exercise **1**. Check (✓) the correct description of each **bold** verb.

	Happening Now	Generally True
1. These women in India **are getting** ready for Diwali.	✓	____
2. People **like** to have new clothes for Diwali.	____	____
3. The women in the photo **are wearing** new saris.	____	____
4. They **are lighting** sparklers . . .	____	____
5. They **want** their family to have a successful future.	____	____
6. The women **hope** that the sparklers attract Lakshmi . . .	____	____

B Work with a partner. Compare your answers from exercise **A**. What do you notice about the verb form that describes actions that are happening now?

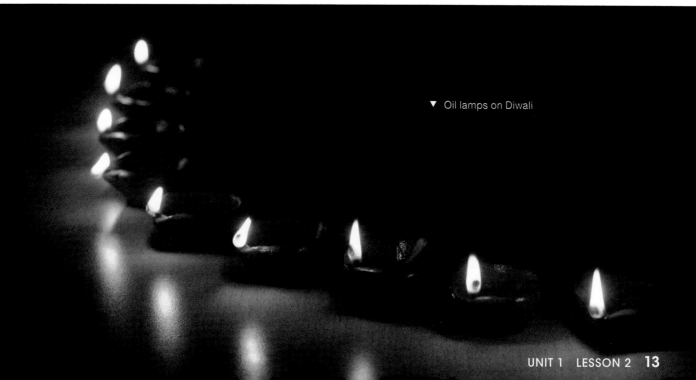

▼ Oil lamps on Diwali

LEARN

1.4 Present Progressive: Affirmative and Negative Statements

Affirmative		
Subject	*Be*	Verb + -*ing*
I	am 'm	studying.
He/She/It	is 's	**working.**
You/We/They	are 're	eating.

Negative		
Subject	*Be + Not*	Verb + -*ing*
I	am not 'm not	studying.
He/She/It	is not isn't / 's not	**working.**
You/We/They	are not 're not / aren't	eating.

1. Use the present progressive* to talk about: 　a. actions in progress now, at the moment 　　of speaking 　b. actions in progress at the present time, 　　but maybe not at the moment of speaking	a. Look! They**'re dancing** in the street. b. My class **is studying** world history 　this semester.
2. **Remember:** Use the simple present to talk about: 　a. habits and repeated actions 　b. facts and things that are generally true 　c. how often something happens	a. Dave and I often **take** a walk after dinner. b. It **snows** a lot in Finland. c. I **meet** with my boss twice a week.
3. Some adverbs and time expressions commonly used with the present progressive are: *now, at the moment, this year,* and *these days.*	It **is raining** <u>at the moment</u>. Susie **is working** hard <u>these days</u>.

* The *present progressive* is sometimes called the *present continuous*.
See page **A1** for spelling rules for the -*ing* form of verbs.

4　Complete each sentence with the present progressive form of the verb in parentheses.

1. The women _____ are lighting _____ (light) sparklers.

2. They _____ (draw) pictures on the floor.

3. Usha _____ (not / celebrate) the holiday with her family.

4. She _____ (study) in England this year.

5. I _____ (not prepare) the food for the party.

6. Alberto _____ (help) in the kitchen at the moment.

7. He _____ (wash) the dishes right now.

8. We _____ (get) the house ready for the party.

5　Circle the correct form of the verb to complete each sentence.

1. Thousands of people **attend** / (**are attending**) the festival this year. The hotels are full!

2. Every November people **celebrate** / **are celebrating** a special holiday in Mexico.

3. My grandmother usually **organizes** / **is organizing** the celebrations in my family.

4. The Chinese New Year **marks** / **is marking** the end of the winter season.

5. Right now I **make** / **am making** a cake for the party.

6. My father **makes** / **is making** beautiful cakes to celebrate special events.

7. We **have** / **are having** a party for my grandparents every summer.

8. Everyone **dances** / **is dancing** right now.

1.5 Present Progressive: Questions and Answers

Yes/No **Questions**				**Short Answers**
Be	Subject	Verb + *-ing*		
Am	I			Yes, you **are**. / No, you**'re not**.
Is	he	helping?		Yes, he **is**. / No, he**'s not**.
Are	you			Yes, we **are**. / No, we**'re not**.

Wh- **Questions**				**Answers**
Wh- Word	*Be*	Subject	Verb + *-ing*	
What	am	I	doing?	You**'re studying**.
	is	he		He**'s singing**.
	are	they		They**'re cooking**.
Why	is	she	crying?	She**'s watching** a sad movie.

Who or *What* **as Subject**				**Short Answers**
Wh- Word	*Be*	Verb + *-ing*		
Who	is	dancing	with Carmen?	Her father.
What		happening?		John**'s leaving**.

1. **Remember:** *Who* or *What* can be the subject in a *Wh-* question. When *Who* or *What* is the subject, the verb is always in the third person singular form (*-s/-es* form).

A: **Who's** playing the piano?
B: Marta.

6 Use the words in parentheses to complete the questions or answers. Use the present progressive.

1. A: Hi, Ana. (1) ___What are you doing___ (what / you / do)?

   B: I (2) _____ (buy) a plane ticket online.

2. A: (3) _____ (where / you / live) these days?

   B: I (4) _____ (rent) an apartment near the university.

3. A: (5) _____ (why / your computer / make) a noise?

   B: (6) _____ (it / not work) properly.

4. A: (7) _____ (your phone / ring)?

   B: Yes, it is. Thanks. My (8) _____ (brother / call) me.

7 SPEAK. Work with a partner. Ask and answer the questions in numbers 1 and 2 in exercise **6**. Use your own answers, not the answers in the book.

1.6 Action and Non-Action Verbs

1. Action verbs describe physical or mental actions.	Action: She **studies** hard every night. Non-Action: I **want** to go to the dance.

2. Non-action* verbs do not describe actions. They describe states, conditions, or feelings. Here are some common categories of non-action verbs:
 	
  a. **Feelings:** *dislike, hate, like, love, miss*
  b. **Senses:** *feel, hear, see, smell, sound, taste*
  c. **Possession:** *belong, have, own*
  d. **Appearance:** *appear, look, seem*
  e. **Desires:** *hope, need, prefer, want*
  f. **Mental States:** *believe, think, understand*
	
	  a. I **love** to dance.
	  b. The soup **smells** delicious.
	  c. He doesn't **own** a car.
	  d. Ted **looks** tired today.
	  e. I **want** some coffee.
	  f. She **understands** Japanese.

3. Non-action verbs are not usually used in the progressive.	✓ They **own** a house and an apartment. ✗ They <u>are owning</u> a house and an apartment.
4. It is possible to use the progressive form with some non-action verbs, but their meaning changes. Some common examples are: *have, think, look, smell,* and *taste*.	Non-Action Action He **has** a headache. He **is having** lunch. I **think** this book is great. I **am thinking** of the answer. The food **tastes** good. She **is tasting** the food.

* *Non-action verbs* are sometimes called *stative verbs*.

8 Complete the conversations with the verbs in parentheses. Use the simple present or the present progressive.

1. **Eric:**   (1) __Do__ you __like__ (like) your new home in Italy?

   Jane: Yes, I really (2) _____ (love) it, but I (3) _____ (think) about the United States a lot.

   Eric: What (4) _____ you _____ (miss) most?

   Jane: Oh, family get-togethers, probably.

2. **Sally:**   Why is Nikki taking so long at the bakery?

   Christina: She (5) _____ (taste) the different kinds of cakes.

   She (6) _____ (want) the perfect cake for her wedding.

3. **Mark:**   That's a nice camera.

   Tim: Thanks, but it (7) _____ (not / belong) to me. It's my sister's.

   Mark: (8) _____ you _____ (have) your own camera?

   Tim: No, I (9) _____ (not own) a camera.

4. **Maria:**   (10) _____ you _____ (have) fun tonight?

   Barbara: Not really, I (11) _____ (have) a headache.

PRACTICE

9 Look at the photos and read the captions. Then complete the conversation with the words in parentheses. Use the simple present or the present progressive form of the verbs.

▲ The New Zealand rugby team does the *haka* before a match.

▲ Maori dancers from New Zealand perform the *haka*, a traditional war dance.

Todd: Hey, Steve, (1) _what are you doing_ (what / you / do)?

Steve: (2) _____ (I / read) a magazine. Look at this photo of the New Zealand rugby team . . . (3) _____ (they / look) scary!

Todd: (4) _____ (what / they / do)?

(5) _____ (they / dance)?

Steve: (6) _____ (they / perform) the *haka*. It's a Maori war dance.

Todd: (7) _____ (they / do) it before every game?

Steve: Yes. (8) _____ (it / help) them get ready for the game mentally, and (9) _____ (they / believe) that it frightens the other team.

Todd: Interesting. (10) _____ (it / work)?

Steve: Maybe in the past, but (11) _____ (it / never / surprise) anyone now. (12) _____

(the other team / usually / pay) no attention. But, (13) _____

(the fans / love) it, and (14) _____

(the *haka* / always / provide) an opportunity for great photos!

10 WRITE & SPEAK.

A Use the words to make *Yes/No* and *Wh-* questions. Use the simple present or the present progressive.

1. what holidays / you / enjoy _What holidays do you enjoy?_

2. what / your classmates / do / right now _____

3. what / you / want / for your birthday _____

4. you / do / anything interesting / these days _____

5. you and your friends / like / soccer _____

6. you / often / work / on weekends _____

7. what / your class / study / this week _____

8. where / you / usually / have / lunch _____

B Work with a partner. Ask and answer the questions from exercise **A**.

A: *Which national holidays do you enjoy?*   B: *I like Thanksgiving. How about you?*

11 Complete the conversations with the words from the box. Use the simple present or present progressive. Then listen and check your answers.

do	have	not believe	not look	talk	think
hate	need	not feel	not want	taste	

Conversation 1

Midori: Hi Sally, how (1) _____ *are* _____ you _____ *doing* _____?

Sally: I'm OK. How about you?

Midori: Great. You know, I usually (2) _____ big crowds, and
I (3) _____ people are too noisy in big groups. Well, guess
what: right now I'm in New York City at the Thanksgiving Day parade!

Sally: You are? I (4) _____ it!

Midori: Yes, I am! And I (5) _____ a wonderful time!

Conversation 2

Angela: Mmm . . . this soup (6) _____ delicious! Do you want some?

Kara: No, thanks.

Angela: Are you sure? It's really good.

Kara: No, thanks. I (7) _____ well, and I (8) _____ you to
get sick.

Conversation 3

Mike: Hi, Kemal. Are you OK? You (9) _____ very happy. What's the matter?

Kemal: Oh, I . . .

Andy: Hey, Mike, do you have a minute? I (10) _____ to ask you something.

Mike: Sorry, but Kemal and I (11) _____ right now. Can I talk to you later?

12 READ & WRITE.

A Read the paragraph. Underline the verbs in the simple present and circle the frequency adverbs.

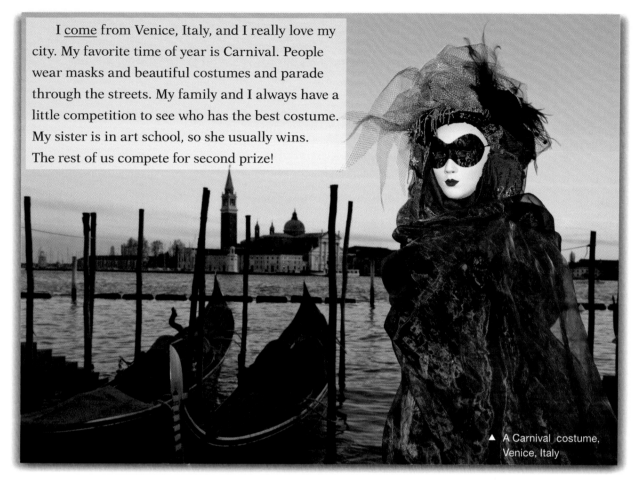

I come from Venice, Italy, and I really love my city. My favorite time of year is Carnival. People wear masks and beautiful costumes and parade through the streets. My family and I always have a little competition to see who has the best costume. My sister is in art school, so she usually wins. The rest of us compete for second prize!

▲ A Carnival costume, Venice, Italy

B In your notebook, write a paragraph of five or six sentences about an event in your country or culture. Use the simple present and frequency adverbs.

13 APPLY.

A Write questions to ask a classmate about what he or she is doing this week, this month, this semester, or this year. Use the present progressive.

Questions	Answers
Where are you living these days?	

B Work with a partner. Take turns asking and answering your questions from exercise **A**. Take notes on your partner's answers in the chart.

C Tell the class about your partner. Use the information from the chart in exercise **A**.

Charts
1.1–1.6

1 Complete the conversation with the words in parentheses. Use the simple present or the present progressive.

Silvana: Hey Christine, it's the 4th of July . . . (1) <u>Why are you sitting</u> (why / you / sit) here in the library?

Christine: I (2) _____ (work). I (3) _____ (have) an important assignment to finish.

Silvana: But Americans (4) _____ (always / celebrate) Independence Day!

Christine: Well, things are different this year. I (5) _____ (usually / visit) my brother and sister, and we (6) _____ (have) a barbecue, but they're not around this year.

Silvana: Oh, (7) _____ (what / they / do) this year?

Christine: Matt (8) _____ (take) a computer course in San Francisco, and my sister Denise (9) _____ (work). She's a doctor.

Silvana: Oh, that's too bad!

Christine: Yeah, and she often (10) _____ (work) on weekends and holidays.

Silvana: Well, listen, I (11) _____ (not do) anything special today. (12) _____ (you / want) to get something to eat later?

Christine: Great idea! I (13) _____ (hear) the new Thai restaurant on Tucker Street is really good. (14) _____ (you / like) Thai food?

Silvana: I (15) _____ (love) Thai food! Give me a call when you are ready.

Charts
1.1, 1.3, 1.4

2 EDIT. Read the paragraph about *La Tomatina*. Find and correct five more errors with the simple present, the present progressive, and frequency adverbs.

La Tomatina

▲ A man lies in tomatoes at *La Tomatina* in Sutamarchán, Colombia.

    In my town, Buñol, Spain, the local people ~~are organizing~~ ^{organize} a festival called *La Tomatina* every year. It always is starting on the last Wednesday in August, and it last for a week. *La Tomatina* is a food fight. Every summer, thousands of local people and visitors gets together to throw tomatoes at each other. Yes, that's right—tomatoes! And I'm not talking about just a few tomatoes. *La Tomatina* is using around a hundred tons of tomatoes every year. These days the festival is becoming so popular that other countries start to organize their own events similar to *La Tomatina*.

3 LISTEN to an excerpt from a lecture about *La Tomatina*. Write the missing words.

🎧
CD1-07

Professor: . . . Now, let's look at the next slide, and you will see what (1) <u>I am talking about.</u> Yes, there we are. Now, look at the young man in this photo. (2) _____ in tomatoes almost up to his waist. And do you see what's happening . . . ?

Student 1: (3) _____ more tomatoes at him!

Professor: Yes, Kim, that's right. And he's smiling about it.

Student 1: Are you sure? (4) _____ he's smiling.

Professor: Hmm . . . well, I guess you're right. But (5) _____ he is complaining?

Student 1: No, (6) _____ to get away. He's just waiting for the tomatoes to hit him.

Professor: Yes, that's right. (7) _____ a good time.

Student 2: So, (8) _____ us that people actually do this for fun? They get covered in tomatoes! What's the point of that?

Professor: You know, Philip, that's a very good question. We live with so many laws and rules. . . . Sometimes, (9) _____ to feel that there are no rules. Many ancient celebrations (10) _____ a time like this. For a few hours or a couple of days, no one (11) _____ to obey the usual rules. I mean, you can't just go to Buñol and start throwing tomatoes in January, right?

4 SPEAK. Work in a small group. Discuss your answers to these questions.

1. Does *La Tomatina* sound like something you would like to go to? Why, or why not?

2. Tell the other members of your group about a special festival or celebration in your town or city.

▼ *La Tomatina*, Buñol, Spain

Connect the Grammar to Writing

1 READ & NOTICE THE GRAMMAR.

A Does your culture have any traditional sports events? Discuss the event(s) with a partner. Then read the text.

The Kila Raipur Sports Festival

In February, my family and I usually go to the Kila Raipur Sports Festival. Kila Raipur is a town near my home in India. It's January now, and we are planning our trip. We are looking forward to this tradition. Each year, thousands of people attend the festival.

At the festival, people race huge tractors.[1] Men sometimes lift bicycles with their teeth. In this photo, men are racing carts pulled by oxen. This is everyone's favorite event.

[1] **tractor:** a vehicle that a farmer uses to pull machinery

GRAMMAR FOCUS

In the text in exercise **A**, the writer uses the simple present to talk about repeated activities and events and facts.

> *In February, my family and I usually **go** to the Kila Raipur Sports Festival.*
> *Kila Raipur **is** a town near my home in India.*

> *At the festival, people **race** huge tractors. Men sometimes **lift** bicycles with their teeth.*

B Read the text in exercise **A** again. Underline the verbs in the simple present. Circle the frequency adverbs. Then work with a partner and compare your answers.

C Complete the chart with information about the Kila Raipur Sports Festival.

When		Where
every year		

| | Kila Raipur Sports Festival | |

Who		What

2 BEFORE YOU WRITE.

A Complete the chart with information about a traditional sports event in your culture. Use the chart from exercise **1C** as a model.

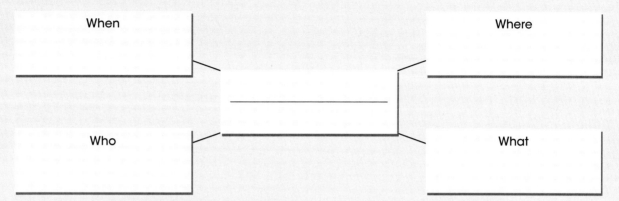

When

Where

Who

What

B Look at the information in your chart from exercise **A**. Place a *1* next to information that you want to include in your first paragraph. Place a *2* next to information that you want to include in your second paragraph.

3 WRITE two paragraphs about a traditional sports event in your culture. Use the information from your chart in exercise **2A** and the text in exercise **1A** to help you.

> **WRITING FOCUS   Capitalizing Proper Nouns**
>
> Proper nouns are the names of specific people, places, and things. Some examples of proper nouns are the names of:
>
> • streets, cities, states, countries, and continents
> • days of the week, months, and holidays
> • people and special events
>
> In **February**, my family and I usually go to the **Kila Raipur Sports Festival**. **Kila Raipur** is a town near my home in **India**.

4 SELF ASSESS. Read your paragraphs and underline the simple present and circle the frequency adverbs. Then use the checklist to assess your work.

☐ I used the simple present for facts. [1.1]

☐ I used the simple present for repeated actions and events. [1.1]

☐ I put the frequency adverbs in the correct place. [1.3]

☐ I capitalized proper nouns. [WRITING FOCUS]

The Past

The Parthenon, Acropolis, Athens, Greece

25

EXPLORE

CD1-08

1 READ the article about a project to protect lions in Kenya. Notice the words in **bold**.

Kenya

The Lion Guardians Project, Kenya

Cattle[1] are basic to the lives of the Maasai people of Kenya. In fact, the Maasai have a saying, "Without the land and the cattle, there are no Maasai people." In 2006, Maasai cattle herders[2] in Kenya **had** a problem. Lions regularly **killed** their cows. The herders **sent** warriors[3] to hunt and kill the lions. Many lions **died**. The Maasai **were** a big threat to the survival of lions in Kenya.

A local organization, Living with Lions, **wanted** to save lions. They **helped** train Maasai warriors to protect lions, not kill them. The warriors **learned** to track the lions with modern technology. They **warned** herders before the lions **got** near their cows. The warriors **didn't kill** any more lions. Instead, they **became** Lion Guardians.[4]

▼ A lion in the Maasai Mara Game Reserve, Kenya

The Guardians **persuaded** the herders not to hunt the lions. They **gave** each lion a Maasai name, and **taught** the herders and villagers about them. Local people **began** to see the lions as individuals. Now, there are more than 30 Lion Guardians. Because of the Guardians' work, the number of lions that die in their part of Kenya is falling fast.

[1] **cattle:** cows and bulls
[2] **herder:** a person who cares for a large group of one kind of animal
[3] **warrior:** a fighter or soldier
[4] **guardian:** a person who protects other people or property

2 CHECK. Read the statements. Circle **T** for *true* or **F** for *false*.

1. Cattle are not important to the Maasai people.   **T** **(F)**

2. The Living with Lions organization wanted to protect the lions.   **T**   **F**

3. Cattle herders educated Maasai warriors about lions.   **T**   **F**

4. Lion Guardians use technology to protect cattle.   **T**   **F**

5. Local people learned more about lions from the Lion Guardians.   **T**   **F**

3 DISCOVER. Complete the exercises to learn about the grammar in this lesson.

A Find the simple past form of these verbs in the article from exercise **1**. Then write them in the charts.

Group A		Group B	
Present	Simple Past	Present	Simple Past
kill	*killed*	have	*had*
die	_____	send	_____
want	_____	get	_____
learn	_____	become	_____
persuade	_____	teach	_____

B Look at the simple past forms of the verbs in Group A. Compare them with the verbs in Group B. How are they different? Discuss your answer with your classmates and teacher.

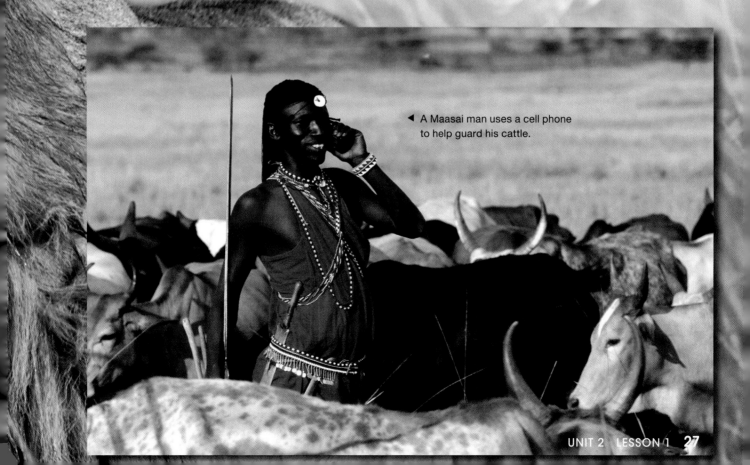

◄ A Maasai man uses a cell phone to help guard his cattle.

LEARN

2.1 Simple Past: Affirmative and Negative Statements

Affirmative		
Subject	Verb	
I/He/She	**helped**	the animals.
You/We/They	**went**	to Africa.

Negative			
Subject	*Did Not/ Didn't*	Base Form	
I/He/She	**did not**	**help**	them.
You/We/They	**didn't**	**go**	to China.

1. Use the simple past for:
   a. a completed action or event
   b. a regular or repeated action or event in the past
   c. past states or feelings
	a. She **called** me yesterday.
	b. I **worked** every day last week.
	c. He **felt sick** this morning.

2. To form the simple past, add *-ed* or *-d* to the base form of most regular verbs.[1]	play ➜ play**ed** dance ➜ danc**ed**
3. **Be careful!** Many common verbs have irregular past forms.[2]	eat ➜ **ate** make ➜ **made** go ➜ **went** see ➜ **saw**
4. The simple past forms of *be* are *was* and *were*. Do not use *did not* or *didn't* with *was* and *were* in the negative.	It **was** warm. It **wasn't** cold. They **were** at work. They **weren't** at home. ✓ I **wasn't** late for class yesterday. ✗ I <u>didn't was</u> late for class yesterday.

[1]See page **A2** for spelling rules for the simple past.
[2]See page **A5–A6** for a list of irregular verbs.

4 Complete each sentence with the simple past form of the verb(s) in parentheses.

1. Herders in Kenya _____*weren't*_____ (not be) able to protect their cattle.

2. For years, lions _____ (kill) many cows in Kenya.

3. The herders _____ (send) warriors to hunt the lions.

4. Living with Lions _____ (start) a new program in 2007.

5. At first, some Maasai _____ (not be) happy about the program.

6. The organization _____ (give) every Guardian a cell phone.

7. When a Lion Guardian _____ (see) a lion nearby, he _____ (call) his neighbor.

8. The Lion Guardians project _____ (not change) the situation in Kenya immediately. It _____ (take) time.

9. Scientists _____ (study) the lion population.

10. The Lion Guardians _____ (not save) all the lions.

2.2 Simple Past: Questions and Answers

Yes/No Questions		
Did	Subject	Base Form
Did	I/he/she/it	help?
	we/you/they	

Short Answers
Yes, she **did**. / No, she **didn't**.
Yes, they **did**. / No, they **didn't**.

Wh- Questions			
Wh- Word	*Did*	Subject	Base Form
When		you	call?
Why	did	she	leave?
Who(m)		they	see?

Short Answers
This morning.
Because she had a meeting.
Nick and Sarah.

Who or *What* as Subject	
Wh- Word	Verb
Who	called?
What	happened?

Short Answers
My sister.
I missed the train.

1. *Whom* is sometimes used as the object in very formal speaking or writing.	**Whom** did you ask?
2. **Remember:** *Who* or *What* can take the place of the subject in a *Wh-* question. When *Who* or *What* is the subject, do not use *did*.	✓ **Who** called? ✗ Who <u>did</u> call?

5 Complete the short conversations with the words in parentheses. Write simple past questions and then write the answers.

1. A: _Did your phone ring_____ (your phone / ring) just now?

   B: Yes, _it did_____.

2. A: _____ (your parents / give) you any money last month?

   B: No, _____.

3. A: _____ (the teacher / send) you an e-mail?

   B: No, _____.

4. A: _____ (your friend / pay) for your lunch yesterday?

   B: Yes, _____.

5. A: _____
   (you / do) anything fun last night?

   B: No, _____.

6. A: _____
   (I / disturb) you?

   B: No, _____.

REAL ENGLISH

Time expressions such as *last night, last week, six months ago,* or *in 2011* are often used with the simple past.

*I saw Kim **two days ago**.*
*She swam every day **last year**.*

7. A: _____ (it / rain) yesterday?

   B: Yes, _____ .

8. A: _____ (we / have) homework last night?

   B: Yes, _____ .

6 **SPEAK.** Work with a partner. Take turns asking and answering the questions from exercise **5**. Use your own answers, not the answers in the book.

7 Complete the conversations. Use the words in parentheses to write simple past questions.

1. A: Why __did you go__ (you / go) to Kenya?

   B: Because we wanted to see the wildlife there.

2. A. How often _____ (you / see) lions when you were in Kenya?

   B: Almost every day.

3. A: Who _____ (the camera / belong to)?

   B: It belonged to our guide.

4. A. _____ (Katya / write) in her journal last night?

   B: Yes, she did.

5. A. Who _____ (give) the presentation yesterday?

   B: Sheila.

6. A. When _____ (the plane / arrive)?

   B: A few minutes ago.

PRACTICE

8 Complete the conversation with the words in parentheses. Use the simple past.

Amy: (1) ____Did you read____ (you / read) Jinny's e-mail about the whale rescue?

Josh: No, I didn't. (2) _____ (what / she / say)?

Amy: Well, the whale (3) _____ (come) too close to the shore, and some fishermen (4) _____ (find) it in their net.

Josh: That's terrible! (5) _____ (it / survive)?

Amy: Yeah, it did, but according to Jinny, the rescue (6) _____ (take) about an hour.

Josh: So, (7) _____ (she / take) any photos of it?

Amy: Yes, (8) _____ (she / take) a lot. (9) _____ (she / send) a few of them with her e-mail. They're amazing!

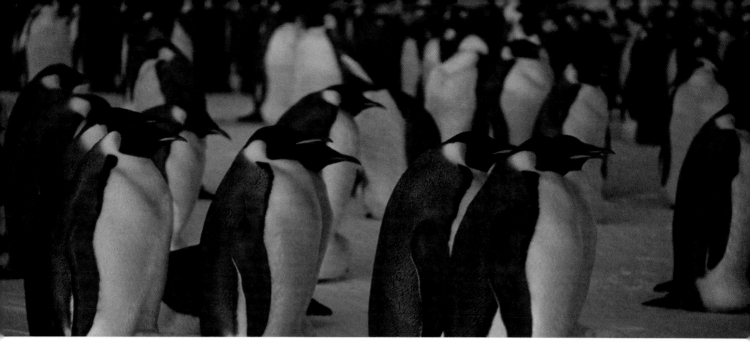

▲ Emperor penguins crowd together to keep warm.

CD1-09

9 LISTEN & WRITE.

A Listen to an interview with a nature filmmaker. Then complete the questions from the interview with the verbs in parentheses. Use the simple past.

1. How long ___did it take___ (it / take) to make your last nature film?

2. Why _____ (you / choose) Antarctica?

3. So, what _____ (you / see)?

4. Why _____ (they / walk) so far?

5. When _____ (the females / return)?

CD1-09

B Listen again and check your answers.

C Read the summary of the last part of the interview. Then complete the paragraph with the verbs in the box. Use the simple past.

begin	~~climb~~	come	crowd	fall	keep	lay	return	survive	walk

The emperor penguins (1) ___climbed___ onto the sea ice and

(2) _____ 50 miles to mainland Antarctica. The females each (3) _____

one egg and (4) _____ to the sea. The males (5) _____ the eggs safe

through the terrible winter. They (6) _____ together to keep warm. The temperature

(7) _____ to –40 degrees Fahrenheit, but the males (8) _____ . In the

spring, the females (9) _____ back. Then the sea ice (10) _____ to

melt.

CD1-09

D Work with a partner. Compare your answers from exercise **C**. Then listen again and check your answers.

▶ A giant panda bear eating bamboo

10 EDIT. Read the conversation. Find and correct seven more errors with the simple past.

Rolf: Hi, Jun. Did you finished your assignment about animal survival yesterday?

Jun: Hi, Rolf. Yes, I did. I write about giant pandas in China.

Rolf: That's an interesting choice. How did it go?

Jun: Oh, it didn't went very well.

Rolf: What did go wrong?

Jun: Well, I did a lot of research, but I didn't found much new information. Everyone else's assignments were at least five pages, but my assignment was only two pages.

Rolf: What Professor Blake said?

Jun: She didn't say anything—she just look at me.

Rolf: Well, don't worry too much. I gave her the shortest assignment last week and got the highest grade in the class. She sayed it was excellent!

11 APPLY.

A Write interview questions to ask a classmate about a recent project or assignment. Use the words in the box to help you.

Did you . . . ?	What did you . . . ?	Where did you . . . ?	Who did you . . . ?
When did you . . . ?	Why did you . . . ?	How did you . . . ?	

B Work with a partner. Ask and answer your questions from exercise **A**. Take notes on your partner's answers in your notebook.

A: *What did you write about?*   B: *I wrote about sports in schools.*

C Write a paragraph of four or five sentences about your partner's assignment or project.

Alain wrote a paper about sports in schools. He did a lot of research. He asked all his friends for their opinions. He also interviewed the football and baseball coaches.

EXPLORE

CD1-10

1 READ a radio interview with a woman who works to help Maya languages survive in Guatemala. Notice the words in **bold**.

Guatemala

Community Radio in Guatemala

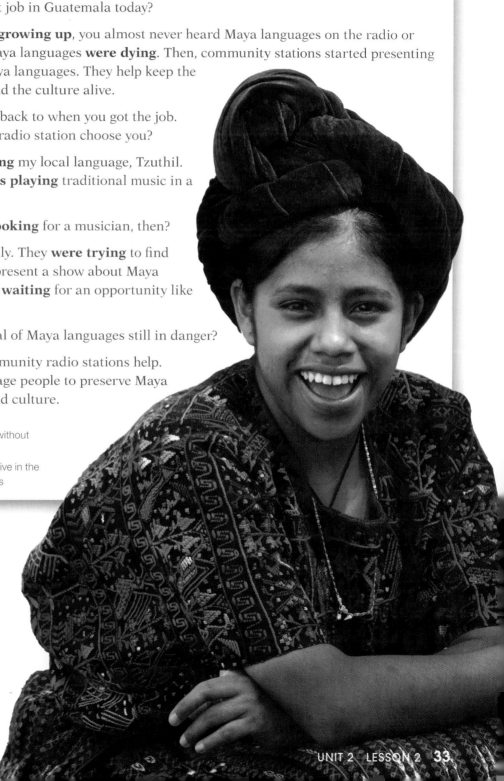

Interviewer: So, Angelica, you work as a volunteer[1] at a community[2] radio station. Why is that an important job in Guatemala today?

Angelica: When I **was growing up**, you almost never heard Maya languages on the radio or TV. Some Maya languages **were dying**. Then, community stations started presenting shows in Maya languages. They help keep the languages and the culture alive.

Interviewer: Now, let's go back to when you got the job. Why did the radio station choose you?

Angelica: I **was teaching** my local language, Tzuthil. Oh, and I **was playing** traditional music in a band.

Interviewer: **Were they looking** for a musician, then?

Angelica: No, not exactly. They **were trying** to find someone to present a show about Maya music. I **was waiting** for an opportunity like that.

Interviewer: Is the survival of Maya languages still in danger?

Angelica: Yes, but community radio stations help. They encourage people to preserve Maya languages and culture.

[1] **volunteer:** a person who does work without being paid for it

[2] **community:** a group of people who live in the same area and have common interests

▶ The Maya have lived in Guatemala for thousands of years.

2 CHECK. Choose the correct answer for each question.

1. Why is community radio important in Guatemala?

   a. It provides jobs for people.

   b. It helps the Maya culture survive.

   c. It plays a lot of music.

2. What was Angelica doing when she got her job on the radio?

   a. studying her local language

   b. traveling around Guatemala

   c. playing traditional music

3. Who was the radio station looking for?

   a. a presenter

   b. a musician

   c. a teacher

4. What was happening to some Maya languages before community radio?

   a. They were growing.

   b. They were changing.

   c. They were dying.

3 DISCOVER. Complete the exercises to learn about the grammar in this lesson.

A Read the pairs of sentences about the interview from exercise **1** and notice the verbs in **bold**. Choose the sentence in each pair that describes an action that was in progress at a certain time in the past.

1. a. The radio station **chose** Angelica.

   b. Angelica **was teaching** Tzuthil in the evenings.

2. a. The radio station **was looking** for a new presenter.

   b. They **decided** to speak to Angelica.

3. a. Several Maya languages **were dying**.

   b. Community radio stations **started** to present shows in Maya languages.

B Work with a partner. Compare your answers from exercise **A**. Which verb form is used to describe actions that were in progress at a certain time in the past?

◄ Two Guatemalan musicians si⁛ with their instruments.

LEARN

2.3 Past Progressive: Affirmative and Negative Statements

Affirmative		
Subject	Was/ Were	Verb + -ing
I/He/She/It	was	working.
You/We/They	were	

Negative		
Subject	Was Not/ Were Not	Verb + -ing
I/He/She/It	was not wasn't	sleeping.
You/We/They	were not weren't	

1. Use the past progressive to talk about an action that was in progress at a certain time in the past.	were studying 9:00 now They **were studying** at 9:00 last night.
2. **Remember:** Use the simple past for completed or repeated past actions, events, states, and feelings.	Yesterday I **rode** my bike to work. She **swam** every day last week. He **didn't like** the movie.
3. **Remember:** *Non-action* verbs are not usually used with the progressive.	✓ I **saw** an accident last night. ✗ I was seeing an accident last night.

See page **A1** for spelling rules for the *-ing* form of verbs.

4 Complete each sentence with the past progressive form of the verb(s) in parentheses.

1. Angelica _____was teaching_____ (teach) her local language in the evenings.

2. At 6:00 p.m. many people in town _____ (listen) to Angelica's show.

3. The radio _____ (play) loud dance music last night.

4. We _____ (talk) to Carlos, but he _____ (not listen) to us.

5. Pedro _____ (look) for a job at a radio station, but he didn't find one.

6. Tom and Karen _____ (live) in Guatemala last year.

7. The people next to us _____ (speak) Spanish. I think they were Mexican.

8. Steve _____ (sit) in the library, but he _____ (not study). He _____ (read) a magazine.

REAL ENGLISH

The past progressive is often used to describe a scene in the past.

*The café was full. A band **was playing**, and people **were talking** loudly. Everyone **was enjoying** the evening.*

5 **WRITE & SPEAK.** Complete the sentences. Use the past progressive. Make two of your sentences negative. Then share your sentences with a partner.

1. Last night at 9:00, _I was having dinner with my friends_ .

2. At 5:00 this morning _____ .

3. Last August _____ .

4. On Sunday morning _____ .

5. Two years ago _____ .

2.4 Past Progressive: Questions and Answers

Yes/No Questions				Short Answers
Was/Were	Subject	Verb + -ing		
Was	I/he/she	listening	to music?	Yes, she was. / No, she wasn't.
Were	you/we/they	eating	dinner?	Yes, they were. / No, they weren't.

Wh- Questions					Short Answers
Wh- Word	Was/Were	Subject	Verb + -ing		
What	was	he	doing	at 3:00?	He was working.
Where	were	you	studying	last night?	At the library.

Who or What as Subject				Short Answers
Wh- Word	Was	Verb + -ing		
Who	was	singing	last night?	Rita.
What	was	making	that noise?	My car.

Remember: *Who* or *What* can take the place of the subject in a *Wh-* question.	A: **Who** was playing that loud music last night? B: Alex and Rui.

6 Use the words in parentheses to complete the questions and answers. Use the past progressive.

1. A: What _____was Berta doing_____ (Berta / do) in the evenings?

   B: _____She was teaching_____ (she / teach).

2. A: _____ (they / speak) Spanish?

   B: No, _____ .

3. A: _____ (you / wait) for me?

   B: Yes, _____ .

4. A: Where _____ (you / go) after class yesterday?

   B: _____ (I / go) home.

5. A: Who _____ (Jane / talk) to?

   B: _____ (she / talk) to her math teacher.

6. A: Why _____ (those people / cheer)?

   B: Because _____ (their team / play) really well.

7. A: What _____ (you / do) at 8:00 last night?

   B: _____ (I / cook) dinner.

8. A: _____ (it / snow) last night?

   B: No, _____ .

7 **SPEAK.** Work with a partner. Take turns asking and answering questions 4, 7, and 8 from exercise **6**. Use your own answers, not the answers from the book.

A: *Where were you going after class yesterday?*   B: *I was going to the gym.*

PRACTICE

8 Circle the correct verb forms to complete each situation.

1. We (1) (were listening) / listened to a great band last night. They (2) **were playing** / **played** three songs, and then they (3) **were stopping** / **stopped.** We (4) **were wanting** / **wanted** them to play more songs, but they didn't. We (5) **were leaving** / **left** and (6) **were asking** / **asked** for our money back.

2. Lily's watch (7) **was breaking** / **broke** yesterday morning. It (8) **was falling** / **fell** off her wrist on her way to work. She (9) **was walking** / **walked** out of the subway station at the time, and someone (10) **was stepping** / **stepped** on it. Last night after work, she (11) **was buying** / **bought** a new one.

3. I (12) **was sitting** / **sat** at the student center yesterday afternoon. Several students (13) **were studying** / **studied**. Others (14) **were using** / **used** their phones. Then I (15) **was seeing** / **saw** my friend, Phil. He (16) **was eating** / **ate** lunch alone, so (17) I **was going** / **went** over and (18) **was sitting** / **sat** with him.

9 Complete each sentence with the past progressive or the simple past form of a verb from the box.

arrive	~~die~~	open	own	see	sleep	think	walk

1. The language _____ was dying _____ . Only a few people spoke it.

2. I saw street musicians when I _____ home last night.

3. Debbie _____ a nice car, but she didn't drive it much.

4. I'm surprised Kumiko is here today. I _____ she was on vacation.

5. Marcia _____ to the meeting 15 minutes late. Her boss was very angry.

6. I _____ Andy yesterday. He was talking to some friends.

7. My sister called me at midnight last night. I _____, and she woke me up.

8. The professor _____ the door and left the room.

10 **EDIT.** Read the information about Dr. Gregory Anderson's work in Siberia. Find and correct five more errors with the simple past and the past progressive.

▲ Dr. Anderson in Siberia

Dr. Anderson and his team made some interesting discoveries during a trip to Siberia in Russia. They were studying Xyzyl (*hizzle*), a local language there. They ~~were visiting~~ *visited* five villages during their trip, and they found that 50 to 60 people in those communities spoke Xyzyl in their daily lives. In one village, they were talking to an eleven-year-old girl called Kristina. She was knowing how to speak Xyzyl. Her grandmother was teaching her. Kristina was the youngest Xyzyl speaker in the village. Most of the other Xyzyl speakers got old. Many of them were 60 years old or older. It was clear that the Xyzyl language died. Dr. Anderson and his team studied the language, and they were making recordings to help it survive.

11 **APPLY.**

A Work with a partner. Write interview questions for Dr. Anderson. Use the information from exercise **10** and the words below to help you. Use the simple past or the past progressive.

1. where / your team go _____ *Where did your team go?* _____

2. how many villages / you / visit _____

3. who / you / talk to in the village _____

4. what / you / do in the village _____

5. your idea: _____

B Role-play a radio interview with Dr. Anderson. Partner A is the interviewer. Partner B is Dr. Anderson. Use your questions from exercise **A**, the information from exercise **10**, and your imagination.

A: *So, tell us about your trip, Dr. Anderson. Where did your team go?*

B: *We went to Siberia.*

EXPLORE

CD1-11

1 **READ** the article about Jimmy Chin, a mountain climber and photographer. Notice the words in **bold**.

Surviving an Avalanche

▲ Jimmy Chin has climbed up and skied down Mount Everest, the world's highest mountain.

Jimmy Chin is one of the few people to survive a Class 4 avalanche—an avalanche big enough to destroy buildings. In 2011, **while he was skiing in the Teton Mountains**, an avalanche started behind him. Chin was going down the mountain **when, in his own words, "the whole mountainside came down."**

The avalanche buried Chin under tons of snow and carried him downhill. Halfway down, the rolling snow threw him to the surface. However, Chin was not safe. **When he looked up**, trees were snapping all around him. The snow was still moving fast. Soon the avalanche buried him again.

"I knew I was going to the bottom of the valley," he remembers. Amazingly,[1] **when the avalanche reached the bottom of the mountain,** Chin was pushed to the surface! He was alive and on top of the snow **when his very surprised friends reached the bottom of the valley**.

After this experience, Chin took a month off from work. "It's important to do what's meaningful to you," he says. "You don't want to take your time for granted."[2]

[1] **amazingly:** (very) surprisingly
[2] **take something for granted:** not be grateful enough for something

▼ An avalanche carries hundreds of tons of snow down a mountain.

2 CHECK. Read the statements. Circle **T** for *true* or **F** for *false*. Then correct the false statements to make them true.

1. A Class ↓4 avalanche can destroy buildings.　　　　　　　T　　(F)

2. Jimmy Chin was skiing alone in the Tetons.　　　　　　　T　　F

3. The avalanche buried Chin at first.　　　　　　　　　　　T　　F

4. Chin's friends had to dig him out of the snow.　　　　　　T　　F

5. Chin decided to take a break after this experience.　　　　T　　F

3 DISCOVER. Complete the exercises to learn about the grammar in this lesson.

A Look at the two underlined events in each sentence from the article in exercise **1**. Write *1* above the event that started first.

1. In 2011, while <u>he was skiing in the Teton Mountains</u>, <u>an avalanche started behind him</u>.

2. When <u>he looked up</u>, <u>trees were snapping all around him</u>.

B Circle the correct answer to complete each statement.

1. The **simple past / past progressive** form is used for the event that starts first.

2. The **simple past / past progressive** form is used for the event that interrupted another event.

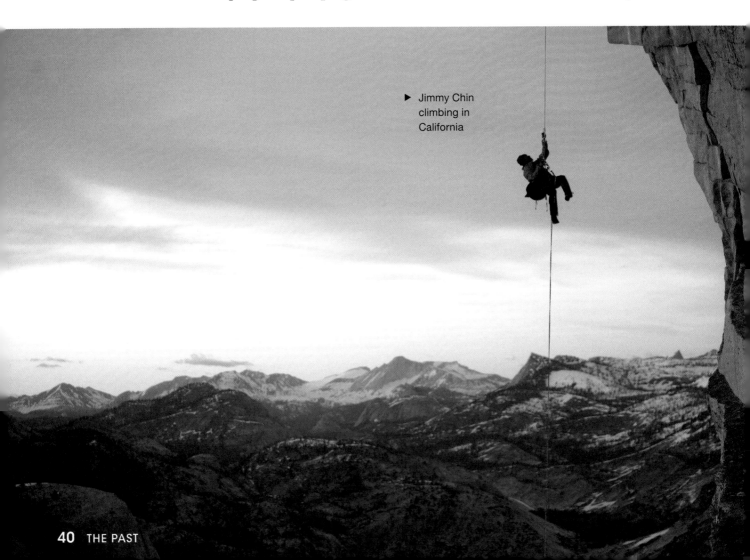

▶ Jimmy Chin climbing in California

LEARN

2.5   Past Time Clauses with *When* and *While*

When	While
The storm began **when I was driving home**. 〔Main Clause〕 〔Past Time Clause〕	The storm began **while we were walking home**. 〔Main Clause〕 〔Past Time Clause〕
When I was driving home, the storm began. 〔Past Time Clause〕 〔Main Clause〕	**While we were walking home**, the storm began. 〔Past Time Clause〕 〔Main Clause〕
I was sleeping **when you texted me**. 〔Main Clause〕 〔Past Time Clause〕	You texted me **while I was sleeping**. 〔Main Clause〕 〔Past Time Clause〕

1. A clause is a group of words with a subject and a verb. A main clause can stand alone as a complete sentence.	Elena called last night **while I was cooking dinner**. 〔Main Clause〕 〔Past Time Clause〕
2. A past time clause tells when an action or event happened. A past time clause can come before or after the main clause.	**When it started to snow**, I was walking home. It started to snow **while I was walking home**.
3. Use *while* or *when* + the past progressive to show that one action was in progress when another action happened.	I broke my leg **when I was skiing**. 〔Second Action〕 〔Action in Progress〕 Iris called **while I was cooking dinner**. 〔Second Action〕 〔First Action〕
4. Use *when* + the simple past for an action or event that happened at a specific point in the past.	I was painting the living room **when I fell off the ladder**. 〔Action in Progress〕 〔Action at a Point in the Past〕
5. Use a comma when the time clause comes at the beginning of a sentence.	**When we were taking the exam**, the lights went out. The lights went out **when we were taking the exam**.

4   Circle the correct form of the verb(s) to complete each sentence.

1. Jimmy Chin **skied** / **was skiing** when the avalanche **began** / was beginning.

2. When Chin's friends **reached** / **were reaching** him, he **lay** / **was lying** on top of the snow.

3. Terry **lost** / **was losing** his watch when he **swam** / **was swimming** in the ocean.

4. Mark and Dan's boat **sank** / **was sinking** while they **fished** / **were fishing**.

5. I **cut** / **was cutting** my finger when I **cooked** / **was cooking** dinner.

6. While Jean **shopped** / **was shopping**, the fire alarm **went off** / **was going off** in the store.

7. Carla **found** / **was finding** fifty dollars when she **walked** / **was walking** home yesterday.

8. Andre **prepared** / **was preparing** for the party when he suddenly **felt** / **was feeling** sick.

9. My pencil **broke** / **was breaking** while I **took** / **was taking** the exam.

10. Padma **heard** / **was hearing** a strange noise when she **hiked** / **was hiking** in the woods yesterday afternoon.

2.6 Past Time Clauses with *When*: Events in Sequence

1. When two actions happened one after the other, use the simple past in the past time clause and the main clause. Use *when* to introduce the past time clause.	When her phone **rang**, she **answered** it. ⎣Past Time Clause⎦ ⎣Main Clause⎦

2. The past time clause can come first or second in the sentence. The action or event in the past time clause happened first.	**When I got home**, I took a shower.
	  ⎣First Event⎦ ⎣Second Event⎦
	
	I took a shower **when I got home**.
	  ⎣Second Event⎦ ⎣First Event⎦

3. **Remember:** Use a comma when the past time clause comes first in the sentence.	**When Joe saw the accident,** he called the police.

5 Read each sentence. Which action or event happened first? Which action or event happened second? Write **1** for *first* and **2** for *second* below each action. Add a comma if necessary.

1. When <u>the storm ended</u>, <u>the workers began to clean up</u>.
   (1)   (2)

2. When <u>Tuan got out of the hospital</u> <u>he made plans for a vacation</u>.
   ( )   ( )

3. <u>We looked out the window</u> when <u>we heard the noise</u>.
   ( )   ( )

4. When <u>she saw the fire in her kitchen</u> <u>Michelle screamed for help</u>.
   ( )   ( )

5. <u>My son called me</u> when <u>his plane landed</u>.
   ( )   ( )

6. <u>The music started</u> when <u>the bride and groom walked into the room</u>.
   ( )   ( )

7. When <u>the phone rang</u> <u>Isabelle turned the TV off</u>.
   ( )   ( )

8. <u>I called my parents</u> when <u>I received my exam results</u>.
   ( )   ( )

6 Complete each sentence with the correct form of the verb in parentheses.

1. Eric finished his assignment when he _____*got*_____ (get) home.

2. When Vicky _____ (put) her bag on the floor, a thief stole it.

3. When Max's car broke down, he _____ (walk) to the nearest gas station.

4. My sister laughed when I _____ (tell) her the joke.

5. Juanita smiled when she _____ (hear) the good news.

6. We _____ (buy) our tickets when we got to the station.

7. Sylvie closed the window when it _____ (start) to rain.

8. I lit some candles when the electricity _____ (go) out.

7 SPEAK. Work with a partner. Complete the sentences.

When I woke up this morning . . . *When I woke up this morning, I called my parents.*

When I got to class . . .

When I finished my homework . . .

PRACTICE

Santiago, Chile

8 Look at the time line about a mine accident in Chile. Then complete each sentence with the simple past or past progressive form of a verb from the box.

0	**Aug 5:** 33 miners were trapped underground in a mine. (Day 1)
10	**Aug 22:** Rescuers discovered that all 33 miners were alive. (Day 17)
20	**Aug 30:** The drills¹ started to work. (Day 26)
30	
40	
50	
60	**Oct 9:** One of the drills reached the miners. (Day 66)
70	**Oct 13:** Rescuers lifted all 33 miners to safety. (Day 69)
80	**Oct 24:** National celebration for the miners in Santiago, Chile (Day 80)

DAY

¹drill: a machine that makes a round hole

arrive	attach	begin	complete	~~fall~~	read	wait	watch

1. On August 5, 2010, when 33 miners were working in a mine in Chile, the roof
    _____*fell*_____ and trapped them.

2. While the miners' families _____ anxiously for news, the mining company
    began its rescue attempts.

3. When those attempts failed, the government _____ a huge rescue
    operation.

4. When the necessary equipment _____ at the scene, the rescue team
    started to search for the miners.

5. When one of the drills reached the miners, the miners _____ a note to it.

6. When the rescue team _____ the note, they discovered that all 33 of the miners were alive.

7. When the rescue team _____ the escape route, they began to lift the miners out of the mine.

8. Millions of people all over the world _____ on TV when the rescue workers lifted the last man out of the mine.

9 LISTEN & SPEAK.

CD1-12

A Listen to the conversation about Ernest Shackleton. Then answer the questions.

1. How many men were with Shackleton on the ship? _____

2. In what year did Shackleton's ship become trapped in the ice? _____

3. Did the men all survive? _____

CD1-12

B Complete each sentence with the simple past or the past progressive form of the verb(s) in parentheses. Then listen again and check your answers.

1. The *Endurance* ____was approaching____ (approach) Antarctica in January 1915 when it _____ (become) locked in the ice.

2. When the ocean water _____ (freeze), ice _____ (surround) the ship.

3. Shackleton and his men _____ (stay) on the *Endurance* at first, and then they _____ (make) a camp on the ice.

4. They _____ (wait) for nine months, but the ice _____ (not release) the ship.

▼ The crew of the *Endurance* plays soccer to pass the time. Their ship is in the background.

5. Then one day, while some of the men _____ (arrange) supplies on the ice, the ship _____ (begin) to break up.

6. When the *Endurance* _____ (start) to sink, Shackleton _____ (decide) to take his men across the ice on foot.

7. While Shackleton and five of his men _____ (try) to reach the island of South Georgia to find help, the others _____ (spend) several more months at the camp on the ice.

8. When Shackleton and his men _____ (arrive) in Chile, they _____ (receive) a hero's welcome.

10 APPLY.

A Read Marta's blog entry. Underline the past time clauses.

You won't believe what happened to me tonight! While I was crossing Newton Street, a truck went through a red light. The driver was texting when the light changed. He wasn't looking at the road. When I jumped out of the way, I fell onto the sidewalk and cut my knee. I was wearing my new jeans, too! When I got home, I took care of my knee and then called the police. Fortunately, I got the truck's license number while I was lying in the street.

B Work with a partner. Close your books and take turns retelling the story about Marta's accident. Use past time clauses.

C Think of an accident that you or someone you know had. Take notes in the chart. Use the questions to help you.

When did the accident happen?	
Where were you?	
What were you doing?	
What happened?	
What happened next?	

D In your notebook, write a paragraph about your accident. Use your notes from exercise **C** and Marta's blog entry as a model. Use at least five past time clauses. When you are finished, read your story to a partner or small group.

EXPLORE

CD1-13

1 **READ** the conversation between two visitors to the British Museum in London, England. Notice the words in **bold**.

London, U.K.

Athens, Greece

Who Owns the Past?

Cho: These statues are beautiful. Where are they from?

Noriko: They're from Athens, Greece. I think they **used to be** a part of the Parthenon.

Cho: Well, it's wonderful to see them, but why are they here in London? They should be back in Greece with the rest of the Parthenon.

Noriko: A lot of people agree with you. Lord Elgin, a British diplomat,[1] brought these statues to London in the early nineteenth century.

Cho: You mean he just took them?

Noriko: Well, I don't know. I'm not sure what really happened. Back then archaeologists[2] **used to do** things like that. They **would explore** a historic site and bring objects from the site back to their home countries. Then, they **would study** them and put them on display in museums. Sometimes, that's the only reason treasures like these survived.

Cho: But didn't the Greek people try to stop Lord Elgin?

Noriko: Sure, there were a lot of complaints. Was it right or wrong to take these statues? It's a difficult question. I love to visit museums and see things from around the world and learn about them.

Cho: Hmm . . . I understand what you're saying, but it still seems wrong to me, somehow.

[1] **diplomat:** a person who acts as the official representative of his or her country in a foreign country
[2] **archaeologist:** a person who studies the past by looking at items such as buried houses, tools, pots, etc.

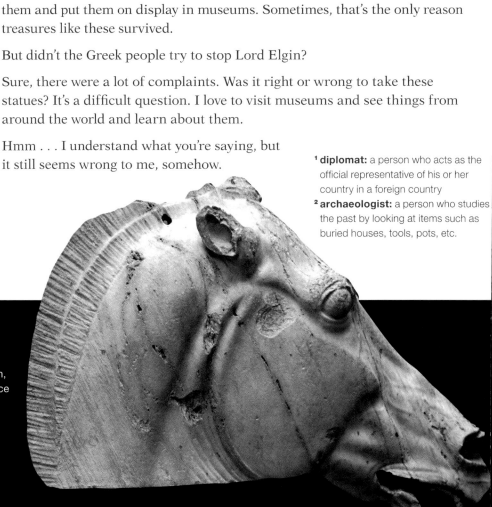

▶ A statue of a horse's head from the Parthenon, Acropolis, Athens, Greece 447-432 B.C.

▲ A carving from the Parthenon, Acropolis, Athens, Greece

2 **CHECK.** Read the statements. Circle **T** for *true* or **F** for *false*.

1. The statues are from Italy.   **T**   **F**

2. The statues came to England in the 20th century.   **T**   **F**

3. Cho thinks the statues should go back to Greece.   **T**   **F**

4. In the past, it was not unusual for archaeologists to bring discoveries home.   **T**   **F**

5. Cho and Noriko agree about the future of the statues.   **T**   **F**

3 **DISCOVER.** Complete the exercises to learn about the grammar in this lesson.

A Look at these sentences from the conversation in exercise **1**. Decide whether the **bold** verb in each sentence refers to a single action **(S)** or a repeated action **(R)**. Write *S* or *R*.

1. _S_ Lord Elgin . . . **brought** these statues to London in the early nineteenth century.

2. _____ You mean he just **took** them?

3. _____ Back then archaeologists **used to do** things like that.

4. _____ They **would explore** a historic site and bring objects from the site back to their home countries.

5. _____ Then, they **would study** them and put them on display in museums.

B Look at the sentences from exercise **A**. Which verb forms are used for repeated actions? Discuss your answer with your classmates and teacher.

LEARN

2.7 *Used To*: Affirmative and Negative Statements

Affirmative			
Subject	*Used To*	Base Form	
I/She/They	**used to**	study	history.

Negative			
Subject	*Didn't Use To*	Base Form	
I/She/They	**didn't use to**	study	math.

1. *Used to* expresses a habit or state in the past that no longer exists.	I **used to run** several times a week. (Now, I don't.) I **used to live** in a small town. (I live in a city now.) I **didn't use to eat** meat. (I do now.)
2. In negative statements use *use to*, not *used to*.	I didn't **use to** love math.

REAL ENGLISH

Use *used to* instead of the simple past to emphasize that the habit or state is not true now.

*When I was young, I **used to go** to the beach every day.*

---

4 Rewrite each sentence with *used to* or *didn't use to* and the verb in **bold**.

1. Archaeologists **removed** objects from historic sites.

   Archaeologists used to remove objects from historic sites.

2. I **went** to museums every weekend when I lived in Berlin.

   _____

3. My cousin **lived** across the street, but I didn't see him much.

   _____

4. Jim **didn't like** math when he was in school.

   _____

5. There **was** a supermarket near my home until last year.

   _____

6. Carole **played** in a band in college.

   _____

7. I **didn't drive** much when I lived downtown.

   _____

8. Mike **worked** in a bank before he got his new job.

   _____

2.8 *Used To:* Questions and Answers

Yes/No Questions				
Did	Subject	*Use To*	Base Form	
Did	he they	use to	get	good grades?

Answers
Yes, he **did**. / **No**, he **didn't**.   **Yes**, they **did**. / **No**, they **didn't**.

Wh- Questions					
Wh- Word	Did	Subject	*Use To*	Base Form	
Where	did	she	use to	live?	
Who		you		study	with?

Answers
In Mexico.
My friend, Felix.

Who or What as Subject			
Wh- Word	*Used To*	Base Form	
Who	used to	teach	this class?
What		be	here?

Answers
Professor Ortiz.
A shoe store.

1. When a question includes *did*, use *use to*, not *used to*.	<u>Did</u> you **use to** live here? Where <u>did</u> she **use to** work?
2. **Remember:** *Who* or *What* can take the place of the subject in a *Wh-* question. **Be careful!** When *Who* or *What* is the subject of the question, use *used to*, not *use to*.	✓ **Who used to live** in that house? ✗ Who <u>use to</u> live in that house?

5 Complete each question with the words in parentheses. Use the correct form of *used to*.

1. _____ Did you use to ride _____ (you / ride) a bike when you were a child?

2. What _____ (you / do) after school when you were a child?

3. _____ (your family / live) in a different place?

4. Where _____ (your mother / work)?

5. What _____ (your family / do) on the weekends when you were a child?

6. Who _____ (be) your English teacher?

7. _____ (you / visit) your friends often?

8. Where _____ (you / go) on vacation?

6 **SPEAK.** Work with a partner. Ask and answer the questions from exercise **5**.

A: *Did you use to ride a bike when you were a child?*

B: *Yes, I did.*

REAL ENGLISH

When the phrases *used to* or *use to* are used to talk about the past, they are often pronounced /yustə/.

2.9 *Would*: Repeated Past Actions

Affirmative and Negative Statements				
	Subject	*Would/ Would Not*	Base Form	
When I was in high school,	I	would 'd	ride	my bike to school.
When Scott was a child,	he	would not wouldn't	eat	any vegetables.

1. *Would* expresses a repeated past action or habit that no longer exists.	In high school, we **would play** soccer every afternoon. As a child, I **wouldn't study**, but I **would get** good grades.
2. **Be careful!** Do not use *would* for past situations or states that no longer exist. Use *used to* or *use to*.	✓ There **used to be** a library on this street. ✗ There <u>would be</u> a library on this street. ✓ He **didn't use to live** on Palm Street. ✗ He <u>wouldn't live</u> on Palm Street.

7 Complete each sentence. Use *would* and the verb in parentheses.

1. When I was a child, my father _____ (take) me to the zoo about once a month.

2. In high school, my brother _____ (not start) his homework until around midnight.

3. When Alicia was a child, she _____ (play) with her friends after school.

4. When my parents were in school, they _____ (eat) lunch at home every day.

5. In college, I often _____ (not go) to bed until 3:00 a.m.

6. My grandfather used to work very hard during the week, but on the weekends he _____ (relax).

7. In college, Sandra _____ (study) for about six hours every day.

8. When I was in high school, I _____ (sit) in the back of the classroom and draw in my notebook.

9. When Kyle was on the soccer team, he _____ (run) five miles every morning before school.

10. We _____ (go) to the market every day when we lived in France.

PRACTICE

CD1-14

8 Complete the article about the Iceman with the words and phrases from the chart. Use each word or phrase only once. Then listen and check your answers.

Used To	Would	Simple Past		
used to hunt	wouldn't come	didn't grow	didn't spend	killed
used to think	would go	~~discovered~~	found	used

The Iceman

Back in 1991, hikers in the mountains near the border of Austria and Italy (1) _discovered_ the body of a man in the ice. Scientists soon learned that the body was over 5000 years old. They called the man the "Iceman."

Scientists (2) _____ that the Iceman died from the cold. Five thousand years ago, people of central Europe (3) _____ wild animals for food. They (4) _____ up into the mountains in all kinds of weather, and sometimes they (5) _____ back. Then, in 2001, scientists found part of an arrow in the Iceman's body. Somebody (6) _____ the Iceman, and we will probably never know why.

After more recent tests, scientists now think the Iceman was not just a hunter. They think he probably had a higher position in society, and (7) _____ a lot of time in the mountains. Before the most recent tests, scientists believed that people in the Iceman's community (8) _____ crops.[1] However, they (9) _____ small pieces of stone in the Iceman's stomach. This suggests that the Iceman's people (10) _____ stones to grind[2] flour for some kind of bread.

Even though the Iceman died over 5000 years ago, we know a lot about his life thanks to scientific research.

[1] **crops:** plants that people grow for food
[2] **grind:** to rub something until it becomes a powder

◄ How the Iceman died used to be a mystery. Now scientists think they have the answer.

9 **WRITE.** Look at the information in the chart about people 5000 years ago and people today. Then write six sentences using *used to, didn't use to,* or *would.*

People 5000 Years Ago	People Today
hunt animals, gather fruit and nuts	buy food in grocery stores
cook over fire	cook with stoves
live in caves or simple shelters	live in houses or apartments
use animal skins for clothing	buy clothing in stores or make clothing from cloth

People didn't use to buy food in a grocery store.

1. _____

2. _____

3. _____

4. _____

5. _____

6. _____

10 **APPLY.**

A A few years ago Brian was not happy, so he made some changes. Look at the chart. What changes did he make? Discuss them with a partner.

Brian used to be unhappy, and he didn't have many friends. He joined a band last year. Now . . .

Brian		
In the Past	Change	Now
lonely, didn't have many friends	joined a band last year	happy, has new friends
unhealthy	bought a bike a few months ago	healthy
always arrived late for class and work	learned to drive last month	always arrives on time

B Think about some changes you have made in your life. In your notebook, make a chart like the one in exercise **A** and write notes about three of these changes.

C Work with a partner. Take turns talking about the changes in your life. Use *used to, didn't use to,* and *would.*

D In your notebook, write a short paragraph of four or five sentences about one of the change you made.

> *A couple of years ago, I used to feel lonely all the time. I would stay home at night and watch TV . . .*

Charts 2.1–2.9

1 Circle the correct word(s) or phrase(s) to complete each sentence.

1. Hundreds of years ago, people **used to believe / would believe** that the Earth was flat.

2. My brother **put / was putting** the phone down while I **talked / was talking** to him.

3. When the plane **landed / was landing** safely, everyone **started / was starting** to clap.

4. When my grandfather was young, he **was walking / would walk** five miles to school every day.

5. How many reports **did Malik write / did Malik use to write** last week?

6. Lisa **used to live / would live** in Miami, but then she **moved / was moving** to Paris.

7. **Were you going / Did you use to go** to Central Park a lot when you **were living / would live** in New York?

8. Yuri **drove / was driving** home when his car **broke down / was breaking down**.

9. I **wanted / used to want** to see the show, but I couldn't get a ticket.

10. **Did you use to play / Were you playing** tennis when you **hurt / were hurting** your arm?

Charts 2.1–2.7

2 Complete each sentence or question with the word(s) in parentheses. Use the simple past, the past progressive, or *used to*. There is more than one correct answer for some items.

1. While I _____was sitting_____ (sit) in the airport lounge, I _____saw_____ (see) a famous actor.

2. Irina _____ (write) poems, but now she writes short stories instead.

3. Martin _____ (try) to turn on his computer, but nothing _____ (happen).

4. When my brother and I _____ (be) young, we _____ (play) games with my parents in the evenings.

5. _____ (you / have) trouble with the alphabet when you _____ (learn) Arabic?

6. We _____ (go) to the movies three times last week.

7. I _____ (work) when you _____ (call), so I _____ (not answer) the phone.

8. When Stephanie was a child, she _____ (visit) her grandparents twice a month.

Charts
2.1, 2.3,
2.5, 2.9

3 EDIT. Read the paragraph about stepped wells in India. Find and correct six more errors with the simple past, the past progressive, and *would*.

Stepped Wells in India

Northern India is very hot. The area gets a lot of rain, but the water disappears very quickly
began
because of the heat. Around 1500 years ago, the people of northern India ~~used to begin~~ to
build stepped wells to provide water for the population. They dug deep holes to reach water
underground, and they were making rock walls for the wells. In each well, they builded stone
steps and passages to help people reach the water easily. They often were decorating the walls of
the passages with beautiful designs.

The stepped wells were long and narrow. They were cool, dark places, and they were often
having special rooms away from the heat. While people were collecting water, they would took
some time out of their busy days and talk with their neighbors. The wells becomed important
social centers.

▶ A visitor walks into
a stepped well in
northern India.

Charts
2.1, 2.3,
2.5

🎧
CD1-15

4 LISTEN & WRITE.

A Look at the photos on page 55. Then listen to the stories of four people who survived attacks
by wild animals. Complete the chart with information about each person's story.

	Eric Nerhus	Ben Nyaumbe	Kootoo Shaw	James Morrow
Activity	diving			
Animal			polar bear	
Place		Kenya		
Reason for Survival				his face mask protected him

▼ an alligator

▼ a python

▼ a shark

▼ a polar bear

B Write sentences about each story from exercise **A**. Use the information in the chart, the simple past, the past progressive, and past time clauses. Then listen again and check your sentences.

While Eric Nerhus was diving in Australia, a shark attacked him. He survived because the shark bit his belt.

_____

_____

_____

_____

_____

_____

_____

Charts
2.1–2.6

5 SPEAK.

A Think of a dangerous situation that you or someone you know was in. What happened? What did you or this person do? How did you or this person survive? Write notes in your notebook.

B Work with a partner. Take turns telling your stories from exercise **A**. Use the simple past, the past progressive, and past time clauses. Ask your partner questions for more information about his or her story.

Connect the Grammar to Writing

1 READ & NOTICE THE GRAMMAR.

A Read the story. What difficult experience did the writer have? How did she survive? Discuss the writer's experience with a partner.

▼ A flooded river in York, England

Remembering a Spring Flood

When I was a young girl, we lived near a river. Every spring when the snow melted, it caused the river to rise a few feet. Then the level of the river would fall again. One spring, however, the river kept rising.

One day that spring, I looked out my window. The river was rising very quickly. My parents came and got me. While the water was rising higher, we climbed onto the roof of our house. From the roof, I looked down at the river. It was covering everything in its path. My family and I waited on our roof for help. I was losing hope when we were finally rescued.

GRAMMAR FOCUS

In the story, the writer uses the simple past to talk about completed actions and events.

> I **looked** out my window.
> My parents **came** and **got** me.

The writer uses the past progressive to describe a scene in the past.

> The river **was rising** very quickly.

The writer uses past time clauses to describe when actions or events happened.

> **When I was a young girl,** we lived near a river.

B Read the story from exercise **A** again. Circle the simple past, underline the past progressive, and double underline the past time clauses. Then work with a partner and compare your answers.

C Complete the chart with information from the story in exercise **A**. Add more boxes to the chart if necessary.

Event 1	Event 2	Event 3	Event 4
One spring, the river near my house kept rising.	My parents came and got me.		

2   BEFORE YOU WRITE.

A   Brainstorm a list of difficult experiences you have had.

B   Choose one experience to write about. Use the chart below to describe your experience. Add more boxes to your chart if necessary.

Event 1	Event 2	Event 3	Event 4

3   WRITE about your difficult experience. Use the information from your chart from exercise **2B** and the story from exercise **1A** to help you.

> **WRITING FOCUS   Identifying and Correcting Sentence Fragments**
>
> A sentence fragment is missing an important part of a sentence, such as a subject or verb.
>
> ✓ <u>My family and I</u> <u>waited</u> on our roof for help.
> ✗ Waited on our roof for help. (no subject)
>
> ✓ <u>It</u> <u>was covering</u> everything in its path.
> ✗ Everything in its path. (no subject and no verb)
>
> Make sure each of your sentences has a subject and a verb.

4   SELF ASSESS. Read your story and underline the simple past, the past progressive, and past time clauses. Then use the checklist to assess your work.

- [ ] I used the simple past to talk about completed actions and events. [2.1]
- [ ] I used the past progressive to describe a scene in the past. [2.3]
- [ ] I used past time clauses to tell when an action or event happened. [2.5, 2.6]
- [ ] I checked for and corrected sentence fragments. [WRITING FOCUS]

Health and Fitness

Nouns

▶ Residents of Shanghai, China, exercise with fans.

EXPLORE

CD1-16

1 **READ** the article about *sangomas*, traditional African healers. Notice the words in **bold**.

Sangomas of Southern Africa

Sangomas are traditional **healers** of southern Africa. They use **plants, songs,** and **dances** to help **people** who are sick. Many people in southern Africa prefer traditional **healers** to modern medicine. **Women,** for example, may see a sangoma instead of a doctor when their **babies** are born. Often, however, modern medicine and traditional medicine work together. Using one kind of medicine doesn't mean ignoring **the other kind**.

A **sangoma's** goal is to make his or her patient[1] feel better. To help their **patients, sangomas** perform different **ceremonies**. In one ceremony, the sangoma throws **shells** and animal **bones** on the ground. The **shells** and **bones** form a pattern. The pattern helps the sangoma understand the patient. **Other methods** of helping **patients** include special **drinks**, drumming, and singing.

Scientists are studying the **methods** used by **sangomas**. They hope to learn new **ways** to keep **people** healthy.

[1] **patient:** a person who is cared for by a doctor

2 CHECK. Read the statements. Circle **T** for *true* or **F** for *false*.

1. Modern medicine has replaced traditional healers in Africa.   **T**   **F**

2. Sangomas perform different kinds of ceremonies.   **T**   **F**

3. The pattern formed by shells and bones helps patients understand the sangoma.   **T**   **F**

4. Sangomas sometimes sing to help their patients.   **T**   **F**

5. Modern scientists don't think traditional medicine is useful.   **T**   **F**

3 DISCOVER. Complete the exercises to learn about the grammar in this lesson.

A In the article, each of these nouns is used in the plural. Find the correct plural form of each noun in the article and write it on the line next to its singular form.

Singular	Plural
1. healer	healers
2. dance	_____
3. person	_____
4. woman	_____
5. baby	_____
6. patient	_____
7. ceremony	_____
8. drink	_____
9. bone	_____
10. scientist	_____

B Notice the different ways the plural nouns in exercise **A** are formed. Discuss them with a partner.

◄ A traditional African healer

LEARN

3.1 Spelling Rules for Regular and Irregular Plural Nouns

	Singular	Plural
1. Add -s to most singular nouns to form the plural.	apple scientist boy	apples scientists boys
2. Add -es to nouns that end in -s, -sh, -ch, or -x.	class, dish, inch, tax	classes, dishes, inches, taxes
3. For nouns that end in a consonant + -y, change the -y to -i and add -es.	party, city	parties, cities
4. For some nouns that end in -o, add -s. For other nouns that end in -o, add -es. Learn the spelling of each noun separately.	photo potato	photos potatoes
5. For most nouns that end in -f or -fe, change the ending to -ves. For other nouns that end in -f, add -s.	leaf, wife belief, roof	leaves, wives beliefs, roofs
6. Some nouns have irregular plural forms.* Irregular plural nouns include nouns with a. a vowel change b. an irregular ending c. no change (often animals)	a. man, foot, tooth b. child c. fish, deer	a. men, feet, teeth b. children c. fish, deer

*See page **A3** for a list of common irregular plural nouns.

4 Complete each sentence with the plural form of the noun in parentheses.

1. _____Scientists_____ (Scientist) are interested in traditional medicine.

2. The healer told _____ (story) about the life of her patient.

3. In some countries, most _____ (baby) are born at home.

4. The mother took her three _____ (child) to the doctor.

5. Healers work to improve the _____ (life) of their patients.

6. The dentist says my _____ (tooth) are in very good condition.

7. The doctor told me to eat more _____ (banana).

8. I think I eat too many _____ (potato).

9. Our school offers healthy _____ (lunch) every day.

10. Different cultures have different _____ (belief) about health.

REAL ENGLISH

A few nouns have n
singular form. They
used only in the plu
Some examples are
clothes, glasses, jea

I'm wearing my n
jeans today.

5 Work with a partner. Partner B closes his or her book. Partner A reads a singular noun from chart 3.1. Partner B says the plural form of the word and spells it. Switch roles after five or six words.

A: *apple*   B: *apples: a, p, p, l, e, s*

3.2 Possessive Nouns

Singular Noun	Possessive Form
girl	The **girl's** bicycle is blue.
child	The **child's** room is messy.

Plural Noun	Possessive Form
girls	The **girls'** bicycles are blue.
children	The **children's** rooms are messy.

1. Use possessive nouns to show ownership or a relationship.	The **writer's** house is in New York. **Mark's** father is very strong.
2. To make singular nouns possessive, add an apostrophe (') + -s ('s).	The **child's** mother is over there.
3. To make plural nouns possessive a. add an apostrophe to regular plural nouns b. add an apostrophe + -s to most irregular plural nouns	a. The **boys'** parents are here. b. The **children's** teacher is kind.
4. To make a noun phrase with two nouns possessive, add an apostrophe + -s to the second noun only.	**John and Tina's** father is sick.

6 Circle the correct word to complete each sentence.

1. (Maria's)/ **Marias'** daughter is in hospital.

2. The **nurses's** / **nurse's** name is Meg.

3. The **students'** / **students's** goal is to become doctors.

4. The **childrens'** / **children's** section of the hospital is bright and cheerful.

5. You can find many **doctor's** / **doctors'** phone numbers online.

6. My **baby's** / **babies'** cold is getting worse.

7. **Peoples'** / **People's** health is getting better.

8. The Internet has increased **parent's** / **parents'** concerns about their children.

7 Write the correct possessive form of the word in parentheses.

1. Is your _____*dentist's*_____ (dentist) office in this building?

2. The _____ (building) elevator is broken.

3. _____ (Mrs. Achebe) house is across the street from the hospital.

4. The _____ (doctors) white coats are in the closet.

5. Julian and _____ (Amy) baby is six weeks old.

6. This _____ (city) hospitals are excellent.

7. Marta is a coach for the _____ (women) swim team.

8. _____ (Mark and Sam) apartment is on the second floor.

8 Work in a small group. Take turns talking about things that belong to members of your group.

Paul's backpack is black.   Ava's hair is long.

3.3   *Another* and *Other*

1. *Another* + a singular noun means one more person or thing of the same group.	I've already had two pieces of pizza, but I'm going to have **another** <u>piece</u>.
Another can also refer to a different person or thing.	This pen doesn't work. I need **another** <u>pen</u>.
Use *another* to refer to a person or thing that is not specific.	My car is very old. I need to buy **another** <u>car</u> soon.
2. *The other* + a singular noun means the second of two people or things of a specific group.	There are two hotels in this area. One hotel is on Main Street. **The other** <u>hotel</u> is on Oak Street.
The other + a plural noun means the rest of the people or things of a specific group.	We had three assignments. I did one last night and did **the other** <u>assignments</u> this morning.
3. *Other* + a plural noun means some, but not all, of the remaining people or things in a group.	Some people like to talk. **Other** <u>people</u> prefer to listen.
4. The pronoun *one* or *ones* can replace the noun after *another* or *(the) other*.	Lydia's watch broke, so she bought **another** <u>one</u>. (*one* = watch)
	These earrings are pretty, but I prefer **the other** <u>ones</u>. (*ones* = earrings)

9 Complete the sentences with *another, other,* or *the other*.

1. I took one pill early this morning. I need to take _____another_____ pill after lunch.

2. Some people exercise every day. _____ people never exercise.

3. Eight nurses work here. Six of them are very experienced. _____ two are new.

4. Many doctors work in hospitals, but _____ doctors have their own offices.

5. My brother had a soccer game on Saturday, and on Sunday he had _____ one.

6. I have two exams tomorrow. One exam is the morning. _____ one is in the afternoon.

7. I saw two movies on Saturday. The first one was great, but _____ movie was terrible.

8. This glass is dirty. Could I have _____ one, please?

> **REAL ENGLISH**
>
> *Another* and *the other* are also used alone as pronouns.
>
> > *These pears are delicious. I'm going to have **another**. (another = pear)*
> >
> > *Ken owns two apartments. One apartment is in Chicago. **The other** is in Miami. (the other = apartment)*

10 Complete the sentences with *one* or *ones*.

1. Leyla takes one vitamin every morning and another _____ *one* _____ at night.

2. There are three hospitals in my city. One is near my apartment. The other _____ are downtown.

3. Brett doesn't like his doctor. He wants to find another _____.

4. I missed my doctor's appointment this morning, so I made another _____ for next week.

5. A few of the articles in that health magazine are about nutrition. The other _____ are about exercise.

6. Dan has two appointments next week. One is on Monday. The other _____ is on Thursday.

7. I prefer these eyeglasses. The other _____ aren't very attractive.

8. Use this elevator. The other _____ are broken.

PRACTICE

11 Circle the correct word to complete each sentence.

1. The (doctor's)/ doctors schedule is very full this week.

2. My **babies** / **baby's** health is very important to me.

3. Doctor Chen has a lot of **patients** / **patient's**.

4. The hospital lost the **men** / **man's** x-rays.

5. The **teacher's** / **teachers** are having a meeting today.

6. Some **person** / **people** watch a lot of TV.

7. The **child's** / **children's** father took them to the park.

8. That building is over 1000 **foot** / **feet** high.

12 PRONUNCIATION. Read the chart and listen to the examples. Then complete the exercises.

CD1-17

PRONUNCIATION	Nouns: *-s* and *-es* Endings
Many plural nouns and possessives end in *-s* or *-es*. The endings have one of three sounds: /s/, /z/, or /əz/.	
1. Pronounce *-s* as /s/ after the consonant sounds /f/, /k/, /p/, /t/, and /θ/.	shop's, tests, beliefs, bike's, months
2. Pronounce *-s* as /z/ after the consonant sounds /b/, /d/, /g/, /l/, /m/, /n/, /ŋ/, /r/, /v/, or any vowel sound.	logs, jobs, head's, songs, wives, day's
3. Pronounce *-es* as /əz/ after /s/, /z/, /ʃ/, /dʒ/, /tʃ/, or /ks/ sounds.	kisses, diseases, wishes, judge's, watches, taxes

A Listen and circle the final sound you hear for each word.

1.	nurses	/s/	/z/	(/əz/)	7.	boy's	/s/ /z/ /əz/
2.	patient's	/s/	/z/	/əz/	8.	beds	/s/ /z/ /əz/
3.	doctor's	/s/	/z/	/əz/	9.	jobs	/s/ /z/ /əz/
4.	cups	/s/	/z/	/əz/	10.	bridges	/s/ /z/ /əz/
5.	book's	/s/	/z/	/əz/	11.	boxes	/s/ /z/ /əz/
6.	hospitals	/s/	/z/	/əz/	12.	dishes	/s/ /z/ /əz/

B Listen again and repeat each word. Pay attention to the endings.

13 Read each situation and complete the sentences about it. Use *another, the other,* or *other* and the noun in parentheses.

1. Situation: *Your father saw one of his two doctors last week.*

   He saw _____the other doctor_____ (doctor) this morning.

2. Situation: *My bottle of vitamins is almost empty.*

   I need to buy _____ (bottle of vitamins) soon.

3. Situation: *You bought six oranges. Four of them were sweet and delicious.*

   _____ (oranges) were sour.

4. Situation: *Emma found three errors on her homework assignment. Then, she found one more.*

   Emma just found _____ (error) on her homework assignment.

5. Situation: *I invited ten people to my party. Seven people came.*

   _____ (people) did not come.

6. Situation: *Carol is a nurse. She doesn't have the same schedule every week. Some weeks she works during the day.*

   _____ (weeks) she works at night or on the weekends.

7. Situation: *My coat is old, and it's not very warm.*

   I need _____ (coat).

8. Situation: *The students at my school study different things. Some students are studying science.*

   _____ (students) are studying history, math, or languages.

14 EDIT. Read the information about the human body in extreme situations. Find and correct eight more errors with plural nouns and possessive nouns.

The human body is amazing, but it has limits. Do you know your ~~bodies~~ _body's_ limits in these extreme situations? Here are some helpful facts:

• **HEAT:** When a person body temperature reaches 107.6 degrees Fahrenheit (42 degrees Celsius), he or she can die. In a burning building, adults can breathe air at 300 degrees F (149 degrees C) for ten minutes. Children's bodys are not as strong.

• **COLD:** Low temperature's are also very dangerous. In cold water, the human body loses heat very quickly. People usually don't survive for more than 30 minute in water that's 40 degrees Fahrenheit (4.4 degrees Celsius).

• **ALTITUDE:** _Altitude_ is the measurement of height above the level of the sea. Many people find it difficult to breathe at 15,000 foot (4572 meters). Mountain climber's sometimes have serious health problemes at very high altitudes.

15 APPLY.

A In your notebook, write six sentences using singular and plural nouns, and possessive nouns. Use the words from the box or your own ideas.

camera	car	children	clothes	diet	dog	health	job	sister	TV

My sister's children are in high school.

B Work with a partner. Share your sentences from exercise **A**. Ask questions to keep the conversation going. Pay attention to possessive nouns and plural nouns.

A: _My sister's children are in high school._

B: _Where do they go to school?_

EXPLORE

CD1-19

1 READ the article about three different superfoods. Notice the words in **bold**.

Superfoods

| Argan Oil | The Acai Palm | Ginseng |

Argan Oil

The **oil** from argan **nuts** is very important to the **people** of southwestern Morocco. It has many different **uses**. It adds **flavor**[1] to **food**, it prevents dry **skin**, and it keeps **hair** soft. Now it is popular in other **countries**, too, and it is becoming more expensive. The **production** of argan **oil** cannot increase very quickly, because argan **trees** don't produce **nuts** until they are about 20 **years** old.

[1] **flavor:** a specific taste

The Acai Palm

The acai palm **tree** of Central and South America has round purple **fruit**. **Acai** is very important to some of the **tribes** in the Amazon **Rainforest**. In fact, it is a very large **part** of their **diet**.[2] **People** make both sweet and salty **dishes** with acai. Now some **companies** say that **acai** helps **people** lose **weight**.

[2] **diet:** a person's regular food and drink

Ginseng

Ginseng is a **plant** that grows in Asia and North America. There are many different **types** of ginseng **plants**. Chinese **medicine** started using **ginseng** **thousands** of **years** ago to treat all **kinds** of **diseases**. According to some scientific **studies**, **ginseng** may help manage **stress**.[3] Be careful, though! Too much **ginseng** can keep you awake at **night**.

[3] **stress:** mental or physical difficulty caused by work, worries, and so on

2 CHECK. Match each statement with the correct tree or plant. Write the letter on the line.

1. You can use it in sweet and salty meals. _b_   a. argan oil

2. It keeps hair soft. _____   b. acai palm

3. Tests suggest it can help you relax. _____   c. ginseng

4. It is becoming more expensive. _____

5. According to some companies, it helps you lose weight. _____

6. Some people don't sleep well because of it. _____

3 DISCOVER. Complete the exercises to learn about the grammar in this lesson.

A Look at these sentences from the article in exercise **1**. Notice the nouns in **bold**. Circle the nouns that name things you can count. Underline the nouns that name things you cannot count.

1. The **oil** from argan **nuts** is very important to the **people** of southwestern Morocco.

2. It adds **flavor** to **food**, prevents dry **skin**, and keeps **hair** soft.

3. Now some **companies** say that **acai** helps people lose **weight**.

B Work with a partner. Compare your answers from exercise **A**.

Goats in Morocco like argan nuts so much that they climb trees to find them.

UNIT 3   LESSON 2   **69**

LEARN

3.4 Count Nouns and Non-Count Nouns

Count Nouns		
	Noun	Verb
A	**doctor**	is coming.
Many	**doctors**	are coming.

Non-Count Nouns		
Noun	Verb	
Health	is	important.
The coffee	tastes	good.

1. Count nouns name things that can be counted. They have a singular and plural form.

   Use *a* or *an* before a singular count noun or an adjective + a singular count noun.

   I ate an **orange** for breakfast.
   I bought four **oranges** yesterday.

   a building
   an apartment
   a small apartment

2. Non-count nouns name things that cannot be counted. They do not have a plural form.

   Do not use *a* or *an* before a non-count noun.

   happiness, beauty, information, science, snow, water
   ✓ Alaska gets a lot of **snow**.
   ✗ Alaska gets a lot of <u>snows</u>.

   ✓ I need **information**.
   ✗ I need <u>an</u> information.

3. Use singular pronouns and verb forms with non-count nouns.

   ✓ Rice <u>is</u> cheap, but I don't like <u>it</u>.
   ✗ Rice <u>are</u> cheap, but I don't like <u>them</u>.

REAL ENGLISH

Some nouns can be count with one meaning and non-count with a different meaning.

*She goes to the gym three **times** a week.* (count)

*I don't have **time** to go to the gym today.* (non-count)

*We had three **exercises** for homework last night.* (count)

***Exercise** is important for good health.* (non-count)

4 Circle the correct word(s) to complete each sentence.

1. Some people use argan oil to keep their (**hair**) / **hairs** soft.

2. Some companies **says** / **say** that acai helps people lose weight.

3. Chinese medicine **is** / **are** over 2000 years old.

4. Science **is** / **are** a difficult subject, but I enjoy **it** / **them**.

5. The **store** / **stores** on that street are sometimes expensive.

6. **Apartment** / **An apartment** is a convenient place to live.

7. Do you have any **time** / **times** to help me with my assignment?

8. Hans goes to Germany three or four **time** / **times** a year.

9. This **information is / informations are** incorrect.

10. Last night's homework **was / were** very difficult.

11. That furniture **is / are** ugly. I don't know why I bought **it / them!**

12. Did you have any interesting **experience / experiences** on your vacation?

3.5 More Non-Count Nouns

Categories of Non-Count Nouns	
1. Some non-count nouns name a category of related items. The related items are often count nouns.	**clothing** (pants, sweaters, shoes) **fruit** (apples, oranges, bananas) **furniture** (tables, chairs, desks) **homework** (essays, exercises, assignments) **jewelry** (necklaces, rings, bracelets) **money** (nickels, dimes, quarters) **mail** (letters, packages, postcards) **weather** (hurricanes, storms, tornadoes)
2. Some non-count nouns name things that do not have separate parts or pieces that can be counted.	air, cheese, coffee, fish, flour, hair, ice, juice, meat, milk, oil, rice, skin, soup, sugar, tea, water, wind
3. Some non-count nouns are abstract nouns. An abstract noun names an idea, a feeling, or a quality.	advice, beauty, energy, experience, fun, happiness, health, help, honesty, intelligence, knowledge, love, nature, work
4. The names of subjects of study are usually non-count nouns.	biology, chemistry, geometry, history, math, science

5 Read the sentences. Circle the non-count nouns. Then write the number of the correct category above each non-count noun. (**1** = a category of related items, **2** = something that does not have separate parts, **3** = an abstract noun, **4** = a subject of study).

1. I'm taking six classes this semester, but I'm not taking (biology). ⁴

2. I have a lot of homework this weekend. I have an essay due on Monday and two exams on Tuesday.

3. Please do not bring food or drinks into the museum, and please turn off your cell phones.

4. My uncle often has cheese and crackers before dinner.

5. I eat a lot of fruit. I usually have a banana, an orange, and two apples every day.

6. The café across the street has great coffee and delicious pastries.

7. For some jobs, experience isn't very important.

8. I usually call my sister when I have a problem. She always gives me good advice.

9. We need to put money in the parking machine. It takes coins and dollar bills.

10. Sarah has a lot of energy. She works six days a week and takes classes at night.

11. Your mail is on the table. You got two letters and a package today.

PRACTICE

6 Circle the correct word(s) to complete the conversations.

Conversation 1

Lori: Did you go to the supermarket?

Stan: Yes I did, but look! (1) The (fruit is) / fruit are rotten.

Lori: Let's see . . . Oh, yes, (2) **it smells** / **they smell** bad.

Stan: The food in that store just (3) **isn't** / **aren't** good anymore. I've been there four or five (4) **time** / **times** recently and there is always a problem.

Lori: Wait a minute, though. The bananas (5) **look** / **looks** all right.

Stan: You're right. (6) **It does** / **They do.** But I'm going to take the rest back.

Conversation 2

Tina: Are you doing your physics (7) **homework** / **homeworks,** Brendan?

Brendan: Yes, but I need some (8) **help** / **helps.** I like physics, but (9) **it's** / **they're** difficult.

Tina: Well, I have some (10) **time** / **times** now. I can help you.

Brendan: Thanks, Tina. I don't understand this (11) **exercise** / **exercises.** These instructions (12) **isn't** / **aren't** very clear.

7 Complete the conversations with the nouns from the boxes. Make the nouns plural if necessary. You will need to use one noun twice.

advice	assignment	class	fun	homework	~~time~~

Alex: Hey, Bruce. Do you want to go to the basketball game tonight?

Bruce: No, sorry. I don't have (1) _____time_____ . I have a lot of
           (2) _____ tonight.

Alex: That's too bad. How many (3) _____ are you taking this semester?

Bruce: Five. And I have an (4) _____ for each of them.

Alex: Ugh! That is a lot. You need to study less and have more (5) _____.

Bruce: That seems like good (6) _____. Enjoy the game tonight!

energy	exercise	health	time

Ellen: Hi, Junko. Where are you going?

Junko: To the gym. I was sitting in a meeting all day today. I need to get some (7) _____

Ellen: Good for you! I'm so busy these days. I don't have (8) _____ to exercise. How often do you go to the gym?

Junko: Oh, about three (9) _____ a week. I often go early in the morning before wor

Ellen: Really? Do you feel tired afterwards?

Junko: No, I actually have more (10) _____ after I work out.

Ellen: That's great. And it's good for your (11) _____, too.

8 LISTEN, WRITE & SPEAK.

A Listen to an interview with a doctor about the health benefits of certain kinds of food. Check the kinds of food you hear.

☐ green vegetables   ☐ beans

☐ apples   ☐ lettuce

☐ oranges   ☐ squash

☐ cabbage   ☐ fish

☐ nuts   ☐ meat

▲ Vegetables provide almost everything the human body needs.

CD1-20

B What are the health benefits of the kinds of food you heard in exercise **A**? Listen again. Then write the name of each kind of food next to the correct health benefit(s).

1. important for our eyes _____

2. good for your skin _____

3. a great source of energy _____

4. strong muscles _____

5. Vitamin K _____

6. strong bones _____

C In your notebook, write five sentences about the different kinds of food in exercise **A**.

Squash is good for your eyes.

D Work with a partner. Compare your sentences from exercise **C**. Do you know of any other kinds of food that have special health benefits? Tell your partner.

A: *Carrots are good for your eyes.*   B: *Milk makes bones strong.*

9 APPLY.

A Think about the kinds of food and drink you buy. Write five items of food or drink in each column of the chart. Next to each item, write **C** if it is a count noun or **NC** if it is a non-count noun.

What items of food and drink do you buy?		
Often	Sometimes	Rarely
coffee (NC)	carrots (C)	soda (NC)

B Work with a partner. Talk about the items in your chart from exercise **A**. Pay attention to the verb forms and pronouns you use with count and non-count nouns.

A: *I sometimes buy carrots. I put them in salads.*   B: *Oh, I never buy them. They taste terrible!*

C In your notebook, write five or six sentences about the items in your chart from exercise **A**. Pay attention to verb forms and pronouns you use with count and non-count nouns.

EXPLORE

CD1-21

1 READ the article about sports science. Notice the words in **bold**.

The Science of Sports

Manchester, United Kingdom

When Manchester City soccer team won the English Premier League in 2012, there were **many** reasons for its success. The owners spent **a lot of** money on star players. The team also had a very good head coach. However, one reason for the team's success was less obvious. **A lot of** teams lose their star players for weeks or months because of injuries.[1] Thanks to sports science, Manchester City players did not get hurt frequently, and did not lose **much** playing time.

During practice each Manchester City player wears a GPS monitor.[2] Sports scientists then use the information provided by the monitor. They analyze each player's movements, effort, and recovery.[3] When practice is over, each player gets **some** vitamins. They also get a large **bottle** of a special drink. Each player's drink is created especially for him. The drinks help keep the players healthy.

Some teams still do not take sports science seriously. However, spending **a little** money on sports science can greatly improve a team's performance. Manchester City's story is proof[4] of this.

[1] **injury:** damage to a person's body
[2] **GPS monitor:** a small computer that records a person's movements
[3] **recovery:** return to usual condition
[4] **proof:** something that shows that something is true

Manchester City is one of the top soccer teams in England. Here the players celebrate their 2012 Premier League success.

2 CHECK. Choose the correct answer to complete each statement.

1. One reason for Manchester City's success in 2012 was _____.

   a. having good luck   b. buying star players   c. playing against weak teams

2. Compared to other teams, Manchester City players _____.

   a. were younger   b. did not play as much   c. had fewer injuries

3. Players wear GPS monitors to _____.

   a. record their performance   b. stop them from getting lost   c. make them work hard

4. After practice, each player gets _____.

   a. his favorite cold drink   b. a bottle of a special drink   c. a large bottle of water

3 DISCOVER. Complete the exercises to learn about the grammar in this lesson.

A Find these sentences in the article from exercise **1**. Write the missing words.

1. . . . there were **many** _____ for its success.

2. The owners spent **a lot of** _____ on star players.

3. **A lot of** _____ lose their star players for weeks or months because of injuries.

4. . . . Manchester City players did not get hurt frequently, and did not lose **much** _____.

5. However, spending **a little** _____ on sports science can greatly improve a team's performance.

B Look at each sentence in exercise **A**. Is the noun after the **bold** word(s) a count noun or a non-count noun? Write **C** for *count noun* or **NC** for *non-count noun* after each sentence.

C Work with a partner. Compare your answers in exercise **B**. Then choose the correct phrase to complete each statement.

1. We use *much* with _____.   a. count nouns   b. non-count nouns

2. We use *many* with _____.   a. count nouns   b. non-count nouns

3. We use *a little* with _____.   a. count nouns   b. non-count nouns

4. We use *a lot of* with _____.   a. count nouns   b. count nouns and non-count nouns

LEARN

3.6 Quantity Words with Count and Non-Count Nouns

Count Nouns		
	Quantity Words	
We have	some a few a lot of many	dishes. flowers. glasses.
We don't have	any a lot of many	

Non-Count Nouns		
	Quantity Words	
We have	some a little a lot of	money. time. work.
We don't have	any a lot of much	

1. Use *some* with count and non-count nouns in affirmative statements.	We need **some bananas**. I left **some fruit** on the table.
2. Use *any* with count and non-count nouns in negative statements.	Maria doesn't want **any oranges**. I don't have **any homework**.
3. Use *a few* and *many* with count nouns.	I have **a few questions**. Did you buy **many apples**?
4. Use *a little* and *much* with non-count nouns.	Give the plants **a little water**. We don't have **much homework** tonight.
5. Use *a lot of* with both count and non-count nouns.	We bought **a lot of vegetables**. She eats **a lot of sugar**.

4 Circle the correct word(s) to complete each statement or question.

1. Manchester City has **some** / **any** star players.

2. **Much** / **Many** soccer teams lose players because of injury.

3. I usually go to **a few** / **a little** soccer games every year.

4. Michel didn't score **any** / **some** goals in the last game.

5. We didn't get **much** / **many** exercise last week.

6. **A lot of** / **Much** people left the game early.

7. Sally bought **any** / **some** new running shoes yesterday.

8. Marie wants to go ride her bike when she has **a few** / **some** time.

9. Were there **much** / **many** people in your yoga class this morning?

10. I didn't find **many** / **much** mistakes in your assignment.

11. There is **a little** / **a few** ice cream left in the freezer.

12. Do you have **much** / **many** homework this weekend?

3.7 Measurement Words with Non-Count Nouns

Container	Measurement	Portion	Shape	Other
a **bag** of rice	a **gallon** of milk	a **piece** of cake	a **bar** of chocolate	a **piece** of jewelry
a **bottle** of juice	a **pint** of ice cream	a **piece** of pie	a **bar** of soap	a **piece** of mail
a **bowl** of cereal	a **pound** of meat	a **slice** of bread	a **loaf** of bread	
a **box** of cereal	a **quart** of oil	a **slice** of pizza	a **sheet** of paper	
a **can** of soda	a **tablespoon** of sugar		a **stick** of butter	
a **carton** of milk	a **teaspoon** of salt		a **tube** of toothpaste	
a **cup** of coffee				
a **glass** of water				
a **jar** of jam				

1. Use a measurement word + *of* to talk about a specific quantity of a non-count noun.	He drank a **bottle of juice**. I bought three **loaves of bread**.
2. Do not use a number before a non-count noun. Use a measurement word.	✓ Put two **bars of soap** in the bathroom. ✗ Put <u>two soap</u> in the bathroom.

5 Circle the correct measurement word to complete each sentence.

1. Clive cut three (**slices**) / **bars** of pizza and put them on his plate.

2. I need to buy a new **bar** / **tube** of toothpaste.

3. Do you have a **sheet** / **slice** of paper? I need to write a shopping list.

4. Would you like a **piece** / **loaf** of pie for dessert?

5. This cake uses six **bars** / **sticks** of butter.

6. We will need three **cartons** / **loaves** of bread for the party.

7. I put a new **bar** / **stick** of soap in the bathroom.

8. Helena had a **glass** / **bowl** of cereal for breakfast.

9. Yoko is wearing five different **slices** / **pieces** of jewelry today.

10. Add two **pounds** / **gallons** of milk to the shopping list, please.

11. I didn't get a single **piece** / **sheet** of mail today.

12. The mechanic put a **quart** / **carton** of oil in my car.

6 **SPEAK.** Work with a partner. Student B closes his or her book. Student A reads measurement words from chart 3.7. Student B says any correct noun for each measurement word. Switch roles after five or six measurement words.

A: *a can of . . .*

B: *a can of beans*

PRACTICE

7 Circle the correct word or phrase to complete the blog post.

Help! What Can I Eat?
[posted by runnergirl at 8:22pm, Jan. 2]

I am a runner, so I take (1) **many** / **much** / (**a lot of**) interest in my diet, but sometimes it can be so confusing! For years, doctors said, "You need to drink eight 8-ounce (2) **cans** / **glasses** / **tubes** of water every day," but now (3) **some** / **a little** / **any** researchers don't agree. Also, I hear about a new diet almost every day. "To lose weight and stay healthy, don't eat (4) **much** / **a few** / **any** grains." Or, "You can eat (5) **a little** / **any** / **some** grains, but (6) **not much** / **not many** / **any**. For example, if you eat a sandwich, use only one (7) **sheet** / **loaf** / **slice** of bread." How do I do that? I already know I shouldn't eat (8) **a little** / **many** / **much** sugar. I won't drink even one (9) **bowl** / **can** / **carton** of soda because there are around nine (10) **teaspoons** / **bars** / **pieces** of sugar in each can. But what about juice? I bought a (11) **jar** / **glass** / **bottle** of juice last week, and it had more sugar than the soda. Is that OK? Please help me.

8 **SPEAK.** Work with a partner. Discuss the advice you might give to the writer. Use quantity and measurement words with the kinds of food and drink she writes about in exercise **7**.

A: *I think it's a good idea to drink a lot of water.*

B: *I agree. The writer shouldn't drink much juice. It's better to eat a piece of fruit.*

9 Complete the sentences with the words or phrases from the box.

a little	any	bowl	much	pound
a lot of	bar	jar	piece	some

1. A calorie is a measure of energy in food. High-sugar foods have _____ a lot of _____ calories.

2. We need to buy food with protein. How about a small _____ of peanut butter and a _____ of sliced turkey from the deli?

3. If you don't want to eat _____ grains, then you can't eat that _____ of cereal or that _____ of cake!

4. There isn't _____ milk left. I'll get _____ later.

5. I used to eat a big _____ of milk chocolate every day. Now I only eat _____ dark chocolate occasionally.

10 LISTEN, WRITE & SPEAK.

A Work with a partner. Look at the different kinds of diets and food listed in the chart. What do you know about them? Tell your partner.

CD1-22

B Listen to three friends talk about their diets. Which kinds of food are OK to eat on each diet? Put ✓ in the chart if it is OK, put ✗ if it is not OK, and put **?** if you are not sure.

Do You Want to Eat Like a Caveman?				
Diet Comparisons	Low-Fat Diet	Vegetarian Diet	Vegan Diet	Paleo Diet
vegetables	✓	✓		✓
fruit		✓		
grain	✓		✓	
meat/protein			✗	
dairy				?
sugar				

C Compare your chart from exercise **B** with a partner. Then write six sentences about the diets in your notebook. Use *much, many, a few, a little, some,* and *a lot of.*

On the Paleo diet, people don't eat any grains. They eat some fruit, but they don't eat candy or other sweets.

D Share your sentences from exercise **C** with a partner. Then discuss any other information you remember from the conversation.

E Work in a small group. Discuss your thoughts and opinions about the different diets.

A: *I don't think low-fat diets are a good idea. I think eating a lot of sugar is a bigger problem.*

B: *I agree. Even organic sweets can have too much sugar. They seem healthy, but they aren't.*

The Paleo diet is sometimes called the "caveman diet." People believe you should eat whole foods, not processed or fast foods. (Graffiti art by Banksy, Los Angeles, CA).

11 EDIT & SPEAK.

A Read the paragraph about a fitness program. Find and correct seven more errors with quantity words and measurement words.

My New Fitness Program

       a lot of

I wasn't always fit. I used to eat ~~many~~ fast food, such as hamburgers and pizza, and I didn't get many exercise. I wasn't very happy. I wanted to lose any weight and feel fit and healthy. I didn't want to go on a special diet. Much diets have a lot of rules, and I want to enjoy a sheet of pizza or a jar of ice cream sometimes. Then, a little months ago, I found a great new fitness plan online. The plan lets me eat different kinds of food. I even have dessert a little times a week. I take a walk or ride my bike every morning. Now I'm fit and healthy, and I feel great!

B Work in a small group. Discuss the following questions.

1. Do you think the writer's fitness plan from exercise **A** sounds like a good one? Why, or why not?

2. Do you know about any special diets or fitness plans? Do you think they work? Why or why not?

12 APPLY.

A How fit and healthy are you? Complete the chart with sentences about some of your healthy and unhealthy habits. Use quantity words and measurement words.

Healthy Habits	Unhealthy Habits
I eat a lot of vegetables.	I have a bowl of ice cream for dessert every night.

B Work with a partner. Share the information from your chart in exercise **A**. Ask your partner questions for more information about his or her healthy or unhealthy habits.

A: *I eat a lot of vegetables.*

B: *What do you usually have for lunch?*

A: *A salad or a bowl of soup.*

C Form a group with another pair of students. Take turns talking about some of your partner's healthy and unhealthy habits. Use quantity words and measurement words.

Antonio gets a lot of exercise. He goes to the gym about five times a week. He also eats a lot of vegetables, but he usually drinks one or two cans of soda every day . . .

Charts **1**
3.4, 3.6

Complete the conversations with *a, an,* or *some.*

Conversation 1

Piet: I just bought (1) _____*a*_____ new bike.

Mauro: Oh, that's (2) _____ good idea.

Piet: Yes, I really need to get (3) _____ exercise.

Mauro: Hmm, well, I have (4) _____ time off tomorrow. Do you want to
             go for (5) _____ ride together?

Conversation 2

June: Would you like (6) _____ cup of coffee?

Belinda: No, thanks. I just had (7) _____ coffee about fifteen minutes ago.

June: Would you like (8) _____ glass of lemonade instead?

Belinda: Yes, that would be great.

June: I also have (9) _____ fruit. I have apples, oranges, and pears.

Belinda: I'd love (10) _____ orange. Thanks, June.

Charts **2**
3.1, 3.4–
3.6

Complete the sentences with one of the nouns in parentheses. Make the noun plural if
necessary.

1. This gym has many new _____*machines*_____ (machine / equipment).

2. My old gym didn't have much _____ (machine / equipment).

3. Taylor's children don't eat much _____ (fruit / apple).

4. How many _____ (fruit / apple) did you use in the pie?

5. I learned an interesting _____ (fact / information) about nutrition yesterday.

6. There was a lot of interesting _____ (fact / information) on the website.

7. My doctor gave me a few good _____ (advice / suggestion) about my diet.

8. Doctor Carson didn't give me much _____ (advice / suggestion) about exercise.

Charts **3**
3.4, 3.6

Circle the correct word(s) to complete each statement or question.

1. Do you play **much** / **many** different sports?

2. My father rides his bike **a few** / **a little** times a week.

3. **Much** / **Many** people like to exercise in the morning.

4. I don't take **any** / **some** vitamins, but I have a healthy diet.

5. Elsie spends **a lot of** / **many** time at the gym. She's very fit.

6. Only **a few / a little** people were at the gym last night. It was almost empty.

7. She gave us **any / some** advice about yoga classes.

8. I found **a few / a little** information about that diet online, but not much.

9. I asked Paula about fitness classes. She gave me **any / some** good suggestions.

10. How **much / many** pieces of fruit do you usually eat a day?

Charts **4**   **EDIT.** Read the information about the health of Siamese crocodiles. Find and correct eight
3.4–3.6   more errors with count and non-count nouns and quantity words.

Cardamom
Mountains,
Cambodia

Why the Health of Siamese Crocodiles Matters

v Many
~~Much~~ species of wild animals are dying out.¹ This is huge problem. The healths of one

group of living things often depends on another group of living things. This is true for

humans, too.

An good example of this is in Cambodia. In 2000, scientist Jenny Daltry took a team of

scientist into Cambodia's Cardamom Mountains. She wanted to make a list of the different

kinds of animals there. Daltry's team discovered much Siamese crocodiles there. There

were 150!

The crocodiles live in marshes. Marshes are soft wet areas of land with much plants.

The crocodiles help keep the marsh areas wet and alive. They dig mud² out of the marshes

and help keep a water there, even during the dry season. As a result, other animals have a

good source of waters. This is also helpful to humans.

¹ **die out:** disappear forever
² **mud:** a mixture of earth and water

▼ Siamese crocodiles are in
danger of dying out.

CD1-23-27

5 **LISTEN & SPEAK.**

A Listen to five people talk about their fitness activities. Match the information in Column B with the correct speaker in Column A. Write the letters on the lines.

Column A	Column B
Speaker 1 _C_	a. plays many different sports
Speaker 2 _____	b. enjoys a dangerous sport
Speaker 3 _____	c. friends do other sports
Speaker 4 _____	d. roommate's father is a coach
Speaker 5 _____	e. is using someone else's bike
	f. gets a lot of injuries
	g. doesn't do much running
	h. isn't interested in team sports

B Work with a partner. Compare your answers from exercise **A**. Then talk about each of the speakers. Use the information from exercise **A** and any other information you remember.

Speaker 1 is starting a new sport. She rode her friend's bike three times last week.

C Look at the list of sports and other fitness activities from exercise **A** in the box below. Which of these activities do you enjoy? Do you like to watch any of these sports or activities? What do you know about them? Discuss your answers with your partner. Use quantity words, *another*, *other*, and *the other* when appropriate.

basketball	football	skiing	volleyball
cycling	running	swimming	yoga

I swim a few times a week. It's really good exercise.
I also like to watch football. It's interesting, but there
are a lot of rules. I don't understand many of them!
I like a lot of other sports, too...

▶ A group of athletes competing in a triathlon

83

1 **READ & NOTICE THE GRAMMAR.**

A Work with a partner. What do you think is the best way to stay fit? Discuss your ideas with your partner. Then read the text.

Staying Fit

Exercise is important if you want to stay fit. You don't need any fancy machines or a lot of expensive clothing. The best exercise, in my opinion, is to take a long walk every day. Walking is inexpensive, easy, and safe.

All you need for a walk are comfortable shoes, appropriate clothing, and 30 minutes to an hour of your time. If it's warm and you live near a beach, you don't even need any shoes! Walking takes very little time and money.

A walk is also a safe way to stay fit. Often people get hurt when they exercise. Some people run several miles a week and then complain of knee or back pain. Other people do a lot of drills[1] and then ache for a week. Walking is relaxing and does not put a lot of stress on your body. It provides exercise without additional pain. Walking keeps your body—*and* your mind—healthy. Go take a walk!

[1] **drill:** a practice exercise that you repeat again and again

---

GRAMMAR FOCUS

In the text, the writer uses singular and plural count nouns and non-count nouns both with and without adjectives and quantity words. Notice the articles and quantity words.

Count Nouns	Singular with *a/an*:	The best exercise, . . . is to take **a** long **walk** . . .
	Plural:	All you need . . . are comfortable **shoes** . . .
	Quantity word:	You don't need **any** fancy **machines** . . .
Non-Count Nouns	(No *a/an*):	**Exercise** is important if you want to stay fit.
	Quantity word:	You don't need . . . **a lot of** expensive **clothing**.

B Read the text in exercise **A** again. Complete the chart with count and non-count nouns. Include possessive adjectives or quantity words. Find at least one more for each category.

Nouns	(Adjective) + Noun (with or without *a/an*)	Quantity Word + (Adjective) + Noun
Count	your body	any shoes
Non-Count	The best exercise	little time

C In exercise **A**, the writer states an opinion and the reasons for it. Then she uses facts to support her reasons. Complete the chart with her reasons and supporting facts.

Opinion: *The best way to stay fit is to take a long walk.*
Reason 1: It's easy and inexpensive.
Supporting Facts: 1. You only need a comfortable pair of shoes and some appropriate clothing.   2.
Reason 2:
Supporting Facts:

2 BEFORE YOU WRITE.

A Work with a partner. What type of exercise or diet do you feel is best? Discuss your ideas with a partner.

B Make a chart in your notebook like the one in exercise **1C**. Complete the chart with your opinion about a good way to stay fit and your supporting facts. Use the ideas you and your partner discussed.

3 WRITE your opinion about a good way to stay fit. Write three paragraphs and give at least two reasons for your opinion. Be sure to give support. Use the information in your chart from exercise **2B** and the text in exercise **1A** to help you.

WRITING FOCUS   Subject-Verb Agreement with Count and Non-Count Nouns

When using nouns in the subject position, be sure to use the correct singular or plural form of the verb. With non-count nouns as subjects, use a singular verb.

Singular Count:	*A **walk is** also a safe way to stay fit.*
Plural Count:	*Often, **people get** hurt when they exercise.*
Non-Count:	***Exercise is** important if you want to stay fit.*

---

4 SELF ASSESS. Read your paragraphs and underline the count nouns, non-count nouns, and quantity words. Then use the checklist to assess your work.

☐   I used *a* or *an* before singular count nouns. [3.4]

☐   I did not use *a* or *an* before plural count nouns and non-count nouns. [3.4]

☐   I used *some* in affirmative statements and *any* in negative statements. [3.6]

☐   I used the correct singular or plural form of verbs. [WRITING FOCUS]

4 Going Places

Pronouns, Prepositions, and Articles

▶ Cars speed past a cowboy in North Dakota, USA.

EXPLORE

CD1-28

1 READ the conversation between Javier and his friends. Notice the words in **bold**.

Getting Around Mexico City

Mexico City, Mexico

Peter: Thanks for meeting **us** at the airport, Javier. **It**'s very kind **of you**.

Javier: No problem, Peter. **I**'m just happy that **you** and Kate are back in Mexico City. How was **your** flight?

Kate: **It** was great, thanks, Javier. The only problem was that **we** wanted to sit together, but at first the airline put the children by **themselves**. **It** took a long time to find a solution, but in the end, **we** sat next to each other. Anyway, **it**'s so good to be here with **you** again.

Peter: The city looks just like **it** did when **we** visited **you** and Alicia a few years ago, but **I** don't remember all these bikes. Where did **they** come from?

Javier: Well, bikes are quite popular here now. People use **them** to commute to work.

Peter: Hmm, I used to ride **my** bike to work, but then **I** had an accident and hurt **myself** quite badly.

Javier: I remember . . . These bikes are mostly pretty basic. **I**'m sure **yours** went a lot faster.

Kate: Yes, **it** did. **I** was glad when **he** stopped riding.

Javier: Well, people here won't leave **their** bikes at home any time soon. Bikes make driving more difficult, but **they** are good for the environment.

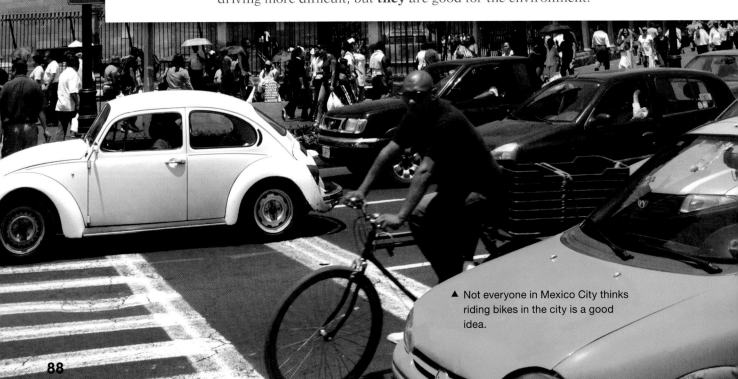

▲ Not everyone in Mexico City thinks riding bikes in the city is a good idea.

▲ Traffic on Paseo de la Reforma, Mexico City, Mexico

2 **CHECK.** Match each person with the correct information from the conversation. Some statements may be true for more than one person.

1. Javier _____   a. was hurt in a bike accident

2. Kate _____   b. was happy when Peter stopped riding bikes

3. Peter _____ _____   c. lives in Mexico City

4. Alicia _____   d. asks about the bikes in Mexico City

3 **DISCOVER.** Complete the exercises to learn about the grammar in this lesson.

A Look at the sentences from the conversation in exercise **1**. Who or what does each underlined word refer to? Write your answer on the line.

1. How was your flight? _____Peter and Kate_____

2. It was great, thanks. . . . _____

3. . . . I don't remember all these bikes. _____

4. People use them to commute to work. _____

5. Well, people here won't leave their bikes at home. . . . _____

B Write each underlined word from exercise **A** in the correct column in the chart.

Position in Sentence		
Subject Pronoun	Object Pronoun	Possessive Adjective
		your

LEARN

4.1 Subject and Object Pronouns

Subject Pronoun	Verb	
I You He She It We You They	arrived	late.

Subject	Verb	Object Pronoun
John	visited	me. you. him. her. it. us. you. them.

1. A pronoun takes the place of a noun or noun phrase. Subject pronouns are used as subjects.	**Elena** enjoys driving. **She** uses her car a lot. **Tom and I** went on vacation together. **We** went to Portugal. **Your suitcase** arrived. **It**'s in your room.
2. Object pronouns are used as objects of verbs or objects of prepositions.	Object of Verb: I bought **a new bike**. Do you like **it**? Object of Preposition: This ticket is for **José**. I bought it for **him**.

4 Circle the correct pronoun to complete each sentence.

1. Javier had a busy day. (**He**)/ **Him** went to the airport to meet his friends.

2. Javier went to school with **they** / **them** years ago.

3. Did you bring your passport? You can't travel without **it** / **them**.

4. Kate couldn't find her suitcase. **Her** / **She** left **it** / **them** at home.

5. Peter and Kate have two children. **They** / **Them** are both girls.

6. Peter visits Mexico City every year. **He** / **Him** likes **it** / **them** a lot.

7. My husband and I ride bikes to work. It saves **us** / **we** a lot of money.

5 Complete the sentences. Use the correct subject or object pronoun.

1. The traffic in Mexico City is heavy. _____It_____ is very slow during rush hour.

2. Some people think cyclists are a problem because there are too many of _____.

3. I drove to work with Kate. Later I met _____ at the gym.

4. These are Mario's car keys. Can you give them to _____, please?

5. I'm going for a bike ride. Do you want to come with _____?

6. This is our new car. _____ was expensive, but we love _____.

7. You look tired, Rosa. Do _____ want to go home now?

8. We were driving to work when the police stopped _____ .

4.2 Possessive Adjectives and Pronouns

Possessive Adjective	Noun			Possessive Pronoun
My Your His Her Its Our Your Their	coat	is black.	This coat is	mine. yours. his. hers. its. ours. yours. theirs.

1. Use a possessive adjective before a noun to show that the noun belongs to someone or something.	Joe bought **his** plane ticket yesterday. The dog pushed **its** bowl across the floor.
2. Use a possessive pronoun in place of a possessive adjective + a noun.	You can use **my bike. Mine** is the blue one. That's not **your coat. Yours** is in the closet.
3. Possessive pronouns can be used as a. the subject of a verb b. the object of a verb c. the object of a preposition	a. A: Where are the bikes? B: **His** is outside. **Hers** is downstairs. b. I found their keys, but I can't find **ours**. c. Our car is nice, but look at **theirs**.
4. **Be careful!** *Its* and *it's* sound the same. *Its* is a possessive adjective, and *it's* is the contraction of *it is* or *it has*.	The team won **its** first game. A: Where is your umbrella? B: **It's** on the table.
5. **Be careful!** *Their, there,* and *they're* sound the same. *Their* is a possessive adjective. *There* refers to a place. *They're* is the contraction of *they are*.	They found **their** coats. **There** are two coats here. A: Where are the coats? B: **They're** on the chair.

6 Circle the correct word(s) to complete each sentence.

1. A: Is this **you** / **your** skateboard?

   B: No, it's not **me** / **mine**. I think it belongs to Gary.

2. **His** / **Him** car wouldn't start yesterday, so Carol let **him** / **he** use **her** / **hers**.

3. We moved here from Ohio last month. **Our** / **Ours** new apartment is beautiful!

4. My friends are unhappy because the neighbors' car is newer than **them** / **theirs**.

5. A: Is this bike **yours** / **you**?

   B: No, **my** / **mine** is green. It's over there.

6. We are going to buy a smaller house. **Ours** / **Our** is too big for us now.

7. Frank arrived here first. I parked my car behind **theirs** / **his**.

7 Complete the conversations. Use *its, it's, their, there,* or *they're.*

Conversation 1

Joan: (1) _____There_____ 's a postcard here from Hawaii.

Steve: Hawaii? I wonder who (2) _____ from.

Joan: Don't you remember? Mick and Tina are (3) _____ now. This year her company is having (4) _____ yearly meeting in Honolulu.

Steve: Oh that's right! Well, I'm sure (5) _____ having a great time. It was always (6) _____ dream to visit Hawaii.

Conversation 2

Phil: I want to e-mail my friends, but I can't remember (7) _____ e-mail addresses. I wrote them in my notebook. Have you seen it?

Mandy: I don't know. What does it look like?

Phil: (8) _____ a small book. (9) _____ cover is light blue.

Mandy: Oh, I think (10) _____ over there, on the shelf by the window.

4.3   Reflexive Pronouns

Subject	Verb	Reflexive Pronoun
I		myself.
You		yourself.
He		himself.
She	hurt	herself.
It		itself.
We		ourselves.
You		yourselves.
They		themselves.

1. Use a reflexive pronoun when the subject and the object of the verb are the same.	✓ I introduced **myself** to the group. ✗ I introduced <u>me</u> to the group.
2. Verbs that are often followed by a reflexive pronoun include *cut, enjoy, feel sorry for, hurt, take care of,* and *tell.*	Did you **cut yourself** on the broken glass? We **enjoyed ourselves** at the party.
3. *By* + reflexive pronoun means "alone" or "without any help."	I live **by myself**. The TV turns off **by itself**.

8 Complete each sentence with the correct reflexive pronoun.

1. Hi, Stella! Did you enjoy _____yourself_____ on your vacation?

2. My brother cut _____ when he was working on his car.

3. Bye, Mike and Linda! It was nice to see you both. Take care of _____!

4. When you are on vacation, set the timer so the lights turn on and off by _____.

5. I felt sorry for _____ when I fell and lost the race.

6. When we got home from the trip, we made _____ comfortable in front of the TV

7. There was an amazing car at the auto show. It actually drives _____!

8. Her friends were busy, so she went to Mexico by _____.

PRACTICE

9 Circle the correct words to complete the conversations.

Conversation 1

Bonnie: Are these keys (1) **your** / **yours**?

Hal: Yes. What's the problem?

Bonnie: (2) **Your** / **Yours** car is blocking the driveway, and I can't get (3) **my** / **mine** out.
I need to move (4) **itself** / **it**.

Hal: Wait a minute, then.

Bonnie: I can't wait. If I'm late for work again, (5) **mine** / **my** boss will fire (6) **me** / **myself**.

Conversation 2

Wendy: Thanks for coming to the airport with me. I don't like to wait by (7) **mine** / **myself**.

Nick: That's OK. When are (8) **you** / **your** parents arriving?

Wendy: (9) **Their** / **There** flight is late, I'm afraid. (10) **Its** / **It's** delayed for another hour.

Nick: No problem. Where do you want to wait for (11) **they** / **them**?

Wendy: Let's get something to eat and enjoy (12) **ourselves** / **yourselves**.

10 Complete the sentences with the correct pronoun(s) or possessive adjective(s).

1. Dale broke ___his___ foot last week. Now _____'s sitting at home and feeling sorry
   for _____.

2. _____ need a photo of _____ for my passport. Can you take one for _____?

3. My car uses much less gas than _____. Why don't you get one like _____?

4. Margaret visits Mr. and Mrs. Cho every Sunday. This Sunday, she knocked on _____ door
   three times, but _____ didn't hear _____.

5. My neighbor's cat isn't feeling well. Yesterday it fell out of a tree and hurt _____. Today it
   didn't eat _____ food.

6. We were on a business trip, so the company paid for _____ hotel. We stay in cheaper
   places when we pay for _____.

7. _____'m sorry. I can't lend you _____ camera. I need _____ tonight. Ask Jim if he
   will lend you _____.

8. A: Do you drive to work by _____?
   B: No, I go with Susan. _____ is a coworker. We drive in my car for a week, and then the
      next week we drive in _____.

11 Complete Eva's story about a cruise she took with her husband and friends. Use a correct pronoun (subject, object, or reflexive) or a possessive adjective.

A Cruise to Remember

A couple of years ago, (1) _____my_____ husband Ricardo and

(2) _____ went on a cruise in southern Europe, on the Mediterranean Sea.

(3) _____ went with (4) _____ friends Aaron and Lara. They

love cruises, so we agreed to try one with (5) _____. The trip was fantastic!

The weather was perfect almost every day. (6) _____ rained only once. Also,

the tour company arranged special activities for (7) _____ at each stop.

From what I remember, (8) _____ enjoyed ourselves very much!

12 LISTEN.

A Look at the map on page 95 and listen to Ricardo tell his story about the cruise. Notice the numbers on the map. After you listen, write the name of the person next to the number where he or she had a problem.

1. _____   3. _____

2. _____   4. _____

B Complete the chart with information from Ricardo's story. Listen again. Then share your sentences with a partner.

Name	What happened? Why?
1. Ricardo	He was seasick. He forgot _____.
2.	
3.	
4.	

13 APPLY.

A Work in a small group. Take turns telling one good or bad thing that happened on a trip you have taken. Complete the chart with information about what happened to each classmate.

Name	What happened?
1.	
2.	
3.	
4.	

B Write two or more sentences about each person in your group. Use the correct pronouns and possessive adjectives.

Dory went to the beach one day with some friends. While they were in the water, they saw a shark. It was swimming near them, but it swam away.

EXPLORE

CD1-34

1 READ this page from a travel website. Notice the words in **bold**.

Diving in the Bahamas

For many years, the Bahamas, a group of islands **in the Atlantic**, has been a popular vacation spot. The islands attract a lot of divers. Divers **from many countries** come to see the wide variety of fish **in the islands' clear waters**. The fish differ **from season to season**. Spring is the best time to see mahi-mahi. **In October**, manta rays are more common. **In the winter**, divers may even see hammerhead sharks.

For experienced divers, the blue holes of the Bahamas are especially interesting. **From above**. these blue holes look like deep blue ponds.[1] In fact, they are entrances **to underwater caves**.

There are over 1000 of these blue holes **in the Bahamas**. They are one of the most unusual environments **on Earth**. **At the surface**, there is a thin layer[2] of fresh rainwater. **Below that**, there is salt water because the caves open **to the sea**.

[1] **pond:** a body of water smaller than a lake
[2] **layer:** a thickness or covering

▼ A great hammerhead shark, Bahamas Islands

2 CHECK. Choose the correct answer for each question.

1. Where are the Bahamas?

   a. in South America   b. in the Pacific Ocean   c. in the Atlantic Ocean

2. In the Bahamas, divers can see _____.

   a. the same fish all year round   b. mahi-mahi in the spring   c. manta rays in the spring

3. The blue holes of the Bahamas are entrances to _____.

   a. caves on the beach   b. caves in the mountains   c. caves under the water

3 DISCOVER. Complete the exercises to learn about the grammar in this lesson.

A Look at the phrases in bold from the website in exercise **1**. Write each phrase in the correct column of the chart.

Phrases about Time	Phrases about Place
for many years	in the Atlantic

B Circle the word at the beginning of each phrase you wrote in the chart. Which words appear in both columns? Which words appear in only one column?

▼ Divers explore an underwater cave in the Bahamas.

LEARN

4.4 Prepositions of Time

1. Prepositions are usually part of a prepositional phrase. A prepositional phrase consists of a preposition and an object of a preposition. The object of a preposition is a noun or noun phrase.	Our train leaves **in the morning**.
2. Prepositions of time tell when something happens.	She took her vacation **in the summer**. **On Sunday** he slept late.
3. Use *at* with clock times and with *noon, night,* and *midnight*.	In some countries, dinner begins **at nine o'clock**. He goes out **at night**.
4. Use *in* with periods of time, including: a. parts of a day (except *night*) b. seasons c. months d. years	a. Sam leaves for work **in the morning**. b. We usually take a vacation **in the summer**. c. School starts **in September**. d. I was born **in 1999**.
5. Use *on* with dates and days of the week.	My sister was born **on July 15**. I'll see you **on Sunday**.
6. Other common prepositions of time are *for, from . . . to/until,* and *during*.	We took lessons **for** three years. Stefan studies **from** six o'clock **until** ten o'clock. She likes to talk **during** class.

4 Circle the correct preposition to complete each sentence.

1. Jenny goes on vacation **for** / **in** two weeks every summer.

2. This year she decided to go **on** / **in** August.

3. She started looking at destinations online **at** / **in** the spring.

4. She took diving lessons **on** / **in** Saturdays from 9:00 **until** / **for** noon.

5. She printed her plane ticket **on** / **in** August 11 **on** / **at** midnight.

6. Her flight left **in** / **at** five **in** / **at** the evening.

7. She was on the plane **for** / **on** almost eight hours.

8. She arrived at her hotel late **in** / **at** night.

5 **SPEAK.** Work with a partner. Complete the statements so they are true about you. Then read your sentences to your partner. Ask your partner questions.

1. Last year, I went to _____. I was there for _____ days.

2. My birthday is on _____. I was born in _____.

3. In my country, students start school in _____. The school day starts at _____ and ends at _____.

4.5 Prepositions of Place and Direction

1. Prepositions of place tell where someone or something is.	The teacher is standing **near the window**. The parking lot is **behind the restaurant**. Let's meet **outside the cafeteria**. My car broke down **under the bridge**. I saw my friend **across the room**.
2. a. Use *in* to talk about a place inside any kind of container. b. Use *in* with names of countries, states, and cities.	a. Put the book **in a box**. I left the keys **in the car**. b. He lives **in China**. They have an apartment **in Shanghai**.
3. a. Use *on* to talk about a position on the surface of something. b. Use *on* with names of streets.	a. Put the book **on the shelf**. I left the keys **on the table**. b. The store is **on Fifth Avenue**. I got lost **on Brookline Street**.
4. a. Use *at* to talk about a specific point. b. Use *at* with addresses.	a. Go left **at the stop sign**. b. My brother lives **at 29 School Street**.
5. Prepositions of direction tell us which way someone or something is going.	We walked **toward the post office**. I drove **from Portland to Seattle**. I saw Mario on his bike **between the art and biology buildings**.

6 Complete the sentences. Use *in, on,* or *at.*

1. Michaela is on vacation __in__ Ireland.

2. The travel guide is _____ the table.

3. I live _____ 21 Millbrook Road.

4. There is a restaurant _____ Walker Street.

5. Your coat is _____ the closet.

6. Barbara was very busy _____ work yesterday.

7. Were you _____ class this morning?

8. Turn right _____ the next traffic light.

> **REAL ENGLISH**
>
> A few common phrases with prepositions do not have *a/an/the* before the noun: *in class, in bed, at home, at school,* and *at work.*
>
> *I stayed **in bed** until 11:00 a.m. I'll call him later. He's **at work** now.*

7 Complete the sentences. Use the correct preposition from the box.

across	~~behind~~	between	from	near	outside	toward	under

1. I want to take your photo with the lake _____behind_____ you.

2. The sun was too hot for Fiona, so she sat _____ a beach umbrella.

3. My last apartment was _____ the street from a restaurant. It was noisy.

4. Nilesh's hometown is _____ two rivers.

5. We couldn't find a taxi, so we started walking _____ the station.

6. This road goes _____ the coast to the top of the mountain.

7. Jill was surprised when someone left flowers _____ her front door.

8. The police station is on Lewis Street _____ the library.

PRACTICE

REAL ENGLISH

In most sentences, 'place' comes before 'time.'

*Jemila went to Brazil **in January**.*

But time expressions can also come at the beginning of a sentence.

***In January**, Jemila went to Brazil.*

8 SPEAK.

A Circle the correct preposition to complete the conversation about Ria's trip.

Kim: Hi, Ria! How was your trip (1)(to)/ at / on Indonesia?

Ria: It was great. Thanks!

Kim: Were you there (2) **during** / **for** / **until** a long time?

Ria: Yes, I was there (3) **from** / **at** / **on** February 28th (4) **for** / **during** / **until** March 15th.

Kim: Wow! What cities did you visit?

Ria: Well, I started (5) **on** / **at** / **in** Jakarta. I stayed (6) **on** / **at** / **in** my friend's place (7) **from** / **until** / **for** a few days. Then I traveled by bus (8) **from** / **toward** / **through** Jakarta (9) **on** / **to** / **until** Bandung. It was beautiful in Bandung, but the traffic was terrible.

Kim: I heard they drive (10) **on** / **at** / **near** the left side of the street. Is that true?

Ria: Yes, and walking (11) **under** / **across** / **between** the street can be dangerous! Cars in the U.S. stop (12) **behind** / **at** / **on** stop lights, but in Bandung I often had to walk (13) **over** / **between** / **under** cars. I was scared until I learned the secret.

Kim: Really? What's the secret?

Ria: Well, first, you put one foot (14) **at** / **on** / **over** the street and wave your hand. Then you walk quickly. People are coming (15) **on** / **toward** / **to** you in their cars, but they slow down when they see you. Easy!

B Work with a partner. Ask and answer the questions about your country. Use prepositions of time and place.

1. Is crossing the street easy? Describe the process.

   Crossing the street is very easy in my country. First, you stop at the corner. Then you wait for a few minutes, until the light is green. When it turns green, you walk to the other side.

2. How do you usually travel to your friends' houses?

3. How do you usually get to another city or town?

9 Complete the phone conversation. Use the words and phrases from the box. Add a correct preposition before each word or phrase.

| a new house | three o'clock | the morning | Monday |
| 24 Oak Road | ~~May 3rd~~ | the airport | night |

Alex: Hi Basma! I'm looking at a flight that arrives (1) _____ on May 3rd _____ .

Can you pick me up (2) _____?

Basma: Sure. What time?

Alex: Well, my plane arrives (3) _____ (4) _____ .

Basma: What? I'll be asleep. Why are you flying so late (5) _____?

Alex: Because the ticket is half price.

Basma: Sorry, but I have to work (6) _____ morning. That might be hard.

Alex: That's OK. I can get a taxi. What is your new address? Didn't you just move

(7) _____?

Basma: I live (8) _____ .

Alex: Great! See you soon. Bye!

10 EDIT. Read the article about an unusual type of vacation. Find and correct seven more errors with prepositions of time, place, and direction.

On the Honey Road

Balyolu (pronounced bal-yoll-oo) is Turkish for "honey road." It is also the name of an unusual tour ~~on~~ ↙in northeast Turkey.

Catherine Jaffee is a woman from Colorado in the United States. At 2008, she went to Turkey and traveled for two years. When she reached Kars, a historic region on Turkey, she thought of an idea for a tour. About 900 years ago, Kars was in the Silk Road, an important trading route from Europe and China. Kars was an important trading center in that time. Jaffee became fascinated by the way people in Kars earn their living: beekeeping and making honey.

Jaffee created a travel experience for visitors that also helped local people. On a Balyolu tour, travelers walked several miles a day at seven days. They passed under many areas with beautiful scenery. Along the way, the walkers met beekeepers and their families and tasted different kinds of honey. It was the perfect trip for anyone with a sweet tooth!

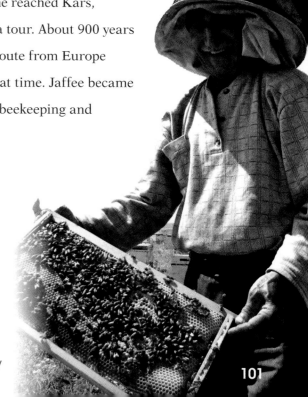

▶ A beekeeper in Turkey

11 **LISTEN** to a student's presentation about a creative- writing vacation in France. Answer each question with a prepositional phrase of time or place.

1. Where did the course take place? _____ in Paris _____

2. When did the course begin? _____

3. How long did the course last? _____

4. Where did Melanie stay? _____

5. When did the students get together? _____

6. Where did they sit to discuss the day's work? _____ or _____

7. Where did the students spend time observing life? _____

8. When did Melanie feel like a student? _____

12 APPLY.

A Work in a group of three. Complete the chart. Ask and answer the questions about a place you have visited. Then ask and answer the questions about your classmates. Use preposition: of time and place.

	You	_____	_____
1. Where did you go?			
2. When did you go?			
3. How long were you there?			
4. Where did you stay?			
5. What was special about your trip?			

B Write about your classmates' trips. Use the chart in exercise **A** as a guide. Be sure to use prepositions correctly.

Martina went to some beautiful mountains in Slovakia a few years ago. She went in the summer. She was there for two weeks While she was there, she stayed in a cabin on a lake and spent her days looking at the beautiful scenery. She also swam, hiked, and had a great time.

EXPLORE

CD1-36

1   READ the article about an adventure in Alaska and the Yukon. Notice the words in **bold**.

Andrew Skurka's Alaska-Yukon Expedition

On March 14, 2010, Andrew Skurka walked out of the town of Kotzebue in northwest Alaska to begin an amazing expedition.[1] He was starting **a** journey of 4678 miles (7528.5 km). He took skis and **an** inflatable raft[2] with him. His plan was to complete **the** journey mostly by hiking and skiing. He used **the** raft to cross rivers. He did not take any trains or ride in any cars or buses on his route. **The** route took him through several national parks, and he saw **some** spectacular[3] sights along **the** way.

Skurka did not carry all of his supplies with him. Instead, he got supplies at villages along **the** way.

▲ Extreme trekker Andrew Skurka in Wrangell-Saint Elias National Park, Alaska

The loneliest part of **the** trip was in **the** north. There, Skurka traveled 657 miles and didn't see **a** single village or road. During his journey, he faced **some** serious challenges. For example, in some places **the** snow was very deep and too soft for skiing. However, he managed to complete **the** journey. On September 5, 2010, he arrived back in Kotzebue. His trip took 176 days.

[1] **expedition:** a well-organized trip taken for a special purpose

[2] **inflatable raft:** a small, flat boat that you fill with air

[3] **spectacular:** wonderful, exciting

2 CHECK. Read the statements about Andrew Skurka. Circle **T** for *true* or **F** for *false*.

1. He used a large boat.   **T**   **F**

2. His journey was 2500 miles.   **T**   **F**

3. He stopped at villages along the way.   **T**   **F**

4. He didn't travel through any national parks.   **T**   **F**

5. There was a lot of snow in some places.   **T**   **F**

6. His journey took a year.   **T**   **F**

3 DISCOVER. Work with a partner. Look at the pairs of sentences from the reading on page 103. Notice the words in bold. Why does the second sentence in each pair use *the* instead of *a* or *an*? Discuss your answer with your classmates and teacher.

a. He was starting **a** journey of 4678 miles. His plan was to complete **the** journey mostly by hiking and skiing.

b. He took skis and **an** inflatable raft with him. He used **the** raft to cross rivers.

▲ Andrew Skurka slides across the ice in his inflatable raft.

LEARN

4.6 Indefinite and Definite Articles

Indefinite Articles: *A, An, Some, (Ø)*			
Singular Count Nouns	She needs	**a**	coat.
	He has	**an**	idea.
Plural Count Nouns	We bought	**some**	peaches.
	I like	Ø	apples.
Non-Count Nouns	She doesn't drink	Ø	tea.

Definite Article: *The*			
Singular Count Nouns	We looked at	**the**	map.
Plural Count Nouns	She opened	**the**	packages.
Non-Count Nouns	I washed	**the**	fruit.

1. Use the indefinite article *a* or *an* to talk about a person, place, or thing that is not specific.	She is at **a party**. (We don't know which party.) Where can I buy **an umbrella**? (I want to buy any umbrella, not a specific one.)
Remember: Use *a* before nouns or adjectives that begin with a consonant sound. Use *an* before nouns or adjectives that begin with a vowel sound.	**a** *college* **an** *adventure* **a** *university* **an** *important point*
2. Use *some* or no article before plural count nouns or non-count nouns to talk about something that is not specific.	There are **some motorcycles** in the parking lot. I need to buy **some gas**. He likes motorcycles. We need gas.
3. Use the definite article *the* to talk about a specific person, place, or thing.	My English course ends next week. I'm studying for **the test**. (We know which test.)
4. Use *the* before a noun when a. there is only one person, place, or thing b. the speaker and listener are thinking about the same thing c. the speaker or listener has mentioned the person, place, or thing before	a. Why are you looking at **the sun**? (There is only one sun.) b. Did you feed **the baby**? (The speaker and listener know which baby.) c. There's a woman with a child outside. **The child** is laughing. (The speaker has mentioned the child before.)

4 Circle the correct article or Ø for *no article* to complete each sentence.

1. Andrew Skurka had problems with **the** / **a** snow during his trip.

2. Skurka took **a** / **some** raft with him.

3. **A** / **The** route of Skurka's expedition went through eight national parks.

4. He bought **some** / **a** supplies for his journey.

5. **Some** / **The** trip took 176 days.

6. A: I'm flying to Alaska tonight.

    B: Really? When do you have to be at **Ø** / **the** airport?

7. **A** / **The** plane tickets to Alaska were very expensive.

8. We need to buy **a** / **some** map of the area.

4.7 Generalizations vs. Specific References

	Generalization	Specific Reference
Singular Nouns	**A bike** is a cheap form of transportation.	**The orange bike** is my sister's.
Plural Nouns	**Bikes** don't use any gas.	**The bikes** are in the garage.

1. A generalization is a statement about all members of a group. To make a generalization, use a singular count noun with *a* or *an* or a plural noun.	**A city** is a great place to live. **Cities** are great places to live.
2. Use *a* or *an* to make a generalization with a singular count noun.	**A car** is the best way to get around. **An icy street** is dangerous.
3. Use no article to make a generalization with a non-count noun or a plural noun.	**Chocolate** is delicious. **Vacations** are relaxing.
4. **Remember:** Use *the* to refer to a specific person, place, or thing.	**The restaurant** on Bay Street is very popular. **The people** at my office are very friendly.

5 Change each generalization from singular to plural.

1. A national park is an interesting place to visit. _National parks are interesting places to visit._

2. A bike is fast and cheap. _____

3. A boat is a slow way to travel. _____

4. A cruise is expensive. _____

5. A taxi is hard to find at night. _____

6. A car is convenient, but it costs a lot. _____

7. A backpack is a useful item. _____

8. An explorer has an interesting job. _____

6 Look at the bold words or phrases. Write **S** for *specific noun* or **G** for *generalization*.

_G_ 1. **Journeys** are often difficult and dangerous.

____ 2. **Train journeys** are often very slow.

____ 3. **The journey** took about six months.

____ 4. **The photos** in this magazine are amazing!

_____ 5. **Photos** are a great way to remember a trip.

_____ 6. **The national parks** in Alaska are beautiful.

_____ 7. **A hike** is a great way to explore, and it's good exercise.

_____ 8. **The hike** up the mountain is very difficult.

PRACTICE

7 Circle the correct article or Ø for *no article* to complete each sentence.

1. **The** / Ⓐ / Ø hiking trip is a good way to relax and enjoy nature.

2. I need **a** / **the** / **some** new bike. The one I have now used to be my grandmother's.

3. When I got on the bus, I looked in my purse for **a** / **the** / **some** change.

4. Please drive carefully. **Ø** / **A** / **The** roads are very icy tonight.

5. **Ø** / **The** / **Some** people do not enjoy traveling by train.

6. **A** / **Some** / **Ø** bus tour is a great way to see the city.

7. Our tour guide showed us **a** / **some** / **an** inexpensive places to eat.

8. The hotel has **a** / **an** / **the** entrance on Water Street.

9. When I'm on vacation, **some** / **a** / **Ø** time seems to pass very quickly.

10. **A** / **The** / **Ø** weather was perfect when we were on vacation.

8 Complete the conversations with *a, an, some, the,* or *Ø* for *no article*.

Conversation 1

Sheila: Are you going out?

Derek: Yes, I'm going to (1) ___the___ train station. I need to buy
            (2) _____ ticket for my trip to St. Louis next week.

Sheila: Oh. Why don't you buy it online?

Derek: I tried to, but there was (3) _____ problem with (4) _____ website.

Sheila: Well, good luck. (5) _____ lines are always very long at the station.

Conversation 2

Derek: Hi there! I'd like (6) _____ information about (7) _____ trains to St. Louis, please.

Clerk: Yes, sir. What's (8) _____ date of your trip?

Derek: March 12th. I want to leave early in (9) _____ morning.

Clerk: Well, there's (10) _____ train at 6:10. Is that too early?

Derek: No, that's perfect. How much is (11) _____ round-trip ticket?

Clerk: Seventy-five dollars. We take (12) _____ credit cards or cash.

9 READ, LISTEN & SPEAK.

A Look at the photo and read the caption and the information in the chart. Then circle the correct article or Ø for *no article* to complete each sentence.

Kent Couch's Balloon Flights, 2006–2010		
Year	Distance/Destination	Other Information
2006	99 miles (159 km)	many balloons exploded
2007	193 miles (311 km)	balloons lost gas
2008	Idaho	reached destination
2010	70 miles (113 km)	raced

▲ Kent Couch and Fareed Lafta prepare for take-off in July 2012.
Their form of transportation? Over 350 balloons and a lawn chair.

1. Kent Couch made **the** / **some** / Øballoon flight every year between 2006 and 2008.

2. Not all of **a** / **some** / **the** flights were successful.

3. In 2006, **some** / **Ø** / **the** balloons exploded, so Couch ended **Ø** / **the** / **an** flight.

4. In 2007, he had **Ø** / **a** / **an** problems with **some** / **a** / **the** gas in the balloons.

5. **The** / **Ø** / **A** 2008 flight was **a** / **some** / **the** success. Couch reached his destination.

6. In 2010, Kent Couch entered **the** / **a** / **Ø** race with another lawn-chair balloon.

7. **A** / **Ø** / **The** race was 70 miles (113 km).

8. **The** / **Ø** / **Some** flights in 2006 and 2007 were not **the** / **Ø** / **some** successes.

B Complete each statement with *a, an, the,* or *Ø* for *no article*.

1. Kent Couch owns _____ Italian restaurant.   **T**   **F**

2. Couch and Fareed used _____ lawn chair for their journey.   **T**   **F**

3. The balloons had _____ gas in them.   **T**   **F**

4. They expected to fly at _____ height of 5000–10,000 feet.   **T**   **F**

5. Each man had _____ small phone.   **T**   **F**

6. _____ weather in the north was perfect.   **T**   **F**

7. _____ weather report that day was not good.   **T**   **F**

8. Their journey was _____ success.   **T**   **F**

C Read the statements from exercise **B**. Then listen to the news reports. Circle **T** for *true* or **F** for *false*. Then correct the false statements to make them true.

D Work with a partner. Compare your answers from exercise **C**. What is your opinion of this form of transportation? Discuss your ideas.

10   APPLY.

A Work with a partner. Decide who will read Activity 1 and who will read Activity 2 and read about the vacation activity. Then close your book and tell your partner about the vacation activity that you read about. Pay attention to articles.

Activity 1

For an amazing undersea adventure, fly to the Maldives in the Indian Ocean and swim with a whale shark. Whale sharks are enormous, so don't swim in front of one!

◀ Swimming with a whale shark in the Maldives

Activity 2

The Nürburgring is a very dangerous racetrack to drive. It costs 35 dollars to drive around the track once. No, there isn't a speed limit!

◀ Racing at the Nürburgring in Nürburg, Germany

B Choose another vacation activity or kind of adventure. In your notebook, write a short paragraph of four or five sentences about the activity.

When I was on my last vacation, I tried scuba diving. For scuba diving, you need to use special equipment . . .

EXPLORE

CD1-40

1 READ the posts from two travel blogs. Notice the words in **bold**.

Greg's Blog   Posted: June 1?

I love photography and I drive all over **the United States** and **Canada** with my camera. I live in **Portsmouth**, **New Hampshire**, so every fall I get some great photos of the leaves changing color in **New England**. I just went on a long road trip and took photos of **the Rocky Mountains**, **Mount Rushmore**, **the Mojave Desert**, **the Mississippi River**, and **San Diego**. . . . I'm posting some of my favorite photos for you to see.

Maya's Blog   Posted: July

I'm staying with my sister Sylvie this month. Last weekend she took me to **New York City**. We took an early train to **Grand Central Station**. Then we walked up **Fifth Avenue** to **Central Park**. Next, we went to **the Museum of Modern Art**. It was wonderful! After a delicious lunch at **the Plaza Hotel**, I wanted to see more sights. I got everything on video: **the Empire State Building**, **th**e **Brooklyn Bridge**, and a lot of other places, too. . . . I'm having a great time!

▼ Mount Rushmore, South Dakota, USA

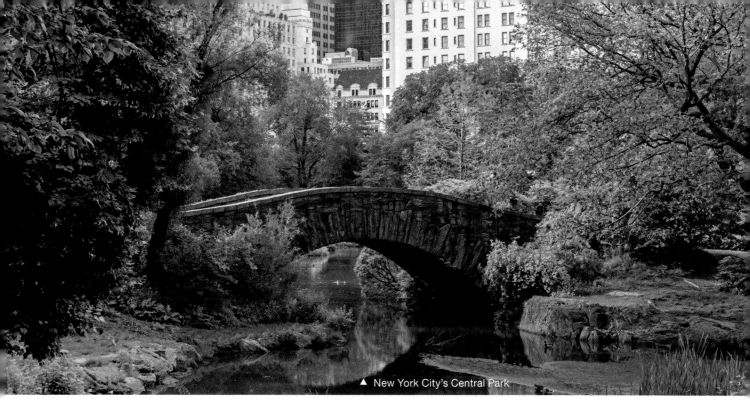

▲ New York City's Central Park

2 CHECK. Answer the questions about the blog posts from exercise **1**.

1. Where is Greg's home? _____

2. Where does he drive with his camera? _____

3. Which desert did Greg just visit? _____

4. Which museum did Maya visit with her sister? _____

5. Where did Maya and Sylvie have lunch? _____

3 DISCOVER. Complete the exercises to learn about the grammar in this lesson.

A Find place names with *the* and without *the* in the blog posts from exercise **1**. Write the place names in the correct column of the chart.

Place Names with *The*	Place Names without *The*
the United States	Canada

B Work with a partner. Compare your charts from exercise **A**. When do we use *the* with place names? Discuss your answer with your classmates and teacher.

LEARN

4.8 *The* and No Article: Geographic Names

The	No Article
Baghdad is on **the** Tigris River. They live in **the** United States.	She is from Brazil. Africa is a huge continent.

1. Use no article before the names of most cities, states, countries, and continents.	Barcelona is a beautiful city. Josh lives in Texas. Morocco is in Africa.
2. Use *the* before the names of places that contain an *of-* phrase or the word *kingdom* or *republic*.	**the** District of Columbia **the** United Kingdom **the** Dominican Republic
3. Use *the* before most plural geographic names.	**the** United States **the** Philippines **the** Alps, **the** Andes **the** Hawaiian Islands
4. Do not use *the* before the names of single mountains or single islands.	Mount Everest, Mount McKinley Long Island, Maui
5. Use *the* before the names of oceans, seas, and rivers. The words *ocean, sea,* and *river* are often omitted.	They live near **the** Caspian Sea. The explorers traveled up **the** Amazon.
6. Use *the* before the names of deserts. The word *desert* is often omitted.	**The** Mojave Desert is in California. **The** Sahara is the world's largest desert.

4 Complete each sentence with *the* or Ø for *no article*.

1. My brother visited ___the___ Rocky Mountains last summer.

2. _____ Luzon is the largest island in _____ Philippines.

3. _____ Andorra is a small country in _____ Europe.

4. Flights from _____ Boston take about six hours to cross _____ Atlantic Ocean.

5. _____ Mount Everest is 29,035 feet (8850 meters) high.

6. _____ Atacama Desert is in _____ Chile between _____ Pacific Ocean and _____ Andes Mountains.

7. _____ Galápagos Islands are the home of many interesting kinds of animals.

8. Millions of tourists visit _____ United Arab Emirates every year.

9. _____ Sardinia and _____ Sicily are islands. They are part of Italy.

10. The city of Riyadh in _____ Saudi Arabia is located in _____ Arabian Desert.

5 **SPEAK.** Work with a partner. Take turns describing the places in chart **4.8** and other places you know. Pay attention to articles.

Mount McKinley is in Alaska. Alaska is in the United States.

4.9   Other Uses of *The* and No Article with Place Names

The	No Article
It's next to **the** Seaside Hotel.	It's near Heathrow Airport.
The Eiffel Tower is in Paris.	We live on Elm Street.

1. Use *the* before the names of most hotels, theaters, museums, and names that end in *tower*, *bridge*, or *building*.	**the** Savoy Hotel **the** Majestic Theater **the** Natural History Museum **the** Golden Gate Bridge **the** Empire State Building
2. Do not use an article before the names of most streets, parks, squares, airports, or bus and train stations.	Third Avenue, North Street, Steamboat Road, Friendship Park, Union Square, Logan Airport, Grand Central Station
3. Use *the* before names of most places that include *of* or *for*.	**the** Statue of Liberty **the** Center for Performing Arts

6 Complete each sentence with *the* or Ø for *no article*.

1. I am staying at ___the___ All Seasons Hotel, on the southwest coast of Bali.

2. When we left Florida, we flew out of _____ Miami International Airport.

3. _____ Eiffel Tower received over seven million visitors in 2011.

4. _____ Museum of Modern Art in Rio de Janeiro has an unusual design.

5. The post office is on _____ Anderson Street.

6. Terry is studying English Literature at _____ University of Mumbai.

7. My brother attends _____ Center for Performing Arts.

8. Traffic was very heavy on _____ Brooklyn Bridge this morning.

9. Do you live on _____ River Road?

10. Heidi took a great photo of _____ Bridge of Sighs in Venice.

11. I'll meet you by the statue in _____ Westridge Park at 2:00 p.m.

12. What's playing at _____ Sherman Theater this week?

PRACTICE

7 SPEAK & WRITE.

A Complete the names of the famous places and locations in the chart with *the* or Ø for *no article*. Then match each famous place with its location. Write the letter of the location on the second line in the first column.

◀ The Burj Al Arab Hotel, Dubai City, Dubai, the United Arab Emirates

Famous Place	Location
1. _the_ Burj Al Arab Hotel _d_	a. ____ Japan
2. ____ Great Pyramid of Giza ____	b. ____ Himalayas
3. ____ Sydney Opera House ____	c. ____ Rio de Janeiro
4. ____ Mount Everest ____	d. _Ø_ Dubai
5. ____ Copacabana Beach ____	e. ____ Egypt
6. ____ Louvre Museum ____	f. ____ Australia
7. ____ Haneda Airport ____	g. ____ Paris

B Work with a partner. Compare your answers from exercise **A**. Then take turns asking and answering questions about the places. Use the information in the chart and *the* or no article

A: *Where is the Burj Al Arab Hotel?*

B: *It's in Dubai.*

C Write five sentences about other famous places and their locations. Use *the* or no article.

The Prado Museum is in Madrid.

_____

_____

_____

_____

8 EDIT. Read the post from a travel blog. Find and correct six more errors with articles.

I just got back from a great business trip to ~~the~~ South America. The trip started in Peru with two sales meetings in the Lima. Then, I flew to Venezuela for a meeting with clients in the Valencia. They also have an office in Philippines. I want to go there someday! The second week I was in Chile. I had some free time, so I went skiing in Andes. The scenery was amazing!

I arrived at the Logan Airport in Boston last night. I like to travel, but it's nice to be home—the New England is really beautiful this time of year. ☺

9 APPLY.

A Complete the e-mail to a friend. Write about a town or city you have visited. Use at least one place name in each numbered line. Use *the* when necessary.

Hi _____ (*name of your friend*),

A big hello from (1) _____ (*town or city*). I'm here for a few days. I decided to stay here because it's near a lot of other places in (2) _____ (*state, region, or country*). Yesterday, I went to see (3) _____ (*interesting building*) in the morning and took some photos of (4) _____ (*an interesting area*).

Today, I went to (5) _____ (*your choice of place*). Tomorrow, I am going to visit (6) _____ (*your choice of place*). Some other places I would like to see while I am here are (7) _____ and (8) _____ (*your own ideas*).

Well, that's all for now!

(9) _____ (*your name*)

B Tell a partner about the places in your email from exercise **A**. Ask and answer questions about each other's city or town. Do you know anything about the places in your partner's email? What do you know about them?

A: *Is Central Park really big?*
B: *Yes, it's the biggest park in New York City.*

Charts
4.1–4.6,
4.8

1 Circle the correct words to complete the conversation. Circle Ø for *no article*.

Gary: Hi, Andrea. It's Gary. Is (1) your / her / yours sister there?

Andrea: Sorry, (2) they're / he's / she's away on vacation (3) at / on / for a month.

Gary: A month? Really? Is she in (4) the / a / Ø Europe?

Andrea: No, South America. She's (5) in / at / on Buenos Aires right now. She's traveling around (6) from / out of / over country to country.

Gary: Is she traveling with (7) the / Ø / a friends?

Andrea: No, (8) Ø / the / some friends wanted to go with (9) she / her / herself, but they decided not to go, so she went (10) with / by / for herself.

Gary: Wow! That sounds exciting. I hope she's having (11) the / some / a great time.

Andrea: She is. I got (12) a / an / some e-mail from her this morning. She's having a lot of fun.

Charts
4.5–4.6

2 **EDIT.** Read the description of a vacation. Find and correct seven more errors with prepositions and articles.

My Favorite Vacation: Singapore

Last year, I took a vacation to ~~the~~ Singapore with my sister Ana. We went at September and had a great time. We stayed at nice hotel, and the food there was delicious. We visited all of a popular tourist places. We also went shopping in

Orchard Road,
one of the main
shopping areas. At
the evenings, we
would sit at a outdoor
café and talk until
late in night. It was a
wonderful vacation.
I want to go back
there someday!

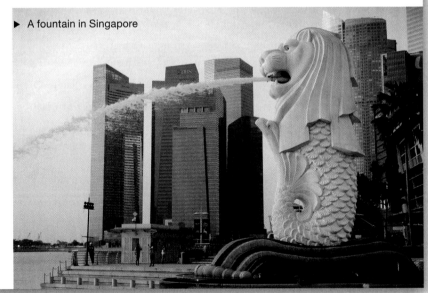

▶ A fountain in Singapore

3 LISTEN & SPEAK.

🎧
CD1-41

A Listen to a woman describe places in Boston. Choose the correct answer for each question.

1. Where does she live?

    a. on Newbury Street

    b. near the Public Garden

2. What is her favorite place in Boston?

    a. The Museum of Fine Arts

    b. Faneuil Hall Marketplace

🎧
CD1-41

B Listen again and take notes about each of the places in the chart.

The Public Garden	Newbury Street	Faneuil Hall Marketplace
beautiful in the spring and summer		

C Work with a partner. Talk about the places from exercise **B**. Use your notes and any other information you remember. Do you know anything else about Boston? Tell your partner.

The Public Garden is beautiful in the spring.

The public transportation in Boston is good.

Harvard University is near Boston. It's in Cambridge.

4 Work in a small group. Take turns talking about your city or hometown. Ask your classmates follow-up questions. Pay attention to articles, pronouns, and prepositions.

A: *My hometown is Tangier in Morocco. I love the Medina, the old part of the city.*

B: *What do you like about it?*

The skyline of downtown
Boston, Massachusetts

Connect the Grammar to Writing

1 READ & NOTICE THE GRAMMAR.

A Read the following description of a writer's favorite place.

My Favorite Place

Last summer I went to Italy with my friends Maria and Beth. One day we woke up early in the morning and drove to a town on the coast. From there, we took a boat to a small island. This island is now my favorite place in the world!

I loved the colorful fishing boats on the beach and the pretty pink houses. The weather was perfect, and the people were friendly. In fact, while we were looking at the boats, a fisherman waved to us. He and his wife invited us to have lunch with them. We had a picnic lunch by the sea. In the afternoon, we walked along the beach and had coffee at an outdoor café. When it was time to leave, I didn't want to go!

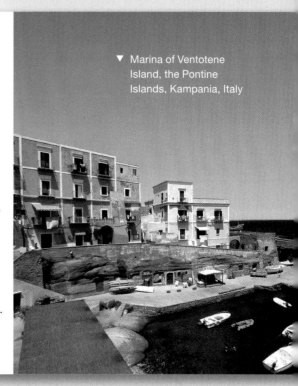

▼ Marina of Ventotene Island, the Pontine Islands, Kampania, Italy

GRAMMAR FOCUS

In the description, the writer uses prepositions of time, place, and direction to describe her favorite place.

*One day we woke up early **in** the morning and drove **to** a town **on** the coast.*
***From** there, we took a boat **to** a small island.*

B Read the description in exercise **A** again. Underline the prepositions of time, place, and direction. Then work with a partner and compare your answers.

C Complete the chart with information from the description in exercise **A**.

Where did she go?	to an island; to Italy
When did she visit this place?	
Who was there?	the writer, her friends, a fisherman and his wife
What did she do there?	
What did she see?	

2 **BEFORE YOU WRITE.** Complete the chart with information about your favorite place. Use the chart from exercise **1C** as a model.

Where did you go?	
When did you visit this place?	
Who was there?	
What did you do there?	
What did you see?	

3 **WRITE** two paragraphs about your favorite place. Use the information from your chart in exercise **2** and the description in exercise **1A** to help you.

WRITING FOCUS   Avoiding Misplaced Prepositional Phrases

When a prepositional phrase is misplaced, the meaning of a sentence is often unclear. Make sure prepositional phrases are correctly placed in your sentences.

✗ *We waited for the boat* <u>*inside the café*</u>*.* (Meaning: The boat is inside the café.)
✓ *We waited inside the café for the boat.*

---

4 **SELF ASSESS.** Read your description. Underline the prepositions of time, place, and direction. Then use the checklist to assess your work.

☐   I used subject and object pronouns correctly. [4.1]

☐   I used prepositions of time, place, and direction correctly. [4.4, 4.5]

☐   I used articles correctly. [4.6–4.9]

☐   I checked for and corrected misplaced prepositional phrases. [WRITING FOCUS]

The Present Perfect

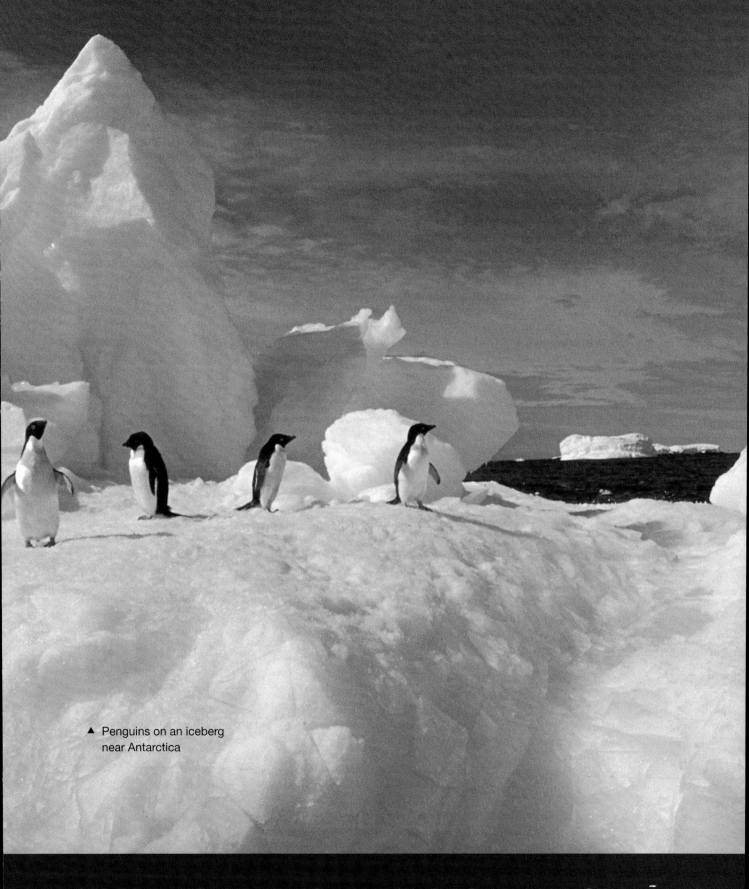

▲ Penguins on an iceberg
near Antarctica

EXPLORE

1 **READ** the excerpt from a lecture about the Aral Sea. Notice the words in **bold**.

Kazakhstan
Aral Sea
Uzbekistan

Asia's Aral Sea

Professor: . . . Now, as we**'ve just seen** in the first slide, the Aral Sea is in central Asia on the border between Kazakhstan and Uzbekistan. It used to be one of the biggest inland seas[1] in the world, but most of its water **has disappeared**. The sea **has shrunk**[2] to 10 percent of its original size.

Some people say that the water level **has gone** down because of climate change. However, we know that in the second half of the twentieth century, agricultural projects used up the water in the Aral Sea. The Aral Sea used to be home to 24 species of fish. Now, people keep cows and camels on the land next to old fishing ships.

Student 1: Have the governments of Kazakhstan and Uzbekistan **ever tried** to save the sea?

Professor: Yes, **they have**. In Kazakhstan, they built a dam[3] to help save the northern part of the Aral Sea, and the water level **has risen** again. A lot of fish are living there again, and birds **have returned**, too.

Student 2: What about the southern part in Uzbekistan? **Has** the situation there **improved**?

Professor: No, I'm afraid it **hasn't**. Unfortunately, most of the southern Aral Sea **has** probably **disappeared** forever.

[1] **inland sea:** a sea that is completely surrounded by land
[2] **shrunk:** gotten smaller
[3] **dam:** a wall that is built to keep water in a certain area

▲ The Aral Sea photographed in 1989 (top) and 2008 (bottom)

2 **CHECK.** Choose the correct answer for each question.

1. Which of these statements about the Aral Sea is true?

   a. It is the biggest inland sea in the world.

   b. It is in two different countries.

   c. It is in eastern Asia.

2. The Aral Sea is smaller now because of _____.

    a. high temperatures   b. agricultural projects   c. building projects

3. The dam in Kazakhstan helped the _____.

    a. northern Aral Sea   b. southern Aral Sea   c. entire Aral Sea

3 DISCOVER. Complete the exercises to learn about the grammar in this lesson.

A Look at these sentences from the lecture in exercise **1**. Notice the words in **bold**. Then choose the correct answers for the questions that follow.

Most of the water **has disappeared**.
The water level **has risen**.
Birds **have returned**.

1. Which statement is true for all three sentences?

    a. The actions happened at some time in the past.

    b. The actions are happening now.

    c. The actions will happen at some time in the future.

2. Do we know the exact time of the actions or events in these sentences?   a. Yes   b. No

B Discuss your answers from exercise **A** with your classmates and teacher.

◀ The Aral Sea has dried up and left behind ships like this one.

LEARN

5.1 Present Perfect: Statements

Statements			
Subject	*Have* or *Has* (*Not*)	Past Participle	
I/We/You/They	have have not/haven't	planned	my trip.
He/She/It	has has not/hasn't	eaten	dinner.

Contractions
I have → **I've** You have → **You've** He has → **He's** She has → **She's** It has → **It's** We have → **We've** You have → **You've** They have → **They've**

1. Use the present perfect:

   a. for a recently completed action

   b. when a time period is not complete, such as *this morning, this afternoon, today, this week*

   c. for an action or event that happened one or more times at an indefinite time in the past

   d. Use the present perfect when the time of the past action or event is not known or important, but the result of or the experience from the action or event is.

   a.
   ```
   ───────────────── the plane arrived ──────────▶
                                  ✕          │
                                            now
   ```
   The plane **has arrived**.

   b. John **hasn't called** today.
   (It's only 4:00 p.m.)

   c.
   ```
   ──────── read that book ────────────│──────▶
          ✕      ✕      ✕               now
   ```
   I **have read** that book three times.

   d. I **have washed** the dishes.
   (They are clean now.)

   Nancy **has lived** in Mexico City.
   (She knows a lot about it.)

2. The present perfect is formed with *have* or *has* + the past participle of the verb. The past participle of regular verbs is the same form as the simple past (the base form of the verb + -*ed*).

   My brother **worked** late yesterday. (simple past)
   He **has worked** late a lot recently. (present perfect)

3. Many verbs have irregular past participles.*

Base	Simple Past	Past Participle
do	did	done
get	got	got/gotten
go	went	gone
have	had	had
make	made	made

*See page **A5–A6** for a list of irregular verbs.

4 Complete each sentence with the present perfect form of the verb in parentheses.

1. The Aral Sea ___has become___ (become) ten times smaller in the last 50 years.

2. The dam _____ (not help) the southern Aral Sea.

3. The Aral Sea _____ (be) the topic of many discussions.

4. We _____ (not hear) the latest news about the Aral Sea.

5. Our professor _____ (go) to Asia many times.

6. Maria _____ (not read) a newspaper for many years. She reads the news online.

7. The students _____ (not speak) to their teacher today.

8. They _____ (do) all of the exercises. Now, they're taking a break.

9. David _____ (call) three times this morning.

10. Joe _____ (see) every James Bond movie twice. He loves them!

11. Ellen _____ (return) from India. I want to hear all about her trip.

12. I _____ (not eat) lunch. Do you want to go to the cafeteria with me?

5 Complete the exercises.

A Write the missing forms of the irregular verbs from exercise **4**.

Base Form	Simple Past	Past Participle
be	was/were	
		become
hear		
	went	
do		
	spoke	
		seen
	read	

B Work with a partner. Compare your charts from exercise **A**. Then check your answers using the irregular verb list on page **A5–A6**.

6 **WRITE & SPEAK.** Complete the sentences. Use the present perfect. Then share your sentences with a partner.

1. I _____ times this week.

2. I _____ many times.

3. I _____, but I want to someday.

A: *I've had pizza three times this week.*
B: *Really? That's a lot!*

REAL ENGLISH

When writing a sentence with two present perfect verbs joined by *and*, do not repeat *has* or *have* before the second verb.

*Aasim **has** recently **graduated** from college and **started** a new job.*

5.2 Present Perfect: Questions and Answers

Yes/No Questions				Short Answers
Have/Has	Subject	Past Participle		
Have	you	**driven**	before?	Yes, I **have**./No, I **haven't**.
Has	he	**worked**	in the past?	Yes, he **has**./No, he **hasn't**.

Wh- Questions				Short Answers
Wh- Word	Have/Has	Subject	Past Participle	
What	have	they	**found?**	A map of the city.
Where	has	she	**gone?**	To the library.

Who or What as Subject				Short Answers
Wh- Word	Has	Past Participle		
Who	has	**been**	to Italy?	I **have**./Maria **has**.
What	has	**happened**	this week?	A lot of things.

7 Put the words in the correct order to make questions.

1. you / visited / South America / have ___Have you visited South America?___

2. this week / what / you / have / learned _____

3. Bill / started / new job / his / has _____

4. the news / you / read / today / have _____

5. have / in Europe / you / where / been _____

6. eaten / today / have / you / what _____

7. this week / absent / has / who / been _____

8. today / she / called / has / who _____

8 Use the words in parentheses to complete each question. Use the present perfect.

1. ___Have you and Scott visited___ (you and Scott / visit) Asia?

2. _____ (he / read) today's newspaper?

3. What _____ (you / do) with the mail?

4. Where _____ (she / go)?

5. _____ (it / stop) raining?

6. What _____ (they / decide) to do tonight?

7. _____ (she / finish) her homework?

8. Who _____ (have) lunch?

5.3 Using Adverbs with the Present Perfect

1. *Already* means "sometime before now." Put *already* before the past participle or at the end of the sentence.	We've **already** seen that movie. We've seen that movie **already**.
2. *Ever* means "at any time before now." It is usually used in questions. *Never* means "at no time before now." *Ever* and *never* usually go before the past participle.	Have you **ever** read that book? I've **never** been to London.
3. *Recently* and *lately* mean "not very long ago" or "in the recent past." Put *recently* after the past participle or at the end of a sentence. *Lately* usually comes at the end of a sentence or a question.	I've read a lot of good books **recently**. Have they **recently** been to China? Have you seen any good movies **lately**? We haven't seen Sonja and Ben **lately**.
4. *Just* means "right before now." Use *just* for recently completed actions. Put *just* before the past participle.	The plane has **just** landed. We've **just** finished dinner.
5. *Still* in negative statements means "up to now." Put *still* before *haven't* or *hasn't*.	She **still** hasn't called me. We **still** haven't found the answer.
6. *Yet* means "until now." *Yet* is often used in negative statements and questions. Put *yet* at the end of the sentence.	He hasn't finished his report **yet**. Have you cleaned the kitchen **yet**?

9 Circle the correct adverb to complete each sentence.

1. Have you sent Mandy's birthday card **just** / **still** / **yet**?

2. I've **already** / **never** / **ever** heard of that restaurant. Where is it?

3. Maria has **already** / **ever** / **yet** finished her math assignment.

4. Have you seen any good movies **still** / **already** / **lately**?

5. Hal has **ever** / **just** / **still** passed his driving test.

6. I've sent Monica three e-mails but she **yet** / **never** / **still** hasn't replied.

7. We took the exam last week but we haven't received our results **never** / **already** / **yet**.

8. I haven't been to the gym **still** / **already** / **lately**.

10 **SPEAK.** Find a classmate who has done each of the activities below. Use questions with *Have you ever . . . ?* and the present perfect. Write his or her name on the line.

A: *Have you ever cooked a turkey?*   B: *Yes, I have./No, I haven't.*

1. cook a turkey _____

2. drive a truck _____

3. paint a picture _____

4. run in a race _____

5. study French _____

6. visit Mexico _____

PRACTICE

11 WRITE & SPEAK.

A Complete each sentence with the words in parentheses. Use the present perfect.

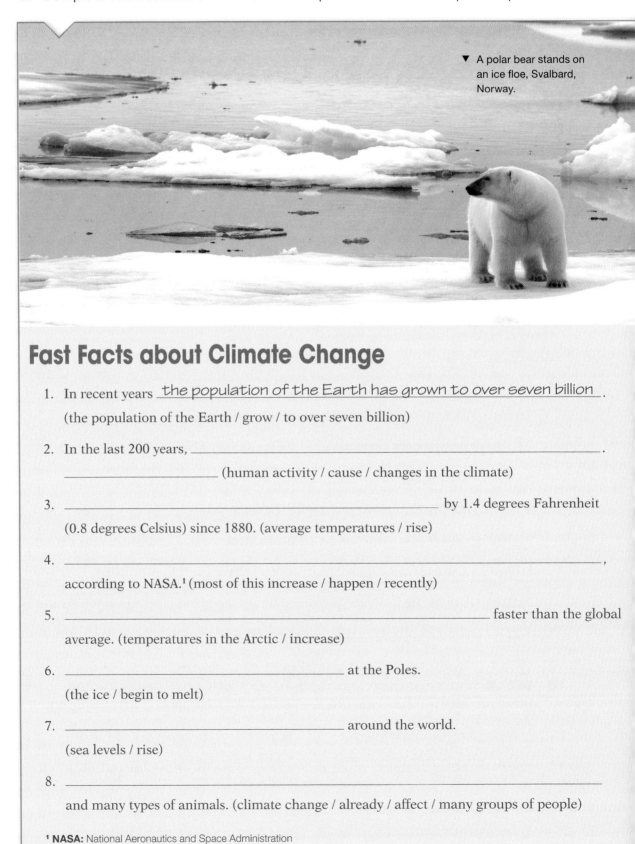

▼ A polar bear stands on an ice floe, Svalbard, Norway.

Fast Facts about Climate Change

1. In recent years <u>the population of the Earth has grown to over seven billion</u> . (the population of the Earth / grow / to over seven billion)

2. In the last 200 years, _____.
   _____ (human activity / cause / changes in the climate)

3. _____ by 1.4 degrees Fahrenheit (0.8 degrees Celsius) since 1880. (average temperatures / rise)

4. _____,
   according to NASA.[1] (most of this increase / happen / recently)

5. _____ faster than the global average. (temperatures in the Arctic / increase)

6. _____ at the Poles.
   (the ice / begin to melt)

7. _____ around the world.
   (sea levels / rise)

8. _____
   and many types of animals. (climate change / already / affect / many groups of people)

[1] **NASA:** National Aeronautics and Space Administration

B Work with a partner. Compare your answers from exercise **A**. Then discuss the questions.

1. Do any of the facts from exercise **A** surprise you? Why or why not?

2. Have you heard or read any other facts about climate change? Tell your partner.

12 LISTEN and write the words you hear.

CD2-03

1. _____ a new apartment.

2. _____ jobs.

3. _____ at that restaurant a few times.

4. _____ all week?

5. _____ the assignment?

6. _____ to Alaska?

7. _____ in a helicopter.

8. _____ their house _____?

13 APPLY.

A Write five questions to ask a partner about activities he or she has done. Use the present perfect. Then ask and answer the questions with a partner. Write your partner's answers.

1. Q: _____

   A: _____

2. Q: _____

   A: _____

3. Q: _____

   A: _____

4. Q: _____

   A: _____

B Form a group with another pair of students. Tell your group about some of your partner's activities. Use the present perfect.

Claudia has learned about climate change this week.

C In your notebook, write eight sentences about your and your group mates' activities.

I've learned about the Aral Sea this week.

EXPLORE

CD2-04

1 **READ** the article about an unusual robot. Notice the words in **bold**.

Paro, the Robot Seal

Factories **have used** robots to build cars and other machines **for many years**. Now, the science of robotics **has reached** a new level. Robots **have now moved** from factories into people's homes.

Paro, for example, is a robot that looks like a baby seal. Paro behaves like a real pet in many ways. It responds to touch and the human voice. It also makes sounds similar to an actual baby seal. **Since Paro first appeared in 2005**, the robot **has found** a place in nursing homes[1] around the world. Nursing homes **have used** dogs and cats in pet therapy[2] **for a long time**. However, it is not always possible to have a live animal in a nursing home. Japanese scientist Dr. Takanori Shibata designed Paro to replace real pets.

▲ Dr. Takanori Shibata with Paro, the robot seal

Paro **has become** very popular in some countries. For example, nursing homes in Denmark **have bought** over a hundred Paro robots **since 2008**. A study found that the robot helped elderly[3] people. They felt calmer and talked more when they spent time with Paro.

Not everyone thinks that the use of robots such as Paro in nursing homes is a good idea. Some psychologists **have pointed out**[4] that relationships with robots are not *real* relationships. They believe that robots such as Paro cannot replace human connections.

[1] **nursing home:** a place where people who are sick or old can live and get care
[2] **pet therapy:** the use of trained animals to help people feel better
[3] **elderly:** old
[4] **point out:** tell someone something

2 **CHECK.** Read the statements. Circle **T** for *true* or **F** for *false*.

1.	Paro first appeared in 2008.	T	F
2.	Sometimes it is not possible to have pets in nursing homes.	T	F
3.	Dr. Shibata designed Paro to help in therapy.	T	F
4.	Paro helps elderly people to move better.	T	F
5.	Some people think it is a bad idea to use robots in nursing homes.	T	F

3 DISCOVER. Complete the exercises to learn about the grammar in this lesson.

A Find these sentences in the article from exercise **1**. Write the missing words.

1. Factories **have used** robots to build cars and other machines _____.

2. Nursing homes **have used** dogs and cats in pet therapy _____.

3. _____, the robot **has found** a place in nursing homes around the world.

4. For example, nursing homes in Denmark **have bought** over a hundred Paro robots _____.

B Look at the sentences in exercise **A**. Then choose the correct answer for each question. Discuss your answers with your classmates and teacher.

1. Which word is used with a length of time?   a. for   b. since

2. Which word is used with a point in time?   a. for   b. since

▼ Nursing homes in the Netherlands have used robot pets since 2008.

LEARN

5.4 Present Perfect with *For* and *Since*

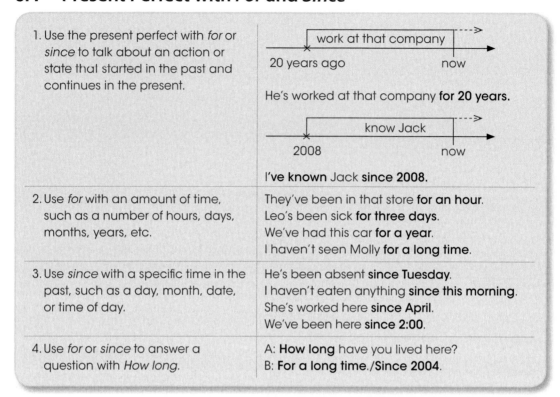

1. Use the present perfect with *for* or *since* to talk about an action or state that started in the past and continues in the present.	work at that company 20 years ago now He's **worked** at that company **for 20 years.** know Jack 2008 now I**'ve known** Jack **since 2008.**
2. Use *for* with an amount of time, such as a number of hours, days, months, years, etc.	They**'ve been** in that store **for an hour.** Leo**'s been** sick **for three days.** We**'ve had** this car **for a year.** I **haven't seen** Molly **for a long time.**
3. Use *since* with a specific time in the past, such as a day, month, date, or time of day.	He**'s been** absent **since Tuesday.** I **haven't eaten** anything **since this morning.** She**'s worked** here **since April.** We**'ve been** here **since 2:00.**
4. Use *for* or *since* to answer a question with *How long.*	A: **How long** have you lived here? B: **For a long time./Since 2004.**

4 Complete each sentence with *for* or *since* and the information in parentheses.

1. Paro has been on sale in the United States ___since 2009___ . (2009)

2. Car manufacturers have used robots in their factories _____ .
   (a long time)

3. The university has had a robotics department _____ . (the 1990s)

4. Nurses in Japan have supported the use of Paro _____ . (several years

5. Robots have performed dangerous jobs in factories _____ .
   (many years)

6. A: How long has Rita owned her car?

   B: _____ . (April)

7. Matt has studied robotics _____ . (two years)

8. A: How long have you known Siri?

   B: _____ . (five years)

5.5 Present Perfect: Past Time Clauses with *Since*

He has been in Japan **since he graduated from college.**
└─── Main Clause ───┘ └──── Past Time Clause ────┘

We have lived here **since we got married.**
└── Main Clause ──┘ └── Past Time Clause ──┘

1. *Since* can introduce a past time clause. The time clause refers to a specific time in the past. Use the present perfect in the main clause and the simple past in the time clause.	I've known Rita **since I was in high school.** └─── Main Clause ───┘ └──── Past Time Clause ────┘
2. **Remember:** A time clause can come first or second in a sentence. Use a comma when the time clause comes at the beginning of a sentence.	She has lived in Mexico **since she was 21.** **Since she was 21,** she has lived in Mexico.

5 Use the words in parentheses to complete each sentence. Use the correct form of the verb. Add a comma when necessary.

1. (life / change / since / a lot) _____Life has changed a lot since_____ the first personal computers went on sale.

2. (since / his cell phone / break) _____ Martin has been without one.

3. Since Yvonne moved into her new apartment, _____
(we / not / speak / to her).

4. (I / not see / Alicia) _____ since she got back from Spain.

5. (since / I get / a smartphone) _____ I haven't bought any CDs.

6. (Jack / be / to Australia / twice) _____
since his parents moved to Sydney.

7. Since the new professor arrived, _____
_____ (the students / enjoy / all of the classes).

8. Since I bought my new car, _____
_____ (I / not have / any / problems / with it).

PRACTICE

6 WRITE & SPEAK.

A Complete each sentence with the present perfect form of the verb in parentheses and *for* or *since*.

1. Personal computers _____have been_____ (be) available __since__ 1980.

2. People _____ (enjoy) television _____ almost 100 years.

3. We _____ (use) social networking sites _____ a long time.

4. Lily _____ (have) a smartphone _____ she was in high school

5. I _____ (not buy) a CD _____ many years.

6. Fabian _____ (take) three online courses each semester _____ he started college.

7. I _____ (not receive) any emails _____ Friday.

8. Dan _____ (send) ten text messages _____ 9:00 a.m.

B Work with a partner. Compare your answers from exercise **A**. Then talk about your own experience with technology. Use the topics below and the present perfect with *for* or *since*.

| laptop | phone | social networking site | TV | DVD |

A: *I've had this phone for six months.*

B: *Really? Do you like it?*

7 LISTEN.

A Listen to three phone conversations with an agent at an electronics company. Write the number of each conversation next to the topics below.

| _____ phone | _____ Internet connection | _____ MP3 player |

B Work with a partner. Complete the excerpts from the conversations. Then listen again and check your answers.

Conversation 1

Agent: I'm sorry to hear that. How long (1) _____ it?

Caller: I bought it in January, so I've only (2) _____ it (3) _____ about two months.

Agent: And what's the problem?

Caller: Well, (4) _____ the last week or two, the sound (5) _____ terrible!

Conversation 2

Caller: . . . (6) _____ some problems with my phone (7) _____ .

Agent: What's the problem, sir?

Caller: . . . Ever (8) _____ I dropped it, the screen (9) _____ really unclear.

Conversation 3

Caller: Finally! (10) _____ on hold (11) _____ twenty minutes.

Agent: Thank you for your patience. (12) _____ a lot of calls today.

Caller: My Internet connection (13) _____ since (14) _____ power yesterday.

8 EDIT. Read the conversations. Find and correct six more errors with the present perfect and past time clauses.

1. A: That's a nice watch, Paulo. I don't think I've s̶a̶w̶ it before.
     ^{seen}

   B: I've only had it since two weeks. It was a birthday present from my parents.

2. A: I've been on a diet for two months ago.

   B: Oh, how much weight have you lost?

   A: Not much, but I felt so much better since I started my diet.

3. A: How long are you interested in music, Anna?

   B: Oh, I've loved music since I am a child. My mother used to sing to me all the time.

4. A: Kazu, you speak French! I didn't know that.

   B: Yeah, I took it in high school. But I don't speak French for several years. I've forgotten a lot.

9 APPLY.

A In your notebook, write five facts about yourself that are true at the present time. Do not write permanent facts such as *I am Japanese*. Use the verbs in the box and the simple present.

be	have	live	own	study	want

I *own a motorcycle.*

B Work with a partner. Share your facts from exercise **A**. Ask questions about your partner's facts with *How long* and the present perfect. Use *for* or *since* in your answers.

A: *How long have you lived on Taylor Street?*

B: *I've lived on Taylor Street since 2010. / I've lived on Taylor Street for several years.*

C Form a group with another pair of students. Share some facts about your partner with the group.

Dalia has been married for nine years.

EXPLORE

CD2-09

1   **READ** the conversation about a website that creates pictures of characters from literature. Notice the words in **bold**.

The Composites

Katya: Hey, Helen, you**'ve been** on the computer for two hours! What are you looking at?

Helen: This website called *The Composites*. **Have** you **seen** it? Brian Davis, the website designer, **had** an interesting idea. He **decided** to use a computer program to create pictures of fictional[1] characters. Last year, he **put** the pictures on the website. Now you can see what the characters from books really look like.

Katya: What kind of computer program does that?

Helen: It's the same program the police use to create pictures of criminals.[2] It's used to help people when they**'ve witnessed**[3] a crime. The program lets them create a composite[4] picture of the criminal for the police. It lets them choose the right eyes, nose, hair, and so on.

Katya: OK, but why is the website using it for characters from books?

Helen: Well, in movies based on books, the characters often look very different from their description in the book, right? I'm often disappointed by that.

Katya: Yes, that's true. **I read** the novel *Dracula* last month. The main character in the book looks completely different in the movie.

Helen: OK, let's see . . . Look, here's a picture of Dracula on the website. Does he look more like the description in the book?

[1] **fictional:** not real
[2] **criminal:** a person who commits a serious crime
[3] **witness:** see or observe an event such as a crime
[4] **composite:** made up of different pieces or elements

► A composite illustration of Count Dracula based on the description in *Dracula* by Bram Stoker

2 CHECK. Choose the correct answer for each question.

1. What does *The Composites* website let people do?

   a. read great literature   b. see interesting pictures   c. write a computer program

2. Who usually uses composite pictures to create pictures of criminals?

   a. authors   b. readers   c. the police

3. Where does the information for the pictures on the website come from?

   a. police witnesses   b. visitors to the website   c. books' descriptions

4. Why is Helen disappointed by some movies that are based on books?

   a. The characters in the movies don't look right.

   b. The movies change the names of the characters.

   c. The movies change the events of the story.

3 DISCOVER. Complete the exercises to learn about the grammar in this lesson.

A Look at each sentence or phrase from the conversation from exercise **1**. Does it refer to a definite or indefinite time in the past? Put a check (✓) in the correct column.

	Definite Time	Indefinite Time
1. **Have** you **seen** it?	☐	✓
2. Last year, he **put** the pictures on the website.	☐	☐
3. . . . when they**'ve witnessed** a crime . . .	☐	☐
4. I **read** the novel *Dracula* last month.	☐	☐

B Look at the sentences from exercise **A**. Which verb form do we use to talk about an indefinite time in the past? Discuss your answer with your classmates and teacher.

◀ Count Dracula as portrayed by Bela Lugosi in the 1931 film *Dracula*

LEARN

5.6 Present Perfect and Simple Past: Indefinite or Definite Past Time

Present Perfect	Simple Past
Luis **has left**.	Luis **left** two hours ago.
I **haven't done** my homework.	I **didn't do** my homework last night.
Have you **seen** the new movie?	**Did** you **see** the new movie last weekend?

1. Use the present perfect to talk about an indefinite past action or situation. The exact time of the action or situation is not known or important, but the result is.	They **have left.** (They are not here now. When they left is not known or important.)
2. Use the simple past for an action or event that happened at a definite time in the past. The past time is stated or understood.	They **left** last night. (The past time is stated.) A: What did you do after dinner? B: I **called** my brother. (The past time is understood.)
3. We often begin a conversation with a general statement or question in the present perfect (indefinite time). Then, we provide details of time, place, and so on in the simple past (definite time).	A: **Have** you **seen** that movie? B: Yes, I **saw** it yesterday. A: What **did** you **think** of it? B: It **was** great!

4 Circle the correct form of the verbs to complete the conversation.

Christine: (1) (**Have you ever visited**) / **Did you ever visit** *The Composites* website?

Rose: Yes, (2) **I've looked** / **I looked** at it this morning!

Christine: What (3) **have you thought** / **did you think** of it?

Rose: It's great! (4) **I haven't seen** / **I didn't see** anything like it before. (5) **I've found** / **I found** a lot of characters on the site from books I've read. In fact, (6) **I've started** / **I started** a new novel last week, and I want to pay more attention to the descriptions from now on.

Christine: Good idea! I love the novel *Jane Eyre*, and I (7) **have read** / **read** it many times. Last year I (8) **watched** / **have watched** a movie based on the book. The actress who played Jane (9) **surprised** / **has surprised** me. She (10) **looked** / **has looked** just like the description in the book. That doesn't happen very often.

5 Complete the conversation. Use the present perfect or the simple past form of the verbs in parentheses.

Drew: (1) _____Have you seen_____ (you / see) any Sherlock Holmes movies?

Joel: Yes, I (2) _____ (watch) several of the old ones when I was in college, but I (3) _____ (not / see) one for a long time now.

Drew: (4) _____ (you / enjoy) them?

Joel: Yes, the stories (5) _____ (be) interesting, and I

(6) _____ (like) the characters a lot.

Drew: Well, it's your lucky day! There's a new TV show with a really good actor as Sherlock

Holmes. (7) _____ (you / see) it yet?

Joel: No, I (8) _____ (not watch) much TV recently. When is it on?

5.7 Present Perfect and Simple Past: Incomplete or Complete Time

Present Perfect	Simple Past
Meg **has had** that job since 2012.	Meg **had** a bad cold last week.
They **have lived** in Texas for a year.	They **lived** in Texas for a year.
He **hasn't texted** me this week.	He **didn't text** me yesterday.

1. a. Use the present perfect for actions or situations that started in the past and continue to the present. Use *for* or *since* to express the time period.	a. She **has worked** at the school for 10 years. (She still works there.)
b. Use the simple past for actions or situations that started and finished in the past.	b. She **worked** at the school for 20 years, but she retired last year. (She does not work there anymore.)
2. a. Use the present perfect for a time period that is incomplete.	a. I **haven't had** breakfast this morning. (It's still morning.)
b. Use the simple past for a time period that is complete.	b. I **didn't have** breakfast this morning. (It's now afternoon.)

6 Complete each sentence with the simple past or present perfect form of the verbs in parentheses.

1. This store __has been__ (be) open for two months. It's already very popular.

2. The store _____ (be) open for 12 years. It closed last August.

3. Carla _____ (use) my laptop yesterday, but she hasn't returned it yet.

4. I _____ (use) my laptop every day since I bought it.

5. We _____ (live) in Florida for ten years. Then we moved to California.

6. My brother and his wife _____ (live) in this house since 2005.

7. Linda _____ (teach) for 15 years. She loves her job.

8. My brother _____ (teach) for six years before he became a pilot.

7 Complete each sentence with the present perfect or the simple past form of the verb in parentheses. Use the time of speaking to help you.

Time of Speaking:

1. `11:00 A.M.` I ___haven't seen___ (not see) George this morning.

2. `5:00 P.M.` I _____ (not see) George this morning.

3. `3:00 P.M.` _____ (you / talk) to Julia this morning?

4. `11:00 A.M.` _____ (you / talk) to Julia this morning?

5. `2:00 P.M.` Lin _____ (answer) the phone three times this afternoon.

6. `10:30 P.M.` Lin _____ (answer) the phone three times this afternoon.

7. `11:00 P.M.` I _____ (eat) two bowls of cereal this morning.

8. `9:30 A.M.` I _____ (eat) two bowls of cereal this morning.

PRACTICE

8 READ & WRITE. Read the information about two science fiction movies. Then complete the paragraphs with the present perfect or the simple past form of the verbs in parentheses.

Science Fiction and Real Life

Science fiction movies sometimes predict the future. We looked at some science fiction movies and asked the question: *What has happened in real life?*

Movie #1: *Blade Runner* (1982)   **Place and Time:** Los Angeles, California, 2019

In the movie:

In the 1982 movie *Blade Runner*, people in Los Angeles speak a combination of European and Asian languages.

What has happened in real life?

The number of Spanish speakers in the Los Angeles area (1) _____

(increase) rapidly since 1980. At that time, the city (2) _____ (be) home to

1.5 million Spanish speakers. Now, that number (3) _____ (grow) to over

3.5 million. In 2012, students in Los Angeles schools (4) _____ (speak) over

90 different languages.

▼ Los Angeles, California, USA

▲ The Terrafugia Transition car-airplane vehicle
on display at the New York Auto Show

In the movie:

In *Blade Runner,* flying cars are a common form of transportation.

What has happened in real life?

Engineers (5) _____ (design) and (6) _____ (build) some flying cars already. A flying car (7) _____ (appear) at the New York International Auto Show in 2012.

Movie #2: *Minority Report* (2002)   **Place and Time:** Washington, DC, 2054

In the movie:

In the 2002 movie *Minority Report,* computers don't have keyboards or mice.[1] Instead, people wear special gloves and make movements with their fingers. They use these movements to control their computers.

What has happened in real life?

Since the movie *Minority Report* (8) _____ (come) out in 2002, touch-screen phones and computers (9) _____ (become) very common. Also, for several years, computer games (10) _____ (allow) users to control the action with hand and body movements.

[1] **mice:** small decives used to control computers

9 Complete the conversation with the words in parentheses. Use the present perfect or the simple past.

Elsa: Last night (1) _____I finished_____ (I / finish) a really good novel about life in the twenty-third century. Do you want to borrow it?

Michel: No, thanks. I'm not very interested in science fiction.

Elsa: (2) _____ (you / read) much science fiction?

Michel: No, not much. (3) _____ (I / read) a few novels by Isaac Asimov

Elsa: Oh, when (4) _____ (you / read) those?

Michel: Um, I think (5) _____ (I / read) the last one about two years ago

Elsa: What (6) _____ (you / think) of them?

Michel: Oh, (7) _____ (I / find) the ideas about the future really interesting.

Elsa: I don't understand. (8) _____ (you / enjoy) them, but

(9) _____ (you / not read) any other science fiction novels

since then.

Michel: That's right. (10) _____ (I / not have) much free time lately.

For the last two years, (11) _____ (I / spend) most of my

time studying. Anyway, I prefer crime novels. (12) _____

(I / borrow) one from the library last week, but (13) _____ (I / no

start) it yet.

10 WRITE & SPEAK.

A Write true sentences about yourself. Use the words in parentheses and a verb in the present perfect or simple past.

1. __I have lived in Wisconsin since 2012.__ _____ (since 2012

2. _____ (this month

3. _____ (since the beginning of the year

4. _____ (last yea

5. _____ (a few years ago

6. _____ (for the past several week

7. _____ (for a few month

8. _____ (when I was ten years old

B Work with a partner. Compare your sentences from exercise **A**. Then use the present perfect or the simple past to ask your partner for more information.

A: *I have lived in Wisconsin since 2012.*   B: *Where else have you lived? / Where did you live before*

11 EDIT. Read about a young software developer in Uganda. Find and correct six more errors with the present perfect and the simple past.

ABDU SAKALALA: SOFTWARE DEVELOPER

Abdu Sakalala is a 22-year-old student in Uganda. His life ~~has~~ changed when a phone company has run a training course for software developers[1] in Uganda last year. Sakalala attended the course and then he has started creating his own apps (programs) for mobile phones. Since then, Sakalala wrote

▲ A man talks on a cell phone west of Kampala, Uganda.

several successful apps for cell phones. For example, he has produced a dictionary app, a translation app, and a sports app for soccer fans. Some of these apps have received international attention, and Sakalala already made almost $400,000 from his work.

But Sakalala is most proud of *Uganda Theme*. This is an app that changes the display on cell phones with pictures and sounds from his country. When it has appeared on the Internet, it immediately has become one of the most popular downloads in the world that week.

[1] **software developers:** people who create computer programs

12 APPLY.

A Read the conversation below. Underline the verbs.

Janice: <u>Have</u> you ever <u>visited</u> Europe?

Logan: Yes, I've been there several times.

Janice: Oh really? Where have you been?

Logan: I've been to Italy, France, and Spain.

Janice: When did you go to Spain?

Logan: I went last summer with some friends.

B Work with a partner. Talk about one of the activities in the box or your own idea. Use the conversation in exercise **A** as a model. Use the present perfect and the simple past.

Visit Europe/Asia/Africa	Take a cruise
Learn to play a musical instrument	Walk more than five miles
Ride a motorcycle	Your idea: _____
Swim in a lake	

EXPLORE

CD2-10

1 **READ** the article about the Inuit people of the Arctic. Notice the words in **bold**.

Good Times and Bad Times for the Inuit

The Inuit are the native people of the Arctic regions of Canada, Greenland, Russia, and the United States. In recent years, climate change **has been making** life difficult for the Inuit people of the Arctic. Their traditional culture **has been** under attack. Sea ice is very important in their lives. Recently, the sea ice **has been melting**. No sea ice means no seal hunting. No seal hunting means no meat for the dogs, and dogs are very important to the Inuit. These changes **have caused** social problems in Inuit communities everywhere.

In some countries, however, life for Inuit people **has been improving**. In Alaska, many Inuit **have been earning** money from shares[1] in local companies. In Canada, changes to the law have given the Inuit more independence from the national government. They live in regions that earn money from mining and pipelines.[2] Russia, however, has no special areas or programs for its Inuit people.

For the Inuit, Greenland is special. Around 85 percent of the island's people are Inuit. The Inuit **have been driving** dog sleds across the icy land for over 700 years. Denmark used to govern Greenland. However, since 2008, the Inuit people of Greenland **have been running** their own country.

[1] **share:** an equal part of the ownership of a company
[2] **pipeline:** a system of connected pipes used to carry gas, water, or oil over long distances

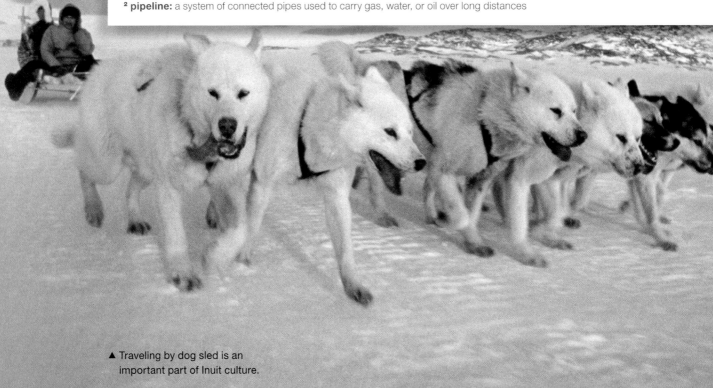

▲ Traveling by dog sled is an important part of Inuit culture.

2 CHECK. Match each Inuit group in Column A with the correct topic(s) in Column B.

Column A

1. All Inuit _____ b, e, g _____

2. Alaskan Inuit _____

3. Canadian Inuit _____

4. Greenlandic Inuit _____

5. Russian Inuit _____

Column B

a. Increased independence

b. Climate change

c. Mining and pipelines

d. Shares in local companies

e. Social problems

f. No special areas or programs

g. Melting sea ice

3 DISCOVER. Complete the exercises to learn about the grammar in this lesson.

A Read the sentences about the article from exercise **1**. Notice the words in **bold**. Is the action finished or still happening? Put a check (✓) in the correct column.

	Finished	Still Happening
1. Climate change **has been making** life difficult for the Inuit people of the Arctic.	☐	✓
2. The sea ice **has been melting**.	☐	☐
3. Canada **has changed** some of its laws.	☐	☐
4. In other countries, life for Inuit **has been improving**.	☐	☐
5. The Inuit **have been driving** dog sleds across Greenland for over 700 years.	☐	☐

B Work with a partner. Compare your answers from exercise **A**. What do you notice about the verb form used for actions that are still happening? Discuss your answer with your classmates and teacher.

▼ Many Inuit depend on seal hunting for food and clothes. The Inuit also sell seal skins to earn money.

LEARN

5.8 Present Perfect Progressive: Statements

Affirmative and Negative Statements			
Subject	*Have* or *Has* (*Not*)	*Been*	Verb + *-ing*
I/We/You/They	have have not/haven't	been	working	for six months. since last year. lately/recently.
He/She/It	has has not/hasn't			

1. Use the present perfect progressive:

   a. to talk about an action or situation that started in the past and continues in the present

   b. to emphasize that a repeated action is only temporary

   c. to emphasize that an action or situation was completed very recently

2. Use *for* or *since* with the present perfect progressive to tell how long the action has been happening.

3. **Remember:** We do not usually use non-action verbs with the progressive.

a. get up early → now

I've **been getting up** early lately.

b. She**'s been walking** to work this week.
(She usually drives, but her car is broken.)

c. A: Why is there paint on your shirt?
B: I'**ve been painting** my living room.
(I just finished painting it.)

I **haven't been thinking** clearly <u>for</u> a few days.
He **has been sleeping** <u>since</u> he got home.

✓ They'**ve known** Ed for a long time.
✗ They'<u>ve been knowing</u> Ed for a long time.

---

4 Complete each sentence with the present perfect progressive form of the verb in parentheses.

1. I ___have been reading___ (read) about the Inuit for my assignment.

2. Inuit people _____ (live) in the Arctic regions for over a thousand years.

3. Their way of life _____ (change) in recent years.

4. In Canada, some Inuit _____ (earn) money as artists.

5. Some schools _____ (not teach) children in their native languages.

6. More tourists _____ (visit) Greenland recently.

7. More people _____ (write) about Inuit culture.

8. Interest in the Inuit _____ (grow).

9. Inuit people _____ (use) dog sleds for hundreds of years.

10. Some governments _____ (not help) the Inuit.

5.9 Present Perfect Progressive: Questions and Answers

Yes/No Questions

Have/Has	Subject	Been	Verb + -ing	
Have	you	been	waiting	for a long time?
Has	he		exercising	lately?

Short Answers

Yes, I have./No, I haven't.
Yes, he has./No, he hasn't.

Wh- Questions

Wh- Word	Have/Has	Subject	Been	Verb + -ing
What	have	they	been	doing?
How long	has	she		sleeping?

Answers

Studying.
About an hour.

Who or What as Subject

Wh- Word	Has	Been	Verb + -ing	
Who	has	been	helping	you?
What	has		happening	lately?

Answers

Maria./Maria has.
A lot of things./Not much.

5 Put the words in the correct order to make questions using the present perfect progressive.

1. recently / been / you / doing / what / have ___What have you been doing recently?___

2. been / long / living / he / how / here / has _____

3. diet / have / healthy / eating / been / you / a _____

4. going / she / been / to class / has _____

5. shouting / he / has / been / why _____

6. the piano / been / for / you / a long time / have / playing _____

7. lately / on weekends / why / Andre / been / has / working _____

8. has / teaching / who / this week / been / the class _____

9. you / been / reading / lately / what / have _____

10. been / a lot / you / have / lately / studying _____

6 SPEAK. Work with a partner. Ask and answer questions using *How long* and the present perfect progressive. Use the phrases below.

do this exercise	drive a car	go to the gym	live here
sit in this classroom	study English	take classes here	wear glasses

A: *How long have you been living here?*   B: *About six months.*

5.10 Present Perfect Progressive and Present Perfect

Present Perfect Progressive	Present Perfect
I've been reading a book on Greenland. (I'm not finished.)	I've read a lot of books on Greenland. (I'm finished.)
A: How long have you been driving? B: About ten years.	A: Have you ever driven in New York City? B: No, I take the subway when I'm there.

1. Use the present perfect progressive for an action or situation that is not complete.	She has been writing a cookbook. (She's not finished.)
Use the present perfect for a completed action or situation.	She has written a cookbook. (She is finished.)
2. Use the present perfect progressive with an action verb to ask a question with *How long*.	A: How long have you been studying? B: I've been studying for two hours.
Use the present perfect with a non-action verb to ask a question with *How long*.	A: How long have you known her? B: I've known her since I was five.
3. Use the present perfect for repeated actions.	I've watched three movies this week. I've watched the news three times today.

7 Complete each sentence or question. Use the present perfect or the present perfect progressive form of the verb in parentheses.

1. Wow! You __have changed__ (change) since I saw you last! You look great!

2. I _____ (work) on my report since this morning. I still have two sections to write.

3. How long _____ (you / own) your car?

4. Margaret _____ (go) to Alaska twice.

5. I _____ (use) Steve's old computer this afternoon. Mine is broken.

6. How long _____ (you / read) that book?

7. This assignment _____ (take) me three hours. It's finally finished!

8. Tamara _____ (have) that coat for 20 years. She needs a new one.

PRACTICE

8 Complete the conversations with the words in parentheses. Use the present perfect or the present perfect progressive.

Conversation 1

Kylie: Judy, (1) __have you seen__ (you / see) my running shoes?

Judy: No, I haven't. I'm not surprised you can't find them. The last few weeks

(2) _____ _____ (you / not exercise)

like you used to.

Kylie: Well, (3) _____ (I / not have) time. (4) _____ _____ (I / work) really hard on my project for school.

Judy: Oh, that's right. How (5) _____ (it / go)?

Kylie: Great, thanks. In fact, (6) _____ (I / just / finish) it. Now I finally have some time to exercise!

Conversation 2

Lori: Come on, Cal, (7) _____ (you / look) at that computer magazine all evening. Why don't we go out and do something fun and interesting?

Cal: (8) _____ (I / already / tell) you. I *am* doing something interesting. I'm finding out about new laptops.

Lori: Well, how many laptops (9) _____ (you / read) about so far? A hundred?

Cal: No, just a few. (10) _____ (I / try) to choose one, and it's a difficult decision.

9 WRITE & SPEAK.

A Write true sentences about yourself. Use the verbs in parentheses and *for* or *since*. Use the present perfect progressive for action verbs and the present perfect for non-action verbs.

1. (study) I've been studying Korean since I was eight years old. _____

2. (own) _____

3. (play) _____

4. (buy) _____

5. (like) _____

6. (eat) _____

7. (sit) _____

8. (see) _____

B Work with a partner. Compare your sentences from exercise **A**.

C Form a group with another pair of students. Tell your group about your partner.

10 LISTEN, WRITE & SPEAK.

CD2-11

A Listen to the conversation. Choose the correct answer for each question.

1. How long has Lars lived in Kiruna, Sweden?

   a. for nine years   b. for his entire life   c. since last year

2. Why does the center of the town need to move?

   a. It's too close to the Arctic.   b. There's a mine nearby.   c. The buildings are very old.

◄ This Sami herder uses a snowmobile to help move his reindeer.

B Use the words to write questions about the conversation from exercise **A** on page 149. Use th[e] present perfect or the present perfect progressive.

1. where / Lars / live / all his life _____

2. what / happen / to the ground under Kiruna / recently _____

_____

3. what / change / in Kiruna / so far _____

4. what / the Sami people / do / for hundreds of years _____

_____

5. how / the Sami people's lives / change _____

CD2-11
C Listen again. In your notebook, take notes on the answers to the questions from exercise **B**.

D Work with a partner. Ask and answer the questions from exercise **B**.

11 APPLY.

A What changes have you and the members of your family made recently? Use the chart to take notes on your ideas.

Changes that have happened	Changes that are still happening
I've made new friends.	My grandmother has been taking classes.

B Work with a partner. Talk about some of the changes you and the members of your family have made. Use the information from your chart in exercise **A**. Use the present perfect and the present perfect progressive.

I've made a lot of new friends this year. My grandmother has been taking computer classes since Augu[st]

C In your notebook, write a paragraph of four or five sentences about your family. Use your notes from exercise **B**. Use the present perfect and the present perfect progressive.

Charts
5.1–5.3, 5.4,
5.6, 5.7

1 Complete the blog post. Use the present perfect or the simple past form of the verbs in parentheses. For some items both forms are correct.

A Change in the American Dream

Sunday, January 25

For years, many Mexicans (1) _____have left_____ (leave) Mexico to come to the United States. However, in recent years, more and more Mexicans in the United States (2) _____ (return) home to Mexico. In 2011, around 400,000 Mexicans (3) _____ (leave) the United States and (4) _____ (return) to Mexico.

The number of people leaving Mexico for the United States (5) _____ (fall) lately, too. According to some research, 404,000 Mexicans (6) _____ (leave) their country for the United States in 2010. Just four years earlier, in 2006, that number (7) _____ (be) over one million. Experts (8) _____ (discuss) the reason for this change, but not everyone agrees on the answer.

Charts
5.1, 5.4,
5.6–5.8, 5.10

2 Circle the correct words to complete the reader's response to the blog post in exercise **1**.

Tuesday, January 27

A very interesting blog post, thank you. I actually have some personal experience with this subject. I (1)(**have known**)/ **knew** my friend Carlos Mendoza (2) **since** / **for** 2005. He (3) **left** / **has left** his hometown in Mexico when he was 18. Like many other young Mexicans, he (4) **crossed** / **has been crossing** the Rio Grande and came to the United States because he wanted to find work. Carlos (5) **settled** / **has been settling** in Arizona in 2004, where he started his own cleaning service. His business was very successful, but Carlos (6) **didn't clean** / **hasn't been cleaning** houses for a year now. While he was in the United States, he (7) **saved** / **has saved** his money. Now, he (8) **has gone** / **has been going** back to Mexico to open his own store. Carlos (9) **sent** / **has been sending** me e-mails regularly (10) **for** / **since** several months. I wish him all the best!

Charts
5.1, 5.4–5.8,
5.10

3 EDIT. Read the article about Brendon Grimshaw. Find and correct eight more errors with the present perfect, the present perfect progressive, and the simple past.

Brendon Grimshaw and Moyenne Island

Moyenne Island in the Seychelles was deserted[1] and forgotten for fifty years. Then, in 1964, British newspaper editor Brendon Grimshaw ~~has~~ bought the island. He moved there nine years later, and lived there ever since.

When Grimshaw moved to Moyenne Island, it has been empty. Small trees and bushes covered the land, and there weren't any paths. Grimshaw wanted to take care of the island, so he asked a local man, Rene Lafortune, to help him. Since the two men have started work, they has planted 16,000 trees. Some of the first trees have now been growing to over 60 feet tall. The two men have also built more than three miles (5 km) of nature paths.

Grimshaw has been working hard on his project since about forty years, and today Moyenne Island is a huge success story. Since Grimshaw bought the island, it have attracted about 2000 new birds. Grimshaw has also raised over 100 giant tortoises[2] on the island.

Since 2008, Moyenne Island was a national park. It is a beautiful example of how one person's dream can change at least a small area of the world.

[1] **deserted:** empty because of no people living somewhere
[2] **tortoise:** a slowly moving land turtle with a high shell

▲ Brendon Grimshaw bought a deserted island in the Seychelles in 1964. Today, Moyenne Island is a beautiful national park.

4 LISTEN.

A Look at the words in the box. Put a check (✓) next to the words you know. Ask your teacher about any words you do not know.

☐ coworker   ☐ cubicle   ☐ social media   ☐ software

CD2-12

B Listen to part of a radio call-in show about changes in the workplace. Which caller is more positive about technological change at work? Circle your answer.

a. Caller 1   b. Caller 2

CD2-12

C Listen again and complete the sentences from the radio show with the words you hear.

Caller 1

1. The way we work _____*has changed*_____ a lot in recent years, but young people like me often feel that it _____ enough.

2. Well, for example, we _____ social media since it first _____ .

3. Some of their programs _____ on the market before I was born!

Caller 2

4. I _____ six e-mails in one hour from the same coworker.

5. The strange thing was that this person was sitting in the cubicle next to mine, and she _____ one word to me the whole time!

6. For one day each week, she _____ down the company's e-mail system.

7. Since the experiment, the change in the office _____ amazing.

5 SPEAK.

A Think about how technology has changed your life. What are some positive and negative changes? Complete the chart with your ideas.

Positive Changes	Negative Changes
easy communication	*not enough face-to-face contact*

B Work in a small group. Talk about how technology has changed your lives. Use your notes from exercise **A** to help you. Ask follow-up questions for more information. Use the present perfect, the present perfect progressive, and the simple past.

Connect the Grammar to Writing

1 READ & NOTICE THE GRAMMAR.

A What kinds of changes have you read about in this unit? Discuss your ideas with a partner. Then read the text below.

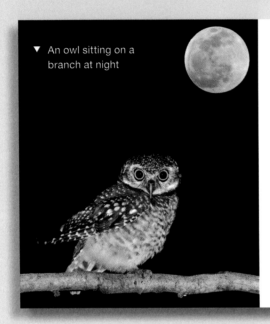

▼ An owl sitting on a branch at night

Since the Sun Went Down

The sun went down three hours ago. Since then, it's gotten very dark. The moon has risen, and the stars have been appearing in the sky.

Many birds, butterflies, and small animals have disappeared for the night. Others have become active. A raccoon is in my yard. It's been coming into my yard every night this winter. I hear an owl. I've heard it a few times before.

Since the sun went down, it's become much colder. The temperature has already dropped six degrees. I've put on a warm sweater, socks, and slippers. I like a lot of things about winter, but not the cold!

GRAMMAR FOCUS

In exercise **A**, the writer uses the present perfect to describe recently completed actions or events.

> It **has gotten** very dark.
> The temperature **has** already **dropped** six degrees.

The writer uses the present perfect progressive to talk about actions that started in the past and continue to the present.

> It **has been coming** into my yard every night this winter.

B Read the text in exercise **A** again. Underline the present perfect verbs and circle the present perfect progressive verbs. Then work with a partner and compare your answers.

C In exercise **A**, the writer begins with a statement about a recent time and event. Then she describes recent changes caused by this event. Complete the chart with information about these changes.

> **Recent Event:** _The sun went down._
>
> **Changes:**
> It's gotten very dark.

2 BEFORE YOU WRITE.

A Think of an event you have recently experienced. When did the event happen? What changes have happened because of the event? Complete the chart with information about the experience. Use the chart from exercise **1C** as a model.

Recent Event: _____
Changes:

B Look at the changes in your chart from exercise **A**. Number each change in your chart 1, 2, 3, etc., to help you plan the order of this information in your writing.

3 WRITE three paragraphs about the changes you have experienced recently. Use the information in the chart in exercise **2A** and the text in exercise **1A** to help you.

> **WRITING FOCUS**   Using Commas between Items in a Series
>
> Use a comma between words or phrases in a series. A series is three or more related words, phrases, or clauses. Use a comma after all items in a series except the last one.
>
> Many **birds, butterflies, and small animals** have disappeared for the night.

4 SELF ASSESS. Read your text. Underline the present perfect verbs and circle the present perfect progressive verbs. Then use the checklist to assess your work.

- [ ] I used the present perfect to talk about recently completed actions. [5.1, 5.4]
- [ ] I used *for* and *since* correctly with the present perfect. [5.4, 5.5]
- [ ] I used the present perfect progressive to talk about an action that started in the past and continues in the present. [5.8, 5.10]
- [ ] I used commas between words or phrases in a series. [WRITING FOCUS]

UNIT 6 Appearances and Behavior

Adjectives and Adverbs

▲ Madagascar's stone forest is home to several kinds of lemurs.

EXPLORE

CD2-13

1   READ the article about an attempt to steal a koala. Notice the words in **bold**.

Queensland

AUSTRALIA

Koalas Fight Back!

In March 2006, thieves broke into a zoo in Queensland, Australia. They planned to steal a koala. Everybody loves koalas, right? With their **big round** eyes, **flat** noses, **thick fur** coat, and **hairy** ears, these **cute** creatures have become a **popular** symbol of Australia. However, appearances can be **deceptive.**[1] The koala at the zoo was very **fierce**. Soon the thieves had **deep** scratches from the koala's **sharp** claws,[2] so they decided to steal something easier. They stole a crocodile instead!

Koalas are **interesting** animals. A **koala** mother carries her baby, called a *joey*, in a **warm** pouch, or pocket, on her stomach. Koalas eat only the **oily** leaves of eucalyptus trees. These leaves are **harmful** to many other animals, but koalas eat about two and a half pounds (just over one kilo) every night. The **water** content of these leaves is **high**, so koalas do not drink very much. In fact, in one **native Australian** language the word *koala* means "no drink."

[1] **deceptive:** causing someone to believe something that is not true
[2] **claws:** the sharp nails of an animal

▶ This baby koala is already covered in **thick** fur.

A saltwater crocodile, Australia

2 CHECK. Read the statements. Circle **T** for *true* or **F** for *false*.

1.	The thieves went to the zoo to steal a crocodile.	**T**	**F**
2.	Koalas have small eyes.	**T**	**F**
3.	The koala at the zoo was very calm.	**T**	**F**
4.	Female koalas have a pouch for their babies.	**T**	**F**
5.	Eucalyptus leaves are bad for many animals.	**T**	**F**
6.	Eucalyptus leaves do not contain much water for koalas.	**T**	**F**

3 DISCOVER. Complete the exercises to learn about the grammar in this lesson.

A Complete the sentences with the words from the article in exercise **1**.

1. . . ., these _____ creatures have become a _____ symbol of Australia.

2. The koala at the zoo was _____ .

3. Soon the thieves had _____ scratches from the koala's _____ claws.

4. These leaves are _____ to many other animals.

5. The _____ content of these leaves is _____ . . . .

B Look at the adjectives you wrote in exercise **A**. Check the three answers that complete the statement *An adjective can* . . .

1. _____ come before a noun   3. _____ come after a form of *be*

2. _____ come after a noun   4. _____ look like a noun

LEARN

6.1 Adjectives

1. Adjectives describe nouns. They usually come before the noun they describe.	Did you see the **beautiful** sunset? Jack told a **funny** story.
2. Adjectives can come after *be* or another linking verb. In this case, they describe the subject. Examples: *appear, be, become, feel, get, look, seem, smell, sound,* and *taste*.	You **are amazing**! You **look tired**. The garbage **smells horrible**.
3. Adjectives do not have a plural form. Do not add *-s* to adjectives that describe plural nouns.	✓ We visited an **ancient** town in Italy. ✓ We visited some **ancient** towns in Italy. ✗ We visited some <u>ancients</u> towns in Italy.
4. Use *a* or *an* before an adjective + a singular count noun. Use *a* before an adjective beginning with a consonant sound. Use *an* before an adjective beginning with a vowel sound.	She goes to **a good** university. We live in **an old** apartment. Climbing Mt. Everest is **a unique** experience.

4 Underline the adjective(s) in each sentence. Then draw an arrow to the noun or pronoun that each adjective describes.

1. Koalas have <u>thick</u> fur.

2. Thieves didn't take the angry koala. They were afraid of its sharp claws.

3. Australia is enormous, and Australian animals are fascinating.

4. The zoo helps sick animals. The koala appeared ill, but it seems healthy now.

5. Crocodiles have sharp teeth and powerful jaws. That crocodile looks hungry.

5 Put the words in the correct order to make sentences.

1. (looks / soft / the bear's fur) _____ The bear's fur looks soft. _____

2. (crocodile / is / enormous / that / an) _____

3. (have / strong / legs / kangaroos) _____

4. (pandas / shy / are / animals) _____

5. (has / exhibit / great / the zoo / a) _____

6. (an / history / interesting / Australia / has) _____

6.2 Nouns as Adjectives

1. A noun can sometimes be used as an adjective. It describes a noun that follows it.	I sat on a bench in the **park**. Noun I sat on a **park bench**. Noun as Adjective
2. When nouns are used as adjectives, they do not change form.	✓ The **plane ticket** was expensive. ✓ The **plane tickets** were expensive. ✗ The planes tickets were expensive.

6 Rewrite each sentence. Use the noun in **bold** as an adjective.

1. My sister works as a nurse in a **school**. My sister is a _school nurse_____.

2. The scissors are in the drawer of my **desk**. The scissors are in my _____.

3. I study the design of **furniture**. I study _____.

4. Her coat is **leather**. She is wearing a _____.

5. Have you seen the keys to my **car**? Have you seen my _____?

6. This store sells **computers**. This is a _____.

7. I need a bag for my **groceries**. I need a _____.

8. This juice was made from **oranges**. It's _____.

7 Circle the correct words to complete the sentences.

1. I need to buy a new pair of shoe / (shoes). I know a very good (shoe) / shoes store.

2. Les enjoys watching **car** / **cars** races. He really likes fast **car** / **cars**.

3. Kate is a **movie** / **movies** star. She's been in a lot of great **movie** / **movies**.

4. Vince is a **mountain** / **mountains** climber. He's climbed seven **mountain** / **mountains** this year.

5. Erin reads a lot of **book** / **books**. Last month she started a **book** / **books** club.

6. Carl is a **restaurant** / **restaurants** manager. He manages three **restaurant** / **restaurants**.

7. My mother makes delicious **vegetable** / **vegetables** soup. She always uses fresh **vegetable** / **vegetables**.

8. We live in a huge **apartment** / **apartments** building. There are 300 **apartment** / **apartments** in our building.

6.3 Word Order of Adjectives

	Opinion	Size	Age	Shape	Color	Origin	Material	Noun as Adjective	Noun
I wore my			new		black		leather		shoes.
We made a	delicious						chocolate		cake.
We sat at a		small		round					table.
I work in an			old		red		brick		building.
We saw some	beautiful					Chinese			paintings.
He gave her a	gorgeous							wedding	ring.
That's a	great					German		soccer	team.

---

1. When more than one adjective is used to describe a noun, they usually follow the order in the chart.

✓ We saw some **ancient Egyptian** sculptures.
✗ We saw some <u>Egyptian ancient</u> sculptures.

2. **Be careful!** We rarely use more than three adjectives together.

✓ They live in a **big brown** house.
✗ They live in a <u>beautiful big old brown</u> house.

3. Use a comma or *and* between adjectives that give the same kind of information. Use *and* when the adjectives come after a linking verb.

He's a **kind, patient** person.
He's a **kind and patient** person.
He's **kind and patient**.

Do not use commas between adjectives that give different types of information.

I have a **big orange** cat.
She has **short curly blonde** hair.

---

8 Put the adjectives in parentheses in the correct order to complete each sentence. Add a comma or *and* where necessary.

1. I live in a ____big apartment____ (apartment / big) building.

2. There are two _____ (Mexican / good) restaurants in my neighborhood

3. Dani keeps her jewelry in a _____ (round / glass) box.

4. Susi bought a _____ (new / winter / nice) coat.

5. Luke knows many _____ (historical / interesting) facts about this town.

6. The restaurant was in a _____ (old / strange / stone) building.

7. Anita is wearing a _____ (silk / beautiful / green) scarf today.

8. We watched a _____ (old / great) movie last night.

9. The animals claws are _____ (long / sharp).

10. My town has many _____ (modern / impressive / beautiful) buildings.

▲ A beautiful male peacock

PRACTICE

CD2-14

9 Complete the conversation with the words from the box. Then listen and check your answers.

amazing attractive brown colorful ~~favorite~~ green nice terrible

Petra: What are you watching?

Alex: It's a documentary about birds. Look, this part is about peacocks.

Petra: Oh, good—peacocks are my (1) _favorite_ kind of bird.

Alex: Really?

Petra: Yes. I love their feathers. The colors are (2) _____ !

Alex: Well, yes, the males are very (3) _____, but the females aren't. Their feather's aren't (4) _____ ; they're (5) _____ .

Petra: I know, but that's the way it is with most birds: the male has beautiful feathers, so he is (6) _____ to females.

Alex: I guess so. Well, they certainly are interesting, beautiful birds, but they make a (7) _____ noise.

Petra: Yes, that's true. When a male calls out to the female birds, he doesn't make a very (8) _____ sound.

10 Put the words in parentheses in the correct order to complete each sentence. Add *a, an, and,* or a comma where necessary.

1. Cows are _common farm animals_
(farm / common / animals)

2. Marta has _____.
(brown / long / hair)

3. Paris is _____.
(exciting / city / interesting)

4. Georgia is _____.
(person / friendly / kind)

5. Pandas eat _____.
(leaves / green / small)

6. There was _____ in the kitchen
(black / scary / spider)

7. We went to _____
(shoe / new / store / wonderful)

8. That restaurant has _____
(food / delicious / Indian)

11 APPLY.

A Work with a partner. Look at the nouns in the box. Each noun can be used as an adjective with all of the nouns in one of the groups below. Match each noun with the correct group.

art	computer	fire	grocery	phone	~~police~~	train	TV

1. _____police_____ officer, station, car

2. _____ show, channel, star

3. _____ class, museum, student

4. _____ call, company, number

5. _____ bag, list, store

6. _____ program, game, system

7. _____ alarm, department, truc

8. _____ schedule, station, ticket

B In your notebook, write five questions. In each, use an adjective + a noun from exercise **A**.

What is your favorite TV show? What art museums have you visited?

C Take turns asking and answering your questions from exercise **B** with your partner. Explain you answers, using adjectives where appropriate.

A: *What is your favorite TV show?*   B: Dr. Who. *It has interesting stories and fascinating character*

EXPLORE

CD2-15

1 **READ** the article about the Maori people, the first people to live in New Zealand, and their traditional tatoos. Notice the words in **bold**.

New Zealand→

Moko—The Art of Maori Tattoos

Dr. Ngahuia Te Awekotuku of New Zealand is a leading writer on Maori issues in New Zealand. On her chin and lips she **proudly** wears a Maori tattoo, or *moko*. The purpose of her moko is to remember the Maori queen who died in 2006.

In the past, young Maori received moko when they became adults. It was an **extremely** painful process. A sharp tool was used to cut the skin. People sat **quietly** and **patiently** to show their courage.

These days, a young Maori might get a moko to mark an achievement[1] such as getting on a sports team or passing an exam. Most young people choose to get a moko using less painful methods than in earlier times.

Some people who are not Maori have also started to get moko. Some Maori don't mind this, but others are not happy about it. For the Maori, moko remains a **very** serious tradition.

[1]**achievement:** something that someone does successfully, usually as a result of much effort

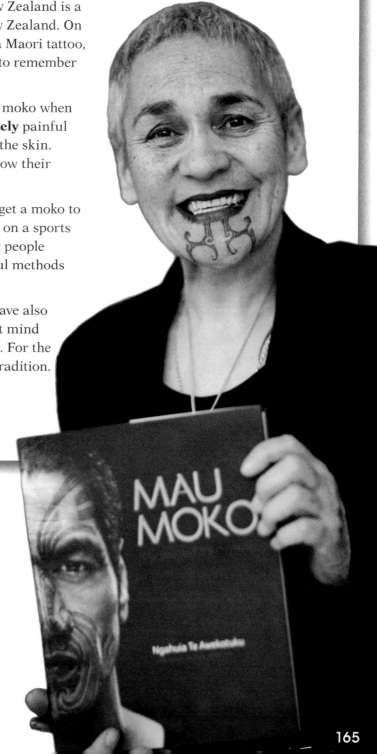

▶ Dr. Ngahuia Te Awekotuku with her book *Mau Moko: The World of Maori Tattoo*.

165

2 CHECK. Choose the correct answer to complete each statement.

1. How does Dr. Te Awekotuku feel about her tattoo? She _____ .

   a. doesn't like it   b. is proud of it   c. doesn't care about it

2. The main reason for Dr. Te Awekotuku's moko is to _____ .

   a. decorate her face   b. mark an achievement   c. honor someone's memory

3. To show their courage when they received moko, young people used to _____ .

   a. watch the sharp tool   b. remain calm   c. choose large designs

4. Some non-Maori people now get moko. The Maori people's feelings
   are _____ about this.

   a. negative   b. positive   c. mixed

3 DISCOVER. Complete the exercises to learn about the grammar in this lesson.

A Find these sentences in the article from exercise **1**. Write the missing words.

1. On her lips and chin she **proudly** _____ a Maori tattoo.

2. People _____ **quietly** and **patiently** to show their courage.

B Work with a partner. Look at the verbs you wrote in exercise **A**. Notice the location of the bold adverbs. With a partner, discuss how to complete the statement *An adverb can come . . .*

▼ A Maori man in New Zealan

LEARN

6.4 Adverbs of Manner

Adjectives		
	Adjective	Noun
They are	**slow**	animals.
She is a	**careful**	driver.

Adverbs of Manner		
	Verb	Adverb
They	move	**slowly.**
She	drives	**carefully.**

1. Adverbs of manner describe action verbs.	He spoke **softly.** She dances **beautifully.**
2. Adverbs of manner usually come after the verb or after the verb + the object. Do not put adverbs of manner between the verb and the object.	✓ He sang **beautifully.** ✓ He sang the song **beautifully.** ✗ He sang <u>beautifully</u> the song.
3. Do not use an adverb after a linking verb. Use an adjective after a linking verb.	✓ She **looks happy.** ✗ She looks <u>happily</u>. ✓ The flowers **smell beautiful.** ✗ The flowers smell <u>beautifully</u>.
4. To form adverbs of manner, add -ly to most adjectives.* **Be careful!** Not all words that end in -ly are adverbs.	beautiful → beauti**fully** cheerful → cheer**fully** happy → happ**ily** soft → soft**ly** Adjectives: friendly, lonely, ugly, lovely Nouns and Verbs: reply, supply
5. Some adverbs of manner have the same form as the related adjective. To create an adverb, do not add -ly to these words: *early, fast, hard, late.*	✓ They eat fast. ✗ They eat fast<u>ly</u>.
6. The adverb form of *good* is *well.*	✓ My new laptop works **well.** ✗ My new laptop works <u>good</u>.

*See page **A4** for spelling rules for adverbs ending in -ly.

4 Complete each sentence with the adverb form of the adjective in parentheses.

1. The professor wears her tattoo _____*proudly*_____ (proud).

2. The young Maori sat _____ (quiet) as they got their tattoos.

3. The tattoo process was painful, but they acted _____ (brave).

4. They started the presentation _____ (early).

5. The professor explained the history of the Maori very _____ (clear).

6. He doesn't speak Maori _____ (good), but he understands it.

7. She answered all our questions _____ (honest).

8. I read her book _____ (quick).

9. She thought very _____ (hard) about her future.

10. He spoke very _____ (fast). I didn't understand everything.

5 Write the adverb form of each adjective. Then place the adverb in a correct place in the sentence. Sometimes there is more than one correct place.

1. My brother doesn't drive. (safe)   ✓ *safely*

2. We worked last semester. (hard)

3. Journalists write their reports. (quick)

4. Martina walked along the beach. (slow)

5. The professor didn't answer my question. (complete)

6. The mail arrived. (early)

7. The children played in the yard. (happy)

8. I held the baby. (gentle)

6.5 Adverbs of Degree

Weaker			Stronger
←			→
somewhat	fairly pretty	really very so quite	extremely

1. Use adverbs of degree to make adjectives or other adverbs stronger or weaker.	The movie was **somewhat** long. The students did **very** well on the test. Our team played **pretty** badly last night.
2. Adverbs of degree usually come before the adjective or adverb.	✓ It was **really** good. ✗ It was good really.
3. Do not use *pretty, fairly,* or *somewhat* in negative statements.	✓ She was **somewhat** tired. ✗ She wasn't somewhat tired.

REAL ENGLISH

Extremely, quite, very, and *somewhat* are more formal. *Really, pretty,* and *kind of* are less formal.

Formal: *The results of the two tests were* **quite** *different.*
Informal: *I'm* **pretty** *sad that my friend moved.*

6 Put the words in the correct order to make sentences.

1. boring / sounds / Steven's assignment / somewhat
   Steven's assignment sounds somewhat boring.

2. extremely / is / this song / popular

   _____

3. expensive / quite / looked / Elsa's shoes

   _____

4. ended / quickly / pretty / the discussion

_____

5. helpful / this software / very / seem / doesn't

_____

6. tired / so / last night / I / was

_____

7. scary / really / was / that movie

_____

8. Russian / Liza / fairly / speaks / well

_____

7 Read each pair of sentences. Does the **bold** adverb of degree make the underlined adjective or adverb stronger or weaker? Put a check (✓) in the correct column.

	Stronger	**Weaker**
1. The article was <u>interesting</u>. The article was **pretty** interesting.	☐	✓
2. The house was in <u>poor</u> condition. The house was in **really** poor condition.	☐	☐
3. Lee studied <u>hard</u> for his exams. Lee studied **very** hard for his exams.	☐	☐
4. Andrea paints <u>well</u>. Andrea paints **fairly** well.	☐	☐
5. I'm <u>hungry</u>. I'm **so** hungry!	☐	☐
6. The professor spoke <u>slowly</u>. The professor spoke **somewhat** slowly.	☐	☐
7. Chen felt <u>tired</u>. Chen felt **extremely** tired.	☐	☐
8. The store was <u>busy</u>. The store was **quite** busy.	☐	☐

PRACTICE

8 Circle the correct word to complete each sentence.

1. Sally came into the room very **sudden** / (**suddenly.**)

2. I love your wedding photos! You both look so **happy** / **happily**.

3. The children are working very **hard** / **hardly** this semester.

4. The team played extremely **good** / **well** in the last game.

5. The new boss spoke **proud** / **proudly** about his plans for the company.

6. This pizza wasn't **cheap** / **cheaply**, but it tastes **good** / **well**.

7. I spoke to the professor **quick** / **quickly**. He explained the assignment very **clear** / **clearly**.

8. Mike had a **bad** / **badly** accident. He hurt his arm very **bad** / **badly**.

9 Complete the text with the correct form of the words in parentheses.

A Person I Admire

I just got back from a really (1) _____ (nice) visit with my grandfather in Montana. He used to live in Florida, but he has been living (2) _____ (happy) in Montana for almost 20 years now. He celebrated his 82nd birthday this summer, and he looks (3) _____ (terrific).

He eats a (4) _____ (healthy) diet and exercises (5) _____ (regular). He's extremely (6) _____ (active) for his age. He hasn't slowed down at all since I last saw him.

My grandfather also has a lot of hobbies and interests. For example, he plays the guitar really (7) _____ (good) and sings (8) _____ (beautiful). When he was young, he was very (9) _____ (curious) and loved to travel. He traveled (10) _____ (frequent), so he has some (11) _____ (interesting) stories. He's a (12) _____ (great) storyteller, too! After a week with Grandpa, I didn't want to leave!

10 EDIT, LISTEN & SPEAK.

A Read the e-mail. Find and correct eight more errors with adverbs and adjectives.

Hi, Jessica and Mark,

    I need some advice. I had an interview for a job as a DJ[1] at my local radio station, but I was
    unsuccessful
~~unsuccessfully~~. I've had a lot of experience as a DJ, and I work very hard. I wore a new nice suit to

the interview, and I felt pretty confidently when I left my house.

    Before the interview, I read some interview tips and techniques online. For example, one said,

"Copy the interviewer's movements close." Well, I tried that technique, but the interviewers didn't seem

to like it very much. Anyway, I didn't get the job. Now I'm real confused. I know I made a few mistakes

in the interview, but nothing really bad. At first, I was nervously, but that was because I arrived lately.

When the interview started, I spoke loud, smiled frequently, and talked a lot—well, until they asked me

to stop. Also, I didn't ask any questions, but in general, I thought it went good. Where did I go wrong?

Thanks,

Kevin in Ohio

[1]**DJ:** a person who plays recorded music on the radio or at live events

B Listen to the first part of the *Helping Hand* radio show and check your answers from exercise **A**.

C Look at the list of Kevin's behaviors in the chart. Then complete the second column of the chart with your opinion of his behaviors. Check (✓) *Good* or *Bad* for each behavior. Then write notes to explain your opinions.

D Listen to the second part of *Helping Hand*. Complete the radio expert's column in the chart.

Kevin's Behaviors	Your Opinion	Radio Expert's (Mark's) Advice
1. wore a suit	Good ✓ Bad ☐ Notes: This shows respect.	Bad choice. Dress appropriately.
2. arrived late	Good ☐ Bad ☐ Notes:	
3. copied the interviewers	Good ☐ Bad ☐ Notes:	
4. spoke loudly	Good ☐ Bad ☐ Notes:	
5. smiled frequently	Good ☐ Bad ☐ Notes:	
6. didn't ask questions	Good ☐ Bad ☐ Notes:	

E Work with a partner. Share the information in your charts from exercise **D** and discuss why you agree or disagree with the radio expert.

11 APPLY.

A Work with a partner. When is it important to make a good first impression, for example, at a job interview, your first day in a new class, your first day at a new job? Brainstorm a list of situations with your partner.

B Choose one of the situations from your list from exercise **A**. Then write a list of ways to make a good impression in that situation. Use adjectives and adverbs.

Situation: first day at a new job → dress professionally, be very polite

C Share your ideas in a small group.

D In your notebook, write five or six sentences about how to make a good first impression in the situation you chose. Use adjectives and adverbs and your ideas from exercise **B**.

On the first day of a new job, it is extremely important to dress professionally and listen carefully. You should also be very polite. . . .

Charts
6.1, 6.3,
6.4, 6.5

1 Circle the correct words to complete the conversation.

Neil: My sister sounded (1) **unhappy** / **unhappily** on the phone last night.

Junko: Oh, what was the matter?

Neil: Well, I think she is a little (2) **angry** / **angrily** about her grades at college.

Junko: Are they really (3) **bad** / **badly**?

Neil: I don't know. My sister works very (4) **hard** / **hardly** and does all of her assignments (5) **careful** / **carefully**. She is an extremely (6) **good** / **well** student.

Junko: So, what happened?

Neil: Well, her math exam didn't go (7) **good** / **well**. She didn't fail it (8) **complete** / **completely**, but she didn't get a (9) **pretty** / **very** good grade. When she took the exam, she didn't feel (10) **very** / **somewhat** confident.

Junko: That's too bad.

Neil: I know, but she's (11) **smart, studious** / **smart and studious**. I'm sure she will become (12) **successful** / **successfully** in the long run.

Charts
6.1, 6.3,
6.4

2 **EDIT.** Read the article about an unusual cat. Find and correct seven more errors with adverbs and adjectives.

Venus, the Two-Faced Cat

Venus is a ~~pet famous~~ ᵥfamous pet cat. She even has her own social networking page. She has also appeared on national TV.

Many people are interested in Venus because she has a unusual appearance, as you can see! One half of her face is black with an green eye, and the other half has stripes orange and a blue eye. How does something like this happen?

According to Leslie Lyons, a professor at the University of California, Davis, cats like Venus are extreme rare. Cats with orange and blacks coats are not unusual. However, cats with different colored eyes are unusually. This means Professor Lyons is much more interested in the real mystery about Venus: her blue beautiful eye.

▲ Venus's face is evenly divided into two colors.

3 LISTEN & SPEAK.

A Look at the photo and read the caption. Listen to the conversation about bowerbirds. Then choose the correct answer for each question.

1. What did Ken think of the film?

   a. It was fairly interesting.

   b. It was very interesting.

2. Why did Ken watch the whole film right away?

   a. He thought the photography was good.

   b. He wanted to watch it alone.

3. Why do male bowerbirds build bowers?

   a. to prove their strength

   b. to attract females

4. The three bowerbirds' stages looked _____ .

   a. similar   b. different

5. What does Marion say about the stage made of garbage?

   a. That sounds terrible!   b. That sounds terribly!

▲ A male bowerbird stands in front of the bower he built.

B Work with a partner. Compare your answers from exercise **A**. Did any of the information about bowerbirds surprise you? Discuss your answer with your partner and then the class.

4 SPEAK & WRITE.

A Think of a person you admire. The person can be someone you know or someone famous. Write notes in the chart about that person. Use adjectives and adverbs. Use the questions in the chart to help you.

	Person: _____
What adjectives describe the person's appearance, character, and abilities?	intelligent, funny
How did/does the person behave? Speak? Move? Laugh? Work? Have fun?	works hard

B Work with a partner. Tell your partner about the person you chose. Use your notes from exercise **A**.

C In your notebook, write a short paragraph of five or six sentences about this person. Use your notes from exercise **A**.

Connect the Grammar to Writing

1 READ & NOTICE THE GRAMMAR.

A Do you know any interesting looking animals? Tell a partner about an animal you think is interesting. Then read the text.

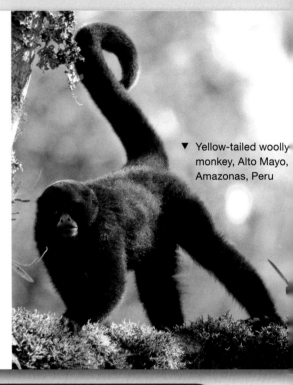

▼ Yellow-tailed woolly monkey, Alto Mayo, Amazonas, Peru

The Yellow-Tailed Woolly Monkey

The yellow-tailed woolly monkey is a very rare animal. It has thick brown fur and white hair around its mouth. The monkey is named for the bright yellow fur underneath its long, curled tail. These monkeys live in a small area in the high mountains of Peru. With their long arms and legs and powerful tail, they move quickly through the forests.

Unfortunately, these monkeys have lost a lot of their natural habitat. Farms and cattle ranches[1] are some of the reasons for this. People are now working hard to protect these amazing animals.

[1] **ranch:** a large farm used for keeping animals

GRAMMAR FOCUS

In the text in exercise **A**, the writer uses adjectives and adverbs to describe a rare kind of monkey.

Adjectives: *It has **thick brown** fur and **white** hair around its mouth.*
Nouns as adjectives: *Farms and **cattle** ranches are some of the reasons for this.*
Adverbs of manner: *. . . they move **quickly** through the forests.*
Adverbs of degree: *The yellow-tailed woolly monkey is a **very** rare animal.*

B Read the text in exercise **A** again. Underline the adjectives and circle the adverbs of manner and degree. Then work with a partner and compare your answers.

C Complete the chart with information about the woolly monkey from exercise **A**. Write adjectives or adverbs and the words they describe.

Appearance	thick brown fur,
Habitat (where it lives)	small area,
Movements or Behavior	

2 BEFORE YOU WRITE. Choose an animal from this unit or another animal that interests you. Then complete the chart. Use the chart from exercise **1C** as a model.

Appearance	
Habitat (where it lives)	
Movements or Behavior	

3 WRITE about the animal you chose. Write two paragraphs. Use the information from your chart in exercise **2** and the text in exercise **1A** to help you.

WRITING FOCUS   Using Adjectives and Adverbs

Good writers use adjectives and adverbs to make their writing more interesting.

Compare:

With their arms and legs and tail, they move through the forests.

*With their **long** arms and legs and **powerful** tail, they move quickly through the forests.*

Good writers also choose their words carefully and do not use too many adjectives or adverbs.

Compare:

*With their **long** arms and legs and **powerful** tail, they move **quickly** through the forests.*

*With their **big long** arms and **strong** legs and **powerful curled** tail, they move **quickly** and **gracefully** through the **beautiful thick Peruvian** forests.*

Make sure to choose your adjectives and adverbs carefully when you write. This is especially important in academic and business writing.

---

4 SELF ASSESS. Read your text. Underline the adjectives and adverbs. Then use the checklist to assess your work.

- [ ] I used adjectives correctly. [6.1–6.3]
- [ ] I used adverbs correctly. [6.4, 6.5]
- [ ] I used the correct word order with adjectives and adverbs. [6.3, 6.4]
- [ ] I used adjectives and adverbs to add interest to my writing. [WRITING FOCUS]
- [ ] I chose my adjectives and adverbs carefully. [WRITING FOCUS]

UNIT 7 Tomorrow and Beyond

The Future

A team of architects has designed a mobile hotel that lets guests sleep in pods hundreds of feet in the air. Each pod is a hotel guest room with power and water.

EXPLORE

CD2-19

1 **READ** the article about space travel for tourists. Notice the words in **bold**.

A Star-Studded Trip You'll Never Forget

Where are you planning to spend your next vacation? **Are** you **going to take** a trip to the beach? Or visit family perhaps? Do you want to travel somewhere new and different for a change? If so, try a trip to space! The following companies provide exciting trips that you **will remember** for a lifetime.

VIRGIN GALACTIC

You**'ll have** a fantastic experience, and you**'ll come back** with great stories to tell. On the VSS *Enterprise*, you and five other passengers **will fly** into space. You **won't orbit**[2] Earth, but you **will experience** zero gravity.[3] How much **will** this trip cost? About $250,000.

SPACE ADVENTURES

You**'ll fly** 250 miles above Earth, and you**'ll orbit** it every 90 minutes. It**'ll be** a spectacular experience! You **will be** the only passenger, but you **will spend** a week on the International Space Station with trained astronauts. How much money **will** you **need** for this trip? Around $50 million dollars.

No, your trip to space **is not going to be** a cheap vacation, but **it will be** a memorable one!

[1] **astronaut:** a person who travels in outer space
[2] **orbit:** to move in a path around another object in space
[3] **zero gravity:** a condition in which people and things float; happens in space

◀ **Virgin Galactic's** special WhiteKnight plane will carry the VSS *Enterprise* to 50,000 feet. Then the *Enterprise (center)* will continue into space alone.

2 CHECK. Read each statement. Is it true for Virgin Galactic, Space Adventures, or both? Put a check (✓) in the correct column(s).

	Virgin Galactic	Space Adventures
1. This trip is expensive.	☐	☐
2. A flight with this company costs $250,000.	☐	☐
3. This company's spaceships circle Earth.	☐	☐
4. Passengers spend a week on the International Space Station.	☐	☐

3 DISCOVER. Complete the exercises to learn about the grammar in this lesson.

A Find these sentences in the article from exercise **1**. Write the missing words.

1. **Are** you **going to** _____ a trip to the beach?

2. You**'ll** _____ a fantastic experience, . . .

3. . . . but you **will** _____ zero gravity.

4. No, your trip to space **is not going to** _____ a cheap vacation, . . .

B Look at the sentences in exercise **A**. Choose the correct answer to complete the statement.

The _____ form of the verb comes after *will/won't* and *be (not) going to*.

a. base   b. simple past   c. the simple present

LEARN

7.1 Future with *Will*

<table>
<tr><th colspan="3">Affirmative Statements</th></tr>
<tr><td>Subject</td><td>*Will*</td><td>Base Form</td></tr>
<tr><td>I/He/We</td><td>will
'll</td><td>win.</td></tr>
</table>

<table>
<tr><th colspan="3">Negative Statements</th></tr>
<tr><td>Subject</td><td>*Will Not/
Won't*</td><td>Base Form</td></tr>
<tr><td>I/He/We</td><td>will not
won't</td><td>win.</td></tr>
</table>

<table>
<tr><th colspan="4">Yes/No Questions</th></tr>
<tr><td>*Will*</td><td>Subject</td><td>Base Form</td><td></td></tr>
<tr><td>Will</td><td>you/she/they</td><td>help</td><td>us?</td></tr>
</table>

<table>
<tr><th>Short Answers</th></tr>
<tr><td>Yes, she **will**. / No, she **won't**.
Yes, they **will**. / No, they **won't**.</td></tr>
</table>

<table>
<tr><th colspan="4">Wh- Questions</th></tr>
<tr><td>*Wh-* Word</td><td>*Will*</td><td>Subject</td><td>Base Form</td></tr>
<tr><td>When</td><td rowspan="3">will</td><td>you</td><td>arrive?</td></tr>
<tr><td>What</td><td>she</td><td>need?</td></tr>
<tr><td>Who(m)</td><td>they</td><td>see?</td></tr>
</table>

<table>
<tr><th>Short Answers</th></tr>
<tr><td>Tomorrow night.</td></tr>
<tr><td>Her passport.</td></tr>
<tr><td>Their parents.</td></tr>
</table>

1. Use *will* for: a. things you are sure will happen in the future b. predictions about the future c. decisions made at the time of speaking d. offers or promises	a. The sun **will rise** at 6:00 a.m. tomorrow. b. I think **you'll do** well on the test. c. A: Someone's at the door. B: **I'll get** it. d. **I'll call** you later.
2. The contractions *'ll* and *won't* are usually used in conversation and informal writing.	A: Do you want anything? B: Sure. **I'll have** a cup of coffee. **I won't** have time for more.
3. To express *there is (not)/there are (not)* in the future, use *there will be/there won't be*.	**There will be** a new teacher next year. A: **Will there be** time for questions? B: I'm afraid **there won't be** extra time.

4 Complete the exercises.

A Complete the information about a new space museum. Use *will* or *won't* and the verbs in parentheses.

The Space Museum
A Fantastic Journey for the Whole Family

Visitors to our grand opening in October (1) _____will get_____ (get) a close look at

several historic spacecrafts. Also, astronauts (2) _____ (visit) the museum

a few times each year. They (3) _____ (talk) about their experiences in

space, and visitors (4) _____ (have) the chance to meet them personally.

You (5) _____ (not be) disappointed with your visit!

The museum (6) _____ (open) on October 16 with an exhibit about space tourism. This exhibit (7) _____ (remain) open until January 15. In addition, there (8) _____ (be) fun activities for the whole family. Your children (9) _____ (not want) to go home!

Next year, the museum (10) _____ (welcome) several new exhibits about the history and future of our journeys to the stars. Buy your tickets for opening day now, so you (11) _____ (not miss) a thing!

B Read the statements. Write questions using *will*. The underlined word or phrase in each statement provides information about the answer.

1. The museum will open in October. _____ *When will the museum open?* _____

2. Astronauts will talk about their experiences in space. _____

3. The new exhibits will be at the museum. _____

4. Visitors will see historic spacecrafts. _____

5. Yes, there will be activities for children. _____

6. This exhibit will close on January 15th. _____

7. Yes, there will be new exhibits every year. _____

8. No, the museum will not be open on major holidays. _____

◄ Astronaut John W. Young drives the Lunar Roving Vehicle (LRV) at the Decartes landing site, April 21, 1972

7.2 Future with *Be Going To*

Affirmative Statements

Subject	Be	*Going To*	Base Form
I	am 'm	going to	stay.
He/She/It	is 's		
We/You/They	are 're		

Negative Statements

Subject	Be Not	*Going To*	Base Form
I	am not 'm not	going to	stay.
He/She/It	is not 's not isn't		
We/You/They	are not 're not aren't		

Yes/No Questions

Be	Subject	*Going To*	Base Form
Am	I	going to	go?
Is	he/she/it		
Are	you/we/they		

Short Answers

Yes, you are. / No, you aren't.
Yes, she is. / No, she isn't.
Yes, we are. / No, we aren't.

Wh- Questions

Wh- Word	Be	Subject	*Going To*	Base Form
What	is	she	going to	do?
Where	are	they		go?

Short Answers

Ride her bike.
To the museum.

---

1. Use *be going to* for
   a. things you are certain will happen in the future
   b. things you plan to do
   c. predictions

   a. It **is going to snow** tomorrow.
   b. I'**m going to watch** the news at 6:00.
   c. Space travel **is going to become** more popular in the future.

2. Contractions are usually used in conversation and informal writing.

   A: What are you going to do this weekend?
   B: I'**m going to visit** my sister in Boston.

CD2-20

5 Complete the conversation with *be going to* and the subjects and verbs in parentheses. Then listen and notice the pronunciation of *be going to*.

Carl: I'm so glad it's Friday. (1) _Are you going to do_ (you / do) anything special this weekend, Valerie?

Valerie: Yes, (2) _____ (I / go) to the opening of the new Space Museum. I'm sure it'll be crowded, but I really want to see it.

Carl: (3) What _____ (you / see) there?

Valerie: Well, (4) _____ (Phil and I / take) the children on some of the rides. There is one called "A Trip to the Moon."

Carl: That sounds fun.

Valerie: Yeah, (5) _____ (they / love) it.

Carl: (6) What _____ (you and Phil / do)?

Valerie: Oh, an astronaut is giving a lecture in the afternoon.

(7) _____ (we / attend) that. How about you?

Are you going to the game on Saturday?

Carl: No, I'm not, unfortunately. I have to study.

Valerie: That's too bad. (8) _____ (you / study) all weekend?

Carl: No, on Sunday (9) _____ (I / not do) any work.

(10) _____ (I / sleep) late and just relax.

Valerie: Oh, good. Well, have a great time.

---

6 SPEAK. Work with a partner. Ask and answer questions about your plans for the future. Use *be going to* and the time expressions in the box. Practice saying *going to* as "gonna."

this weekend	tonight
next year	after class

A: *What are you going to do this weekend?*

B: *I'm going to relax. How about you?*

REAL ENGLISH

In speaking, *going to* is often pronounced "*gonna*" when it comes before a verb. Use *going to*, not *gonna*, in writing.

Say: *We're **gonna** be late.*
Write: *We're **going to be** late.*

PRACTICE

7 LISTEN and write the words and contractions you hear. *(CD2-21)*

1. This book about the planets looks great. I ___'m going to buy___ it.

2. My brother enjoyed the astronaut's lecture. He _____ to another one next month.

3. Governments _____ much money on space research in the near future.

4. The astronauts _____ on the space station until the end of the month.

5. A: Don't wait for me. I _____ here for a long time.

   B: I'm not in a hurry. I _____ for you.

6. The museum gift shop _____ at 10:00 a.m.

7. There _____ any lectures next week.

8. Sarah _____ that movie. She doesn't like science fiction.

8 WRITE & SPEAK.

A Read the statements. Write questions using *will* or *be going to*. The underlined word or phrase in each statement provides information about the answer.

1. <u>Yes</u>, I'm going to take classes here next semester.

   Are you going to take classes here next semester?

2. I'm going to <u>hang out with friends</u> this weekend.

   _____

3. <u>No</u>, I won't be in class on Wednesday.

   _____

4. <u>Yes</u>, people will visit Mars someday.

   _____

5. People will travel <u>by flying car</u> in the future.

   _____

6. I'm going to call my parents <u>tonight</u>.

   _____

B Work with a partner. Take turns asking and answering the questions from exercise **A**. Use your own ideas.

A: *Are you going to take classes here next semester?*

B: *No, I'm not. I'm going to go back to Colombia.*

9 LISTEN, WRITE & SPEAK.

A Listen to three people who want to become astronauts. Complete the notes in the chart.

	Glenn	Sylvia	Mark
Two Years	be _____	finish _____	join the _____
Five Years	start *astronaut training*	be _____	be *a flight engineer*
Ten Years	be _____	go on her *first space mission*	work for _____

B Write five questions about the information from the chart in exercise **A**. Use *When* or *What* and *will* or *be going to*.

When will Sylvia go on her first mission? What is Sylvia going to do in ten years?

1. _____

2. _____

3. _____

4. _____

5. _____

C Work with a partner. Take turns asking and answering the questions from exercise **B**. Use the information from the chart in exercise **A** in your answers.

10 **EDIT.** Read about home life in the future. Find and correct seven more errors with *will* and *be going to*.

Home Life in the Future

I grew up in a house with a big yard and a lot of room to play. However, I don't think
that children of the future going to be so lucky. The world's population will continues to
increase, and this means all of us will live in smaller homes. I think some big cities in
Asia, such as Seoul and Singapore, will be serves as models for the cities of the future.
People are going live in high-rise apartment buildings. These apartment buildings going
to be cheaper, safer, and more practical than separate houses.

There are going be more advances in electronics. Also, people have more
entertainment choices in their homes in the future. We won't to go out very often to
watch movies or concerts. Movie theaters will go out of business in the future.

11 **APPLY.**

A Write six predictions about the future with *will* or *be going to*. Use the topics from the box or your own ideas.

education	fashion	shopping
entertainment	food	work

Cars will use hydrogen for fuel.

1. _____

2. _____

3. _____

4. _____

5. _____

6. _____

B Work in a group. Share your predictions from exercise **A**. Give reasons for your ideas.

Cars will use hydrogen for fuel, because there won't be any gas in the future.

EXPLORE

CD2-23

1 READ the conversation and the excerpt from a lecture. Notice the words in **bold**.

The Future of Work

10:00 a.m.

Stuart: Hey, Bob. **Are you coming** to the lecture on the future of work?

Bob: Yes, but it **doesn't start** until twelve, so **I'm leaving** around eleven.

Stuart: No, it *was* at twelve, but Professor Miller**'s going** on vacation tonight, so she changed the schedule. The lecture **begins** at ten-thirty. Hurry up, or we'll be late!

10:50 a.m.

Professor Miller: . . . so you see, in the future, companies are not going to pay people to drive to a central building. With the money they **save**, they're going to be able to hire more qualified workers. And it probably isn't going to matter where you live. In fact, workers in different time zones[1] are going to be popular with companies.

Stuart: Why is that?

Professor Miller: Well, let's take an example, Stuart. Imagine you're a manager in the United States. It's late afternoon on Thursday. The financial[2] year **finishes** tomorrow, and you**'re giving** a presentation in the morning. You need some new information, but everyone around you is going home. You contact your researcher in Australia, and because of the time difference, you **have** the information first thing the next morning . . .

[1] **time zone:** one of 24 areas the world is divided into as measured from Greenwich, England
[2] **financial:** having to do with money

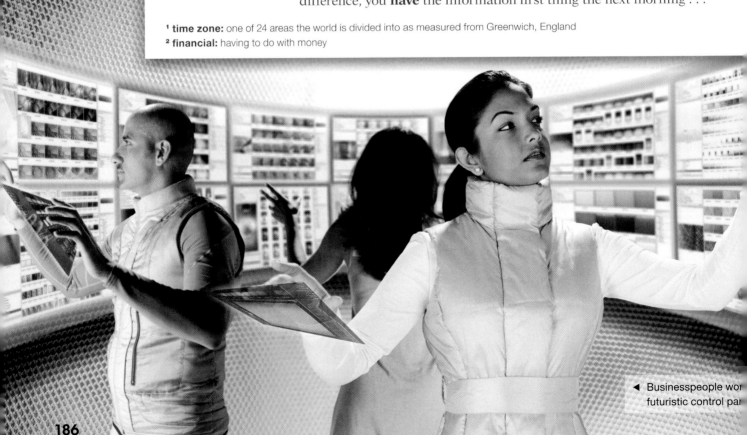

◀ Businesspeople wo[r]
futuristic control pa[r]

186

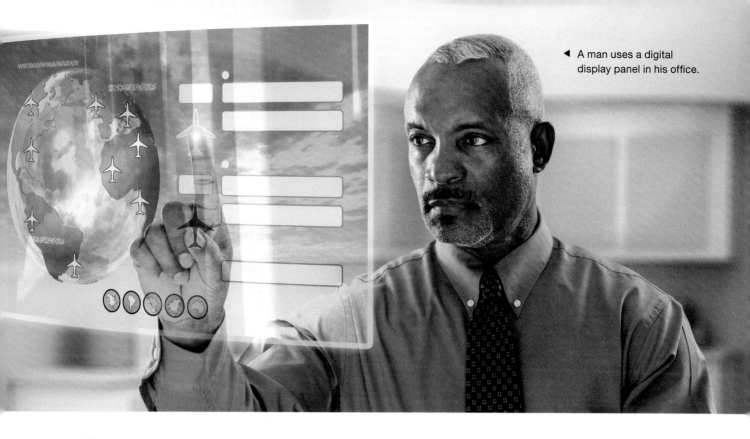

◄ A man uses a digital display panel in his office.

2 CHECK. Read the statements. Circle **T** for *true* or **F** for *false*.

1. Bob isn't going to go to the lecture.   T   F

2. The lecture is about work in the future.   T   F

3. Professor Miller changed the class schedule.   T   F

4. The class is usually at 10:30.   T   F

5. Professor Miller is going to take a vacation.   T   F

3 DISCOVER. Complete the exercises to learn about the grammar in this lesson.

A Look at the verb forms in **bold** in the conversation and excerpt in exercise **1**. Write the verbs in the correct column of the chart.

Simple Present	Present Progressive
doesn't start	

B Work with a partner. Discuss your answers to the questions.

1. Do the verb forms from exercise **A** refer to the present or future?

2. How does the meaning differ between the forms in the two columns?

LEARN

7.3   Simple Present: Future Schedules

Statements	Questions
My train **leaves** at 4:00 this afternoon. The game **doesn't start** until 3:00.	**Does** the train **leave** at 5:00? **When does** the game **start**?
The stores **close** at 6:00 this evening. They **don't close** late tonight.	**What time** do the stores **close**? **Do** the stores **close** late tonight?

1. Use the simple present to talk about future events that are scheduled or on a timetable.	Next semester **starts** on January 15. Our flight **leaves** at 10:45.
2. The simple present is often used to talk about the future with these verbs: *arrive, begin, close, end, finish, leave, open,* and *start*.	A: What time **does** the concert **end** tomorrow night? B: I think it **ends** around ten.

4 Complete the conversations with the verbs in parentheses. Use the simple present.

1. A: What time _____*does*_____ the lecture _____*begin*_____ (begin)?

    B: It _____*begins*_____ (begin) at ten-thirty.

2. A: When _____ Professor Miller _____ (leave) for vacation?

    B: She _____ (leave) tonight.

3. A: Excuse me, what time _____ flight 225 from Chicago _____ (arrive)?

    B: It _____ (arrive) at 1:45.

4. A: When _____ fall classes _____ (start)?

    B: They _____ (not start) until September 20.

5. The stores _____ (not open) until noon on Sunday.

6   A: What time _____ Martha's train _____ (get) to Miami?

    B: It _____ (get) there at ten-fifteen.

7. Hurry up! The cafeteria _____ (close) in 20 minutes.

8. Our bus _____ (not leave) until one-thirty. Let's get something to eat.

9. A: When _____ Linda _____ (start) her new job?

    B: She _____ (start) next Monday.

10. A: I _____ (finish) work at six tomorrow. Do you want to have dinner?

    B: No, sorry. My son _____ (have) an important hockey game tomorrow night

7.4 Present Progressive for Future Plans

Statements
I'm **going** to the beach tomorrow.
She's **not traveling** to Norway this summer.
They **are finishing** later.
We **aren't working** tomorrow.

Questions
Is Olga **going** to the party tonight?
What are you **doing** this weekend?
Are they **finishing** by 5:00?
What are we **eating** for dinner?

1. Use the present progressive for definite future plans. The plan is often in the near future, or the details of the plan, such as place or time, are specific.	She's **meeting** us at the airport. I'm **not going to** the concert tonight.
2. When the present progressive is used for the future, we often include a future time expression, such as *tonight, tomorrow, next month, this summer*, etc.	Future: I'm **working** <u>this weekend</u>.
When there is no future time expression or future context, the present progressive refers to the present.	Present: I'm working.

5 Complete each statement or question with the words in parentheses. Use the present progressive for future.

1. _____I'm working_____ (I / work) late tonight.

2. _____ (when / they / leave) for Rio?

3. _____ (we / go) a party on Friday night.

4. _____ (Craig / graduate) in June?

5. _____ (he / not have) dinner with us tonight.

6. _____ (I / meet) Marla at 2:30.

7. _____ (where / you / go) after class?

8. _____ (what / you / do) tomorrow night?

9. _____ (you / visit) your family this weekend?

10. _____ (how / you / get) home today?

6 SPEAK. Work with a partner. Take turns asking and answering questions 7–10 from exercise **5**.

A: *Where are you going after class?*

B: *To the dentist.*

PRACTICE

7 Circle the correct words to complete the conversations. Then listen and check your answers.

Conversation 1

Alison: Sue, (1) **do you do / are you doing** anything tomorrow evening?

Sue: No, (2) **I just spend / I'm just spending** a quiet evening at home. Why?

Alison: Well, I bought tickets to a lecture called "Working Smart." for my sister and me, but now (3) **she doesn't come / she's not coming**. Would you like to go with me?

Sue: I'd love to! Who (4) **speaks / is speaking**?

Alison: A guy called Tim Ferriss. He (5) **talks / is talking** about ways to work less and enjoy life more. I can't wait!

Sue: I definitely need to hear that! What time (6) **does it start / is it starting**?

Alison: At eight.

Conversation 2

Terri: Hey, George, I don't really understand this week's assignment.

(7) **Do you hand / Are you handing** it in tomorrow?

George: No. (8) **I don't understand / I'm not understanding** it either, and Professor Doyle's vacation (9) **starts / is starting** tomorrow. Jerry and I (10) **meet / are meeting** him tonight for coffee to discuss it. Do you want to join us?

Terri: Sure. Where (11) **do you meet / are you meeting him**?

George: At the Bridge Street Cafe at seven-thirty.

8 **LISTEN** to each statement or question. Is it present or future? Check (✓) present or future. Then listen again and write the words or phrases that helped you choose your answers.

CD2-24

1. ☐ present   ✓ future   Helpful words: _____*tomorrow*_____

2. ☐ present   ☐ future   Helpful words: _____

3. ☐ present   ☐ future   Helpful words: _____

4. ☐ present   ☐ future   Helpful words: _____

5. ☐ present   ☐ future   Helpful words: _____

6. ☐ present   ☐ future   Helpful words: _____

7. ☐ present   ☐ future   Helpful words: _____

8. ☐ present   ☐ future   Helpful words: _____

9 APPLY.

A Look at Pedro's calendar for next week. In your notebook, write five questions about his schedule and plans. Use the present progressive and simple present for future.

When is he going to New York City?

What time does his train to New York leave?

12 Monday		Thursday 15
math exam 10:30 a.m. meet Professor Allen—Room 204 4:00 p.m.		Spanish exam 3:00 p.m. dinner with Mom and Dad—7:00 p.m. China Garden Restaurant—28 Brown St.
13 Tuesday		**Friday 16**
dentist appointment 8:30 a.m. study for Spanish exam with Yuri and Keiko—library 2nd floor 5:00 p.m.		work at bookstore 10:00 a.m. – 4:00 p.m. New York City with Ted get tickets at train station train 431 6:15 p.m.
14 Wednesday	**17 Saturday**	**18 Sunday**
tennis with Rick—sports center 4:00 p.m. watch game—Todd's house 7:00 p.m. bring snacks	museum concert—8:00 p.m.	1:00 p.m. baseball game go home—train 432 6:45 p.m.

B Work with a partner. Ask and answer your questions from exercise **A**.

A: *When is he going to New York City?*

B: *On Friday.*

A: *What time does his train leave?*

B: *It leaves at 6:15.*

C In your notebook, create a calendar with notes about your schedule and plans for next week. Use Pedro's calendar from exercise **A** as a model.

D Work with a partner. Take turns asking and answering questions about your partner's week. Use the simple present and the present progressive for future.

A: *I'm having dinner with Alex on Wednesday night.*

B: *That's nice. Where are you going?*

EXPLORE

CD2-25

1 **READ** the blog post about Fatima's experience in South East Asia. Notice the words in **bold**.

Fatima's Blog: Ocean News and Views

Hi everyone! I'm on a diving tour of Southeast Asia. The diving is breathtaking! **I'll post** some photos **when I have more time.**

In this blog I **will share** photos of my trip as well as ideas about the ocean and ways to protect it. I'm **going to write** about a new topic each week. My first post is about the future of coral reefs. *Sharks are Not Your Enemy!* **is coming** next week, so stay tuned! My goal is for everyone to enjoy the photos and learn ways to help protect our oceans and the animals in them. I hope, for example, that **after you read this first post**, you **will never use** another plastic bag and you **will avoid** all toxic sunscreens. Enjoy!

Post 1: The Future of Coral Reefs

Coral reefs are one of the most beautiful and colorful sights in nature, but according to scientists, they are in danger. We must change our behavior if we want them to survive. Some experts predict that a large percentage of the world's coral reefs **will not exist** in the year 2050. **Will** people **change** their behavior **before it's too late**? Here are some facts about coral reefs, and a few things you can do to help protect our oceans:

▼ A coral reef looks like an underwater garden, but corals are animals not plants.

2 CHECK. Choose the correct answer to complete each statement.

1. Fatima is in _____. a. Asia b. Africa

2. Her goal is to _____ the ocean. a. enjoy b. protect

3. Coral reefs are _____. a. in danger b. dead

4. She thinks plastic bags are _____. a. good b. bad

5. According to some experts, only _____ of coral reefs will exist in 2050. a. 50 percent b. 30 percent

3 DISCOVER. Complete the exercises to learn about the grammar in this lesson.

A Look at these sentences from the blog post in exercise **A**. Circle the subject + verb that comes after each underlined time word.

1. I'll post some photos <u>when</u> I have more time.

2 . . . <u>after</u> you read this first post, you will never use another plastic bag . . .

3. Will people change their behavior <u>before</u> it's too late?

B Look at the verbs you circled in exercise **A**. What verb form is used in the clauses?

LEARN

7.5 Comparison of Future Forms

1. Use *will* or *be going to* for predictions and things you are certain about in the future.	Ana is smart. She**'ll get** a good job. Ana is smart. She**'s going to get** a good job.
Be careful! Use only *be going to* when you are certain about something because of evidence or information you have now.	✓ The score if 5-0. We **are going to** win! ✗ The score is 5-0. We <u>will</u> win!
2. Use *will* for decisions made at the time of speaking, offers, and promises.	A: You didn't mail the letter. B: I forgot! I**'ll do** it tomorrow.
3. Use *be going to* for plans or intentions.	I**'m going to play** soccer on Sunday afternoon. Lisa **isn't going to teach** next semester.
4. Use the present progressive for plans. The plans are often in the near future.	Jason **is leaving** for Hong Kong tomorrow. Rita **isn't coming** to the party tonight.
5. Use the simple present for future events that are scheduled or on a time table.	The train **leaves** at 10:35 tomorrow morning.

4 Circle the correct future form to complete each sentence.

1. Don't carry that heavy suitcase. **I'll carry** / **I'm carrying** it for you.

2. I'm going to Australia this summer. **I'm going to visit** / **I visit** the Great Barrier Reef.

3. I heard the weather report. **It's snowing** / **It's going to snow** tonight.

4. According to experts, coral reefs **are** / (**will be**) in serious trouble by 2050.

5. Tricia **will go** / **is going** to a concert tonight.

6. We **are going** / **go** to Alaska next month.

7. I'm tired. **I'm staying** / **I stay** home tonight.

8. Darlene **has** / **is going to have** her baby in a few months.

9. Do you need money? **I'm lending** / **I'll lend** you some.

10. **I'll take** / **I'm going to take** a photography class next semester.

5 Choose all possible correct answers to complete each sentence.

1. In the future, people _____ to Mars.

   a. travel   (b.) will travel   (c.) are going to travel

2. Ten years from now, I _____ a doctor.

   a. will be   b. am   c. am going to be

3. Don't forget. We _____ dinner with my grandparents tonight.

   a. have   b. are having   c. will have

4. Louis _____ to Puerto Rico to study Spanish next semester.

   a. goes   b. is going   c. is going to go

5. My friends and I _____ our own business after college.

   a. start   b. will start   c. are going to start

6. Are you going to class now? _____ you a ride.

   a. I'm giving   b. I'll give   c. I give

7. My family _____ a vacation in Florida next week.

   a. will take   b. is taking   c. takes

8. _____ early tomorrow morning. I have a meeting at 7:30 a.m.

   a. I'm getting up   b. I get up   c. I'll get up

9. Oh, no! Look at this traffic! _____ late.

   a. We're   b. We'll be   c. We're going to be

10. When _____ Friday? Let's do something afterward.

    a. does your class end   b. will your class end   c. is your class ending

7.6 Future Time Clauses with *After, As Soon As, When, Before*

1. A future time clause tells when an action or event will happen. The time clause can come before or after the main clause.	**After I eat lunch,** I will take a nap. Time Clause Main Clause I will take a nap **after I eat lunch.** Main Clause Time Clause

2. Future time clauses begin with *before, after, as soon as,* or *when.*
 	
   a. Use *after, as soon as,* or *when* to show that the action or event in the time clause will happen first.
 	
   b. Use *before* to show that the action or event in the time clause will happen second.
	a. **When** we **get married,** we'll buy a house.
	
	Time Clause (First Event) Main Clause (Second Event)
	
	b. **Before** we **get married,** we'll buy a house.
	
	Time Clause (Second Event) Main Clause (First Event)

3. Use the simple present, not *will* or *be going to,* in the time clause.	✓ After I **graduate,** I will get a job. ✗ After I <u>will</u> graduate, I will get a job.
4. **Remember:** Use a comma when a time clause comes at the beginning of a sentence.	**As soon as I get a job,** I'm going to move. **When I get to the office,** I'll call you.

6 Look at the underlined clauses in each sentence. Write *1* above the action that will happen first. Write *2* above the action that will happen second. Then add a comma if necessary.

1. <u>After I finish my homework</u>, <u>I'm going to bed</u>.
   (1 above "After I finish my homework", 2 above "I'm going to bed")

2. <u>When I finish this book about coral reefs</u> <u>I am going to write my essay</u>.

3. <u>Lulu is going to call the office</u> <u>as soon as she receives the information</u>.

4. <u>My sister will read all the instructions</u> <u>before she uses her new phone</u>.

5. <u>I'll start cooking dinner</u> <u>when you get home</u>.

6. <u>My brother is going to buy a new computer</u> <u>when he receives his next paycheck</u>.

7. <u>After I go to the gym</u> <u>I'm going to go to the supermarket</u>.

8. <u>I'll clean the living room</u> <u>before our guests arrive tonight</u>.

9. <u>I'll help you</u> <u>as soon as I send this e-mail</u>.

10. <u>After she graduates from college</u> <u>she's going to move to Toronto</u>.

7 Circle the correct form of the verb to complete each sentence. Then add a comma if necessary.

1. After the rain **(stops)** / **will stop**, we we're going to take a walk.

2. Louise **goes** / **will go** back to work as soon as she feels better.

3. I'll let you know as soon as my plane **lands** / **will land** in Paris.

4. Andy **is** / **will be** surprised when I arrive at his birthday party.

5. Before I leave I **show** / **will show** you that website.

6. They're going to take some photos of the Alps when they **visit** / **will visit** Switzerland.

7. When my sister saves enough money she **buys** / **is going to buy** a car.

8. He'll call you as soon as he **finishes** / **is going to finish** his homework.

9. When I **see** / **will see** Sam I'll invite him to the party.

10. I'll say goodbye to you before I **leave** / **am leaving** tonight.

PRACTICE

8 Circle the correct form of the verbs to complete the conversation.

Ria: Hey Joan, what (1) **are you doing** / **do you do** this evening?

Joan: (2) **I'm going to watch** / **I'll watch** TV.

Ria: What (3) **are you going to watch / will you watch**?

Joan: There's a documentary about wildlife in Africa on tonight. It (4) **starts / will start** at nine.

Ria: Oh, that sounds interesting. What time (5) **will it end / does it end**?

Joan: Let's see . . . It (6) **ends / is ending** at ten-thirty. Why? (7) **Are you going to go / Will you go** to bed early?

Ria: Yeah, I (8) **'ll give / 'm giving** a presentation in the morning . . . but, I (9) **'ll watch / 'm watching** the first half of it with you.

Joan: Oh, good. I (10) **'m recording / 'll record** the rest of it, so you can watch it tomorrow.

9 Combine the pairs of sentences with the words in parentheses. Add a comma when necessary.

1. First: I'm going to talk to Hans. Second: I'm going to write my assignment.

   (after) <u>After I talk to Hans, I'm going to write my assignment. OR</u>

   <u>I'm going to write my assignment after I talk to Hans.</u>

2. First: Rui and Fatima are going to arrive. Second: We're going to have dinner.

   (when) _____

3. First: Barbara is going to buy a few things. Second: She's going to go home.

   (before) _____

4. First: Mary is going to call. Second: I'm going to ask about the test.

   (when) _____

5. First: She is going to finish law school. Second: She is going to move to Ohio.

   (as soon as) _____

6. First: I'm going to finish my homework. Second: I'm going to go for a run.

   (when) _____

7. First: He is going to paint it. Second: He is going to sell his house.

   (before) _____

8. First: I'm going to make dinner. Second: I'm going to watch the news.

   (after) _____

10 SPEAK. Work with a partner. Complete the sentences about yourself.

After I finish this English course . . .   When I retire . . .

As soon as class ends today . . .   . . . before I go home today.

After I finish this English course, I'm going to take a vacation.

11 EDIT. Read the article about the Great Bear Rainforest. Find and correct six more errors with future forms.

The Future of the Great Bear Rainforest

A Canadian company wants to build an oil pipeline[1] in central Canada. It ~~carries~~ *will carry* oil from Alberta to the coast of British Columbia, over 700 miles (1120 km) away. The pipeline will carrying oil to the coast, where big ships will to collect the oil for the next stage of its journey. The pipeline will create a new market for Canadian oil in China and other Asian countries.

Unfortunately, the plan going to take the pipeline through the Great Bear Rainforest. Many people do not want this to happen. The building of the pipeline will threatens animals such as the Kermode bear. Also, some of the local people think that the ships are going cause problems. They are afraid that one of the ships will spill[2] oil when it will travel along the coast of British Columbia.

[1] **pipeline:** a large pipe for carrying oil or gas across a country
[2] **spill:** to drop liquid by accident

◄ A Kermode bear, also known as a spirit bear, in the Great Bear Rainforest, British Columbia, Canada

12 APPLY.

A Work with a partner. Read Judy's *To Do List* for tomorrow. With a partner, take turns talking about her plans for tomorrow.

At eleven o'clock, she's going to check the monkey house.

TO DO LIST

- check monkey house 11:00
- answer e-mail 1:00
- call Frank – ask about lions and their new diet 2:00
- interview zookeeper applicant 3:00 – use new question sheet for the interview
- leave office 4:00
- buy Mom's birthday present
- get birthday cake—Sam's Bakery

B Complete each sentence with the correct form of the verbs in parentheses. Then add a comma if necessary. For some items, there is more than one correct answer.

1. Judy _is going to answer_ (answer) her e-mail before she _____calls_____ (call) Frank.

2. When she _____ (speak) with Frank she _____ (ask) him about the lions' diet.

3. She _____ (call) Frank before she _____ (interview) the zookeeper applicant.

4. Judy _____ (use) the new question sheet when she _____ (talk) to the zookeeper applicant.

5. After she _____ (finish) the interview she _____ (leave) her office.

6. As soon as she _____ (leave) her office she _____ (go) to the store.

7. When she _____ (go) to the store she _____ (buy) her mother's birthday present.

8. Judy _____ (get) a birthday cake after she _____ (do) everything else.

C In your notebook, write five or six sentences about your schedule for tomorrow. Use *before, after, as soon as,* and *when.*

After I finish class, I'm going to meet Luisa and Daniela for coffee.

D Work with a partner. Take turns talking about your schedules for tomorrow. Ask follow up questions.

A: *What are you doing after class?*

B: *I'm going to study for a grammar test.*

A: *Oh, who's your grammar teacher?*

Charts
7.1–7.6

1 Complete the conversations with the words in parentheses. Use *will, be going to,* the present progressive for future, or the simple present for future. In some cases, more than one answer is possible.

1. **Vera:** What's wrong with Erik today?

   Deng: He's upset about last month's sales report. _____ (I / talk)
   to him after _____ (I / send) this e-mail.

2. **Jamal:** What time _____ (you / finish) work tonight?

   Larry: At six-thirty. _____ (I / call) you when
   _____ (I / leave) the office.

3. **Student:** Excuse me, _____ (the library / close)
   at ten tonight?

   Librarian: No, _____ (it / close) at eleven tonight.

4. **Scott:** Hey, Mike. _____ (you / go) to the meeting this afternoon?

   Mike: No, _____ (I / leave) for China today. My flight
   _____ (be) at three o'clock.

Charts
7.1, 7.2, 7.6

2 **EDIT.** Read the article about a new form of identification for zebras. Find and correct five more errors with future verb forms.

Barcodes for Zebras

Counting zebras in the wild has always been difficult. However, counting zebras
will become
~~becomes~~ much easier in the future thanks to a new computer program called *Stripespotter*. In the future, scientists will just take photos of zebras. After they will take photos of the zebras,

▲ A zebra in the Okavango Delta, Botswana

Stripespotter is doing the rest of the work. It will to examine the stripes on each zebra.
The pattern of a zebra's stripes is like the barcode on a product at the supermarket. Each
one is different. After scientists are going to collect enough photos, they are having an
accurate record of the zebra population.

3 LISTEN, WRITE & SPEAK.

A Listen to two people talk about one of their future goals. Check (✓) the correct goal for each speaker.

Speaker 1: Matt

Goal: ☐ learn to cook Thai food   ☐ learn to play the guitar   ☐ own a music store

Plans:

_____ at a music store

_____ every day

_____ music a lot

Predictions:

_____ famous _____ very good

Speaker 2: Tammy

Goal: ☐ meet new people   ☐ get in shape   ☐ run a marathon

Plans:

_____ a new pair of running shoes

_____ a running club

_____ some short races

Predictions:

_____ really hard _____ in great shape

B How do the speakers plan to achieve their goals? What predictions do they have about their goals? Listen again and complete the notes for each speaker.

C Work with a partner. Compare your answers from exercises **A** and **B**. Then take turns asking and answering questions about the speakers' goals, plans, and predictions. Discuss anything else you remember about the speakers. Use future forms.

A: *Is Matt going to take a class?*   B: *Yes, he is.*

4 WRITE & SPEAK.

A Think of one of your own goals for the future. Then, in your notebook, write notes to answer these questions: How do you plan to achieve your goal? What are your predictions about your goal?

B Work with a partner. Take turns talking about your goals. Use your notes from exercise **A**.

1 READ & NOTICE THE GRAMMAR.

A What are some of your predictions about the future? Discuss your predictions with a partner. Then read the text.

Personal Transporters

In the future, more people will use personal transporters, like the one in this photo. Personal transporters will take us places quickly and safely. When they become cheaper, everyone is going to want one!

Personal transporters will also be good for the environment. They'll use less fuel than cars. They'll also take up less space, so we won't need as many large parking lots. This will mean more space for parks and trees.

We'll soon see more personal transporters at airports and in large factories. When workers at these places try them, I'm sure they will find them very helpful and convenient. Police officers, letter carriers, and security guards will also find these vehicles very useful in their work. Personal transporters are going to make the commute to work more fun. I'm going to buy one as soon as I can!

GRAMMAR FOCUS

In the text in exercise **A**, the writer uses *will* and *be going to* to make predictions.

> In the future, more people **will use** personal transporters like the one in this photo.
> When they become cheaper, everyone **is going to want** one!

The writer uses *future* time clauses to specify the time of future events.

> **When they become cheaper,** everyone is going to want one!

B Complete the chart with four more predictions about personal transporters from the text in exercise **A**.

Topic: Personal Transporters

Predictions:

1. more people will use them

C Read the text from exercise **A** again. Underline two more future time clauses.

2 BEFORE YOU WRITE.

A Work with a partner. Brainstorm topics about the future. Write a list of your ideas in your notebook.

B Choose one of the topics from your list in exercise **A**. Then complete the chart with your predictions about this topic. How will it change life in the future?

Topic:
Predictions:

3 WRITE about your predictions for the future. Write three paragraphs. Use your topic and your notes from exercise **2B** and the text in exercise **1A** to help you. Use future time clauses.

WRITING FOCUS   Using Gender-Neutral Language

Use gender-neutral language in your writing. This shows respect for both men and women. Here are some tips for using gender-neutral language in writing:

- Do not use words with *man* or *mankind* when referring to people in general or all people. For example, in the text in exercise **1A**, the writer uses *people* instead of *man* or *mankind*.

- Use job titles that refer to both men and women. For example, in exercise **1A**, the writer uses *police officers* instead of *policemen*. Here are some other examples:

Original Term:	Gender Neutral Term:
fireman	*fire fighter*
mankind, man	*humanity, people*
businessman	*businessperson*
policeman	*police officer*
stewardess	*flight attendant*

---

4 SELF ASSESS. Read your text. Underline your predictions. Then use the checklist to assess your work.

☐   I used *will* or *be going to* to make predictions [7.1, 7.2]

☐   I used future forms correctly. [7.1–7.4]

☐   I used the correct verb forms in main clauses and time clauses. [7.6]

☐   I used gender-neutral language. [WRITING FOCUS]

Consumer Society

Comparatives and Superlatives

▲ Cars in a scrap yard in Canada.

EXPLORE

CD2-28

1   READ the article about consumer societies. Notice the words in **bold**.

What is a Consumer Society?

A *consumer* is a person who buys things, and a *consumer society* is a society that encourages people to buy and use goods.[1] Some people think that a consumer society provides people with **better** lives. People in consumer societies tend to live **more comfortably**. They eat a **wider** variety of food. They go to restaurants **more often**. They also buy a lot of products, maybe more than they need.

Products such as TVs, cell phones, and computers used to be luxuries.[2] Today people can buy these things **more easily than** ever before. The market for these goods is growing **faster** all the time. Consumer societies encourage people to buy **bigger** and **better** products. For example, "smarter" phones come out every year. In a consumer society, people are often buying **newer** and **more advanced** products. This creates a lot of waste. Nowadays, many people are thinking **more seriously** about the effects of consumer societies on the environment, and they are trying to become **more responsible** consumers.

[1] **goods:** items that can be bought or sold
[2] **luxury:** something that is expensive but not necessary

2 CHECK. Read each statement. Circle **T** for *true* and **F** for *false*.

1. Everyone agrees that consumer products improve their lives.   **T**   **F**

2. These days, consumer goods are hard to find.   **T**   **F**

3. Many people want luxury products these days.   **T**   **F**

4. Consumer societies help the environment.   **T**   **F**

3 DISCOVER. Complete the exercises to learn about the grammar in this lesson.

A Find these sentences in the article from exercise **1**. Write the missing words.

1. They eat a _____ variety of food.

2. . . . ., and they are trying to become _____ consumers.

B Look at the words you wrote in exercise **A**. Then circle the correct word to complete each rule.

1. For **long** / **short** adjectives, put *more* before the adjective to form the comparative.

2. For **long** / **short** adjectives, add *-er* to the end of the adjective to form the comparative.

LEARN

8.1 Comparative Adjectives

	Comparative Adjective	Than	
The blue car is	newer	than	the gray car.
	more expensive		

1. Use a comparative adjective + *than* to compare two people, places, or things. You can use a comparative adjective + noun when the comparison is clear from context.	Lydia is **taller than** Alex. Gorillas are **more intelligent than** cows. The **bigger house** is mine. The **more interesting shows** are on cable TV.
2. Add -*er* to the end of most one-syllable adjectives to form the comparative.* If the adjective ends in -*e*, add -*r*.	small → small**er** low → low**er** large → large**r** nice → nice**r**
3. Use *more* before most long adjectives (adjectives that have two or more syllables).	Jack is **more serious than** Nikki. Do you think math is **more important than** music?
4. Some two-syllable adjectives are used with either -*er* or *more* to form the comparative.	quiet → quiet**er** / **more** quiet simple → simple**r** / **more** simple
5. Some adjectives have an irregular comparative form.	good → **better** bad → **worse** far → **farther, further**

*See page **A4** for more information on speling rules for comparative adjectives.

REAL ENGLISH

Words such as *a little, a lot, much,* and *not much,* are often used to quantify comparative adjectives.

*Tina is **a little** taller than Nick.*

4 Complete each sentence with the correct comparative form of the adjective in parentheses. Add *than* when necessary.

1. New cars are much <u>more quiet than / quieter than</u> (quiet) old cars.

2. Do you think money is _____ (important) good health?

3. This coat is _____ (nice) that one.

4. My old laptop was a lot _____ (big) my new one.

5. Gas is so expensive! I want a _____ (efficient) car.

6. Many people think modern life is _____ (good) life in the past.

7. Communication is a lot _____ (easy) it was 50 years ago.

8. The pollution in my city is much _____ (bad) it used to be.

9. I prefer _____ (hot) temperatures. That's why I love summer.

10. My new school is a little _____ (far) my old one.

COMPARATIVES AND SUPERLATIVES

8.2 Comparative Adverbs

Gas prices are rising	Comparative Adverb	Than	
	faster	than	food prices.
	more rapidly		

1. Use a comparative adverb + *than* to compare two actions.	Mark works **harder than** Jeff. Carol drives **more carefully than** Peter.
2. Add -*er* to the end of one-syllable adverbs to form the comparative.	fast ⟶ fast**er** hard ⟶ hard**er** long ⟶ long**er** high ⟶ high**er**
3. Use *more* before adverbs that end with -*ly*.	quickly ⟶ **more** quickly frequently ⟶ **more** frequently
4. Some adverbs have an irregular comparative form.	well ⟶ **better** far ⟶ **farther, further** badly ⟶ **worse**

5 Complete the sentences with the comparative form of the adverbs in parentheses + *than*.

1. My new oven works a lot ____better than____ (good) my old oven. It heats up

   much _____ (quick) my old oven, but it also burns food

   _____ (often) my old one!

2. Now that he's a manager, Gerry works a lot _____ (hard) he used to.

   He also travels _____ (frequent) he did before, and his trips

   last _____ (long) they used to.

3. People are creating garbage _____ (rapid)

   they used to. They are throwing away their old things because they can buy new goods

   _____ (easy) before. In the past, people treated their belongings

   _____ (careful) they do now.

6 Use the words in parentheses to complete each sentence. Use the comparative form of the adverb and the correct form of the verb.

1. This computer __works more efficiently than__ (work / efficiently) that computer.

2. My new watch _____ (keep time / accurately)
   my old watch.

3. My sister _____ (call / often) my brother.

4. My phone _____ (ring / loudly) your phone.

5. Tara _____ (shop / frequently) Lori.

6. Brad _____ (type / quickly) Lynn.

7. Kate _____ (sing / badly) Deb.

8. Lila _____ (study / hard) Nora.

8.3 Completing Comparisons

1. You can use an object pronoun to complete a comparison. But in more formal speaking and writing, use a subject pronoun + an auxiliary verb.	Ed is six feet tall. Bob is taller than **him**.
	                     Object Pronoun
	Ed is six feet tall. Bob is taller than **he is**.
	           Subject Pronoun + Aux. Verb

2. Use an auxiliary verb after *than*. Do not repeat the main verb.	✓ Ana runs faster **than** Pat **does**. ✗ Ana runs faster than Pat <u>runs</u>.
3. A possessive noun or possessive pronoun can be used after *than*.	My car was more expensive **than Ellen's**. My car was more expensive **than hers**.
4. If the comparison is clear, *than* and the second part of the comparison are not necessary.	Nowadays, smart phones are **cheaper**.
5. **Be careful!** Use *than*, not *then*, in a comparison.	✓ I work harder **than** I used to. ✗ I work harder <u>then</u> I used to.

7 Circle the correct word(s) to complete each sentence.

1. My computer is more efficient **than your** / **than yours.**

2. The white coat is warmer **then** / **than** the gray one.

3. Ellen buys nicer clothes **than I do** / **than I am**.

4. Cars are expensive, but houses are **more expensive** / **more expensive than**.

5. Does your new stereo play music more loudly than your old one **was** / **did?**

6. Harry's motorcycle is newer than **my** / **mine**.

7. Cho's package arrived more quickly **than Kelly's did** / **than Kelly's was**.

8. Dave is 27 years old. His sister is older **than he is** / **than he does**.

8 Complete each comparison using the information in parentheses. Do not repeat the same noun.

1. Irina's car is bigger _____than mine (is)_____ (my car).

2. Tom takes better photos _____ (his father).

3. Miguel's suit is more fashionable _____ (Chad's suit).

4. You finished your shopping more quickly _____ (she).

5. Jeff's kitchen is larger _____ (our kitchen).

6. This printer prints more quickly _____ (your printer).

7. My apartment is more comfortable _____ (their apartment).

8. Alison studies harder _____ (her sister).

PRACTICE

9 Use the words in parentheses to complete the conversation with comparative adjectives or adverbs. Add *than* where necessary. In some cases, more than one answer is possible.

Matt: My phone is working (1) <u>worse than</u> (badly) ever! And it's

(2) _____ (old) all the other phones I see, too.

I want a (3) _____ (modern) phone.

Lara: Take a look at my phone. It was (4) _____ (cheap) my

last phone, and I'm much (5) _____ (happy) with it. When I'm

traveling, I listen to music (6) _____ (often) I do when I'm at

home, so I wanted a phone with a (7) _____ (big) memory card.

Matt: Wow, it's much (8) _____ (nice) mine! The screen is a lot

(9) _____ (large), too. I want one like that!

Lara: Yeah, you need a big screen, because you watch videos on your phone

(10) _____ (frequently) I do.

10 Look at the charts comparing three laptop computers. Then complete the sentences with the comparative form of the adjectives and adverbs in parentheses.

Product Details	T400	XJ7	A-50
Screen size	15 inches	17 inches	14 inches
Weight	5.5 pounds	6 pounds	6.5 pounds
Amount of time on the market	18 months	3 months	9 months
Cost	$565	$650	$499

Customer Ratings	T400	XJ7	A-50
Starts quickly	★ ★ ★	★ ★	★ ★ ★ ★
Runs reliably	★ ★ ★ ★ ★	★ ★ ★ ★	★ ★ ★
Operates quietly	★ ★ ★ ★	★ ★ ★	★ ★ ★ ★ ★
Displays pictures well	★ ★ ★	★ ★ ★ ★ ★	★ ★ ★ ★

1. (large / small) The screen of the T400 is <u>larger than</u> the A-50's, but it is
   <u>smaller than</u> the XJ7's.

2. (light / heavy) The XJ7 is _____ the A-50, but it is _____
   the T400.

3. (new / old) The A-50 is _____ the T400, but it is _____
   the XJ7.

4. (cheap / expensive) The T400 is _____ the XJ7, but it is
   _____ the A-50.

5. (quickly / slowly) The T400 starts _____ the XJ7, but
   _____ the A-50.

6. (reliably) The T400 runs _____ the XJ7 or the A-50.

7. (quietly) The A-50 operates _____ the T400 or the XJ7.

8. (well) The XJ7 displays pictures _____ the T400 or the A-50.

🎧 **11** **LISTEN** to six people deciding what to buy. Circle the choice each speaker makes. Then
CD2-29   write the reason for each decision. Use comparative adjectives or adverbs.

	Speaker's Choice	Reason for Decision
Speaker 1	blue coat / (green coat)	It is more comfortable.
Speaker 2	sports car / family car	
Speaker 3	yellow roses / red roses	
Speaker 4	downtown / suburbs	
Speaker 5	brown boots / black boots	
Speaker 6	big TV / small TV	

12 APPLY.

A Imagine that you are going on vacation soon. Brainstorm a list of vacation ideas, for
example, a camping vacation, a resort vacation, a safari, etc. Write your list of ideas in your
notebook.

B Choose two of your vacation ideas from exercise **A** to compare. In your notebook, make a
chart like the one below. Write notes about your vacation ideas in your chart.

A Camping Vacation	A Resort Vacation
cheap	expensive
sleep on the ground	comfortable bed
fun	relaxing
simple food	good food
close to nature	gym, pool

C In your notebook, write five sentences comparing your two vacation choices. Use the
information from your chart from exercise **B** and comparative adjectives and adverbs.

A camping vacation is cheaper than a resort vacation.
Your sleep will be more comfortable at a resort.
Camping is more fun than a resort.

D Choose one of your vacation ideas from exercise **C**. In your notebook, write two or three
sentences to explain why you prefer it.

I want to go on a camping vacation. It's cheaper than a resort vacation, and it
closer to nature. . . .

E Work with a partner. Share your ideas from exercise **C** and explain your decision from
exercise **D**. Did your partner make a good choice? Why, or why not?

EXPLORE

CD2-30

1 READ the excerpt from a discussion between the professor of a business class and a guest speaker. Notice the words in **bold**.

Online Reviews: ★ or ★★★★?

Professor: So, Dennis, what changes have you seen in marketing recently?

Dennis: Well, as you know, customers love to post online reviews of products these days. These reviews are now just **as important as** traditional advertising. Maybe even more important. TV advertising is **as useful as** it was before, of course. On the other hand, newspaper ads[1] are much **less effective than** they used to be.

Professor: Hmm. That's interesting. . . . I've spoken to some marketing people who are**n't as positive as** you are about online reviews.

Dennis: Really? I'm surprised. There are certainly some concerns with online reviews. For example, satisfied customers are **less likely** to write reviews **than** people who have had a problem. This means there might be more negative reviews than positive ones. But online shoppers are wiser now. A few negative opinions are **not as harmful as** they used to be. Also, the positive reviews can be **as valuable as** ads. If a customer loves a product, he or she will endorse[2] it just **as enthusiastically[3] as** a TV ad does!

[1] **ad:** short for advertisement
[2] **endorse:** to say that you support or approve of someone or something
[3] **enthusiastically:** to do something in a way that shows a lot of interest and excitement

A billboard, a traditional form of advertising

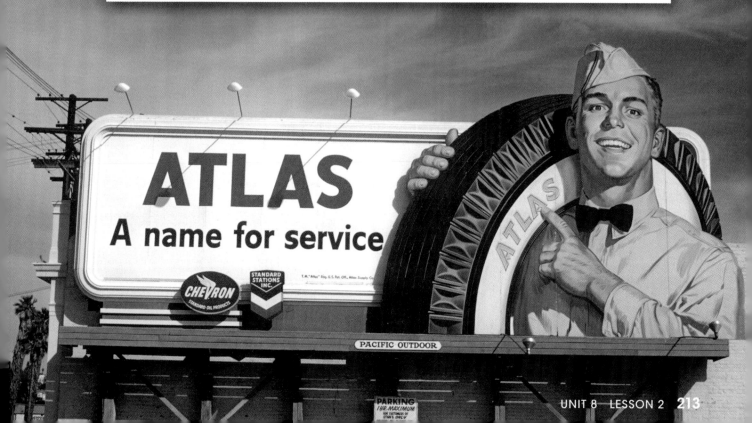

2 CHECK. Read each statement. Circle **T** for *true* or **F** for *false*.

1. Dennis thinks that online reviews are not very important in marketing.   **T**   **F**

2. Newspaper ads used to be more effective.   **T**   **F**

3. Some marketing people have a negative opinion of online reviews.   **T**   **F**

4. Customers with problems are more likely to write online reviews.   **T**   **F**

5. Online shoppers won't buy a product if they see a negative review.   **T**   **F**

6. Positive online reviews aren't very valuable.   **T**   **F**

3 DISCOVER. Complete the exercises to learn about the grammar in this lesson.

A Look at each phrase from the discussion in exercise **1** on page 213. Does the phrase mean *equal* or *not equal*? Circle the correct answer.

1. as useful as   equal / not equal
2. less effective than   equal / not equal
3. aren't as positive as   equal / not equal
4. not as harmful as   equal / not equal
5. as valuable as   equal / not equal
6. as enthusiastically as   equal / not equal

B Look at the phrases from exercise **A**. Then answer the questions.

1. What word follows comparisons beginning with *as* + adjective? _____

2. What word follows comparisons beginning with *less* + adverb? _____

◄ Neon signs in Nanjing Lu, Shanghai's main shopping street, China

LEARN

8.4 Comparisons with *As . . . As*

	As	Adjective	As	
My car is	as	big comfortable	as	your car.

	As	Adverb	As	
I drive	as	well carefully	as	you do.

1. Use *as* + adjective/adverb + *as* to compare two people, places, or things that are the same or equal in some way.	Adjective: Your car is **as old as** mine. Adverb: I can run a mile **as fast as** you can.

2. To complete a comparison with *as . . . as*, you can use
   a. a noun (+ verb)
   b. a subject pronoun + verb or an auxiliary verb
 	
   c. a possessive noun or possessive pronoun
	
	a. I dance as well as **my brother (dances).**
	b. I dance as well as **he dances.**
	   I dance as well as **he does.**
	c. My computer is as old as **Rita's.**
	   My computer is as old as **hers.**

3. In informal speaking, object pronouns are often used to complete comparisons with *as. . . . as*.	Formal: He's as tall as **I am.** Informal: He's as tall as **me.**

4 Complete each sentence with *as . . . as* and the adjective or adverb in parentheses.

1. Magazine ads are _____as effective as_____ (effective) newspaper ads.

2. Mark plays the guitar _____ (well) Nancy does.

3. Online reviews are _____ (useful) asking friends about products.

4. I read online reviews _____ (carefully) he does.

5. The coat was just _____ (warm) it looked.

6. Your sofa is just _____ (comfortable) Diane's.

7. My computer is _____ (fast) the newer models.

8. He shops online _____ (frequently) I do.

5 Use the words to make comparisons with *as . . . as*.

1. Desktop computers / be / popular / laptops

   Desktop computers are as popular as laptops (are).

2. Microwave ovens / work / well / regular ovens

   _____

3. Motorcycles / go / fast / cars

   _____

4. This hotel room / be / big / my apartment

   _____

5. A smartphone / send messages / quickly / a laptop

_____

6. My mother / speak English / well / my father

_____

7. Gabi / go shopping / often / Linda

_____

8. Trains / be / comfortable / airplanes

_____

8.5 Comparison with *Less* and *Not As . . . As*

	Less	Adjective/Adverb	*Than*	
This phone is	less	expensive	than	that one.
This old fan works	less	efficiently	than	the new fan.

Less + Adjective or Adverb + *Than*

	Not As	Adjective/Adverb	*As*	
This phone is	not as	expensive good	as	that one.
This old fan does	not work as	efficiently well	as	the new fan.

Not As + Adjective or Adverb + *As*

1. The opposite of *more* is *less*. *Not as . . . as* and *less* have the same meaning.	My old car was **less efficient than** my new car. My old car was **not as efficient as** my new car.
2. Use *not as . . . as* with one-syllable adjectives or adverbs.	My apartment is **not as big as** yours. Tom does**n't** run **as fast as** Steven.
3. Use *less . . . than* or *not as . . . as* with adjectives or adverbs that have two or more syllables. The meaning is the same.	My son visits **less frequently than** my daughter. My son does**n't** visit **as frequently as** my daughter.
4. **Remember:** If the comparison is clear, the second part of the comparison is not necessary.	The food at Joe's cafe is**n't as good as** the food at Chez Claude, but it's **less expensive**. The food at Joe's cafe is **less expensive than** the food at Chez Clause, but it is**n't as good**.

See Chart 8.3 for more information completing comparisons.

6 Complete the conversations with *less* or *not as . . . as* and the words in parentheses. Do not use *not* unless it is included in the parentheses. Use *than* and the second *as* only where necessary.

1. Anita: The clothes in this store (1) _____ *aren't as nice as* _____ (not be / nice) they

used to be. Look at this coat! It's much (2) _____ (fashionabl

the coat I bought here last year.

Jackie: Well, that's true. It (3) _____ (not be / stylish), but it's also

(4) _____ (expensive).

2. Chris: Check out this new coffee machine! It looks great! Ours

(5) _____ (not be / fancy) this new one.

Mike: Well, it's definitely fancier than ours, but it (6) _____

(not be / efficient). It (7) _____

(not make coffee / quickly), and the coffee (8) _____

(not taste / good).

7 Rewrite each sentence with the word(s) in parentheses.

1. My watch is less attractive than yours. (not as . . . as)

   My watch isn't as attractive as yours.
   _____

2. Sally's shoes aren't as fancy as Jill's. (less)

   _____

3. Adam exercises less frequently than he used to. (not as . . . as)

   _____

4. This supermarket isn't as expensive as the one across the street. (less)

   _____

5. The actor's new movie isn't as exciting as his last one. (less)

   _____

6. This gym is less convenient than the one near my house. (not as . . . as)

   _____

7. This review is less positive than that one. (not as . . . as)

   _____

8. The new tablet doesn't start up as quickly as the old one. (less)

   _____

PRACTICE

8 Complete the conversation with *less* or *(not) as . . . as* and the words in parentheses. Make the verbs negative only when *not* is given. Use *than* and the second *as* only where necessary.

Tina: Your new camera (1) _____ isn't as big as _____ (not be / big) your old one.

Dawn: I know. It (2) _____ (not be / heavy) my old X-2000, and it was

(3) _____ (expensive), too.

Tina: But you took great photos with your old one! Why did you decide to change?

Dawn: Well, my old camera was really difficult to use, so I

(4) _____ (not take photos / often)

I wanted to. This new camera is (5) _____ (not be / complicated)

my old one, so it's much (6) _____ (difficult) to use.

Tina: And what about your photos? Are they (7) _____ (nice) the ones from your old camera?

Dawn: Oh yes, they're just (8) _____ (good) my old ones.

9 EDIT. Read the online reviews of a play house for children. Find and correct seven more errors with comparisons with *less* and (*not*) *as . . . as.*

THE JOLLY ROGER PIRATE SHIP

Customer Reviews

★★★★★ **A Huge Success!**

Our family loves this! Our last
playhouse was much less exciting ^{than}
the Jolly Roger. It was also less
attractive as this one. And this is
really an important point: it wasn't
as safe as. –**Maria**

★★★ **Hard to Build**

My kids enjoyed this, but for me, putting it together was just as hard building a real
pirate ship! It's true that I probably don't build things as quickly as a lot of other people
do. And maybe I'm not as good with tools as they do, but I still think this product should
be less complicated than! –**Sam**

★★★★ **Fun for Younger Kids**

My four-year-old son says this play structure is fun as a real pirate ship! He plays in it
as often as he can, but my six-year-old daughter isn't as enthusiastic as he is about it. I'm a
little disappointed because she uses it less often then I expected. –**Lin**

10 Look at the chart comparing three Internet movie services. Then complete each sentence with the words in parentheses. Use *less* and *(not) as . . . as*. For some sentences, more than one answer is possible.

	C-Movie	MyScreen	FAB
Membership fee	$9.95	$5.00	$5.00
Monthly rate	$7.95	$8.50	$9.95
New movies	every month	every two weeks	every week
Easy to use	★ ★ ★	★ ★ ★	★ ★ ★ ★
Customer service	★ ★ ★	★ ★ ★ ★	★ ★ ★ ★

1. FAB's membership fee _____is as cheap as_____ (be / cheap) MyScreen's.

2. Becoming a member of MyScreen _____ (be / expensive) joining C-Movie.

3. C-Movie's monthly rate _____ (be / high) the others'.

4. C-Movie _____ (add new movies / frequently) FAB.

5. Using FAB _____ (be / difficult) using the others.

6. On C-Movie, you can _____ (find movies / easily) on MyScreen. They are both pretty easy to use.

7. MyScreen's customer service _____ (be / good) FAB's.

8. C-Movie's customer service _____ (be / helpful) the other two services.

11 APPLY.

A Use the chart below to compare two or three similar products or services you have used. For example, transportation services, restaurants, shopping websites, etc. Choose five categories to compare. Use the chart from exercise **10** as a model.

	1: _____	2: _____	3: _____

B In your notebook, write five sentences comparing the products or services from your chart in exercise **A**. Use *less* and *(not) as . . . as*. Use the sentences in exercise **10** as models.

The TRIMET bus is less expensive than the subway or a taxi. It's not as comfortable as a taxi. . . .

C Work with a partner. Talk about how the products or services you chose compare with each other. Use *less* and *(not) as . . . as*. Does your partner agree with you?

EXPLORE

CD2-31

1 **READ** the article about a problem on Mount Everest. Notice the words in **bold**.

Mount Everest:
The Highest Garbage Dump in the World?

Most people know that Mount Everest is **the highest** mountain in the world. However, there is another fact that many people don't know: it has become one of **the dirtiest** mountains in the world.

Mount Everest is one of **the toughest** and **most exciting** mountains to climb on Earth. It is not **the coldest** or **the windiest** place on Earth, but it comes close! These challenges make it one of **the most attractive** mountains for serious climbers. Since 1952, over 3500 climbers have reached the top. Unfortunately, most of them have left equipment and trash on the mountain.

In fact, trash is now one of **the biggest** threats to the environment on Mount Everest. Local organizations have brought tons of trash down from the mountain. One of **the most interesting** projects handed over more than a ton of tin cans, glass bottles, and old climbing tools to artists in Nepal. The artists used the trash to create works of art. Then, they sold the art to raise money for local charities.[1] **The least expensive** work of art cost $17, and **the most expensive** one cost $2400.

[1] **charity:** an organization that raises money to help people

▶ The consumer society produces a lot of waste, even in the Himalayas. Here, a climber collects trash on Mount Everest.

2 **CHECK.** Circle the correct word to complete each statement.

1. According to the reading, Mount Everest is very **clean** / **dirty**.

2. Climbing Mount Everest is very **difficult** / **easy**.

3. Mount Everest is **an unusual** / **a popular** mountain for serious climbers.

4. Climbers **rarely** / **often** leave trash on Mount Everest.

5. People create **art** / **charities** from the trash on Mount Everest.

3 **DISCOVER.** Complete the exercises to learn about the grammar in this lesson.

A Look at the bold phrases in the reading from exercise **1**. Then write three more examples in each column of the chart.

Adjectives with *-est*	Adjectives with *most*
tall	exciting

B Which adjectives add *most*? Circle the correct answer.   a. long ones   b. short ones

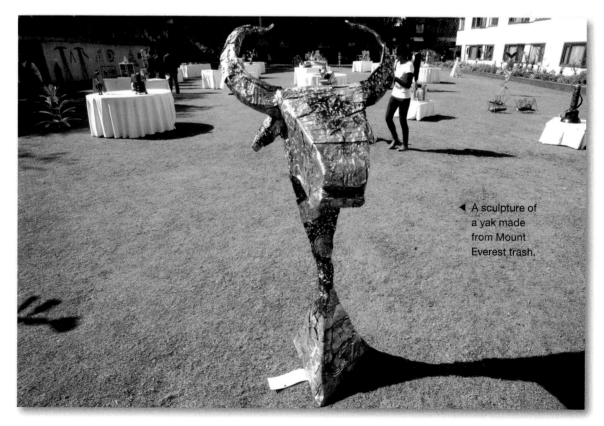

◀ A sculpture of a yak made from Mount Everest trash.

LEARN

8.6 Superlative Adjectives and Adverbs

	Superlative Adjective	
The red car is	the nicest the most expensive	car in the parking lot.

	Superlative Adverb	
She runs	the fastest the most slowly	of all the players on the team.

1. Use a superlative adjective to compare three or more people, places, or things.	Ali is **the tallest** student in our class. Prague is **the most beautiful** city I've ever seen. What's **the most interesting** book you've ever read?
2. Use a superlative adverb to compare the action of three or more people or things.	Of all my friends, Alicia calls **the most frequently**. My red shoes fit **the most comfortably** of all my shoes.
3. Add -est to the end of most one-syllable adjectives or adverbs to form the superlative.* Use the before superlative adjectives. It is not as common before adverbs.	Adjective: I bought **the longest** couch in the store. Adverb: Steve works **hardest** of all the students.
4. Use the most before most adjectives that have two or more syllables and adverbs ending in -ly.	Maria is **the most careful** climber of the group. The Grand Canyon is **the most amazing** sight I've ever seen. Of all the girls, Brenda sings **the most beautifully**.
5. For some two-syllable adjectives and adverbs, either -est or the most can be used to form the superlative.	stupid ⟶ the stupid**est**/the **most stupid** cruel ⟶ the cruel**est**/the **most cruel**
6. Some superlatives are irregular.	good/well ⟶ **the best** bad/badly ⟶ **the worst**

*See page **A4** for more information on spelling superlative adjectives and adverbs.

4 Complete the sentences with the superlative form of the adjective or adverb in parentheses.

1. _____The biggest_____ (big) piles of trash on Mount Everest are on the lower areas.

2. Trash is one of _____ (bad) problems on Mount Everest now.

3. Many climbers consider K2, a mountain between Pakistan and China, to be _____ (difficult) mountain to climb, not Mount Everes[t]

4. Ted was _____ (experienced) climber on the expeditio[n]

5. Which climber is _____ (far) from the top?

6. That was _____ (easy) mountain I've ever climbed.

7. Danny climbs _____ (quickly) of all of us.

8. Mount Everest is _____ (high) mountain on Earth.

9. That company has _____ (good) guides.

10. Climbing Mount Everest in a snowstorm is one of _____ (stupid) thing you can do. It's extremely dangerous!

5 LISTEN & SPEAK.

CD2-32

A Listen and complete each question with the superlative form of the adjective or adverb you hear.

1. At what time of day do you work ___*most efficiently*___ ?

2. Who is _____ person in the world?

3. What is _____ movie you've ever seen?

4. What kind of books do you read _____?

5. What is _____ thing to do in a storm?

6. What is _____ to watch?

7. What is _____ place to have lunch in this area?

8. Who is _____ person in your family?

B Work with a partner. Take turns asking and answering the questions from exercise **A**.

A: *At what time of day do you work most efficiently?*

B: *In the afternoon.*

> **REAL ENGLISH**
>
> A possessive adjective can replace *the* in a superlative comparison.
>
> Zara is **the best** friend I have.
> Zara is **my best** friend.

8.7 More on Superlative Adjectives and Adverbs

1. The opposite of *the most* is *the least*.	This is **the least expensive** phone in the store. All the other phones cost a lot more. She drives **the least carefully** of all my friends. All my other friends drive much more carefully.
2. A prepositional phrase with *in* or *of* is often used to complete a superlative.	The Nile is **the longest river in the world**. This hat is **the prettiest of the three**.
3. **Remember:** If the comparison is clear, it is not necessary to complete it.	This sentence is **the longest**. She won because she ran **the fastest**.
4. *One of the* often comes before a superlative adjective. The superlative adjective is followed by a plural noun.	China is **one of the biggest countries** in the world.

6 Use the words in parentheses to write superlative sentences. Use *least* when *not* is included in the parentheses. Make the nouns plural if necessary.

1. This is a state park. (not popular / in California)

   This is the least popular state park in California.

2. Canada is a country. (large / in North America)

   _____

3. Tokyo has a population. (big / in Japan)

   _____

4. This is an apartment. (not expensive / in the building)

   _____

5. Alan drives. (fast / of my three brothers)

   _____

6. Jane is a student. (one of the / intelligent / in her class)

   _____

7. That was a class. (one of the / not interesting / I've ever taken)

   _____

8. Mel works. (not efficiently / all the people in this office)

   _____

9. This is a computer. (cheap / in the store)

   _____

10. That's a street. (one of the / pretty / in this city)

    _____

7 **SPEAK.** Work with a partner. Talk about people, places, and things you know about. Use the superlative form of the adjectives and adverbs from the box or your own ideas.

carefully	fast	hard	large	popular
crowded	good	interesting	old	well

My grandmother is the oldest person in my family. She's 91.

PRACTICE

8 Complete the sentences with the superlative form of the adjectives and adverbs in parentheses. Use *least* if *not* is included in the parentheses.

1. Kelly: I think people are too concerned about having (1) _____the most modern_____

(modern) cell phones. Cell phones contain some of (2) _____

(rare) minerals on Earth, but many people just throw their old cell phones away

when they buy a new one. This is (3) _____

(one of the / bad / thing) you can do! But if you recycle your old cell phones,

it's (4) _____ (one of the / good / thing) you can do.

2. Amir: My cell phone is (5) _____ (important / thing) I own. It's

(6) _____ (convenient / place) I have to keep information.

3. Brad: My new cell phone is a piece of junk! It was (7) _____

(not expensive) phone in the store. What a mistake! Also, the salesperson in that

store was one of (8) _____ (not helpful /

salesperson) I've ever spoken to.

9 **EDIT.** Read the article about trash in the desert. Find and correct eight more errors with superlatives.

Cameron's Camels

The Arabian Desert in the Middle East is one of the ~~most hot~~ ^hottest environments on Earth, and it has

the less amount of rainfall. But to the camel, it is home. The camel is one of the most strong animals

in the world. Camels can go for many days with only a little food and water. When they do find water,

they probably drink the most quick of any land animal. Adult camels can drink about 25 to 30 gallons

(95–114 liters) in ten minutes. Unfortunately, finding water is not the seriousest problem camels face.

Most dangerous threat to camels comes from humans. Tourists in the desert leave trash behind. Camels

think the trash is food and eat it. This is very dangerous for the camels, because it can kill them.

One of the most polluted part of the desert is outside the city of Abu Dhabi. Each year, many

camels die there from eating trash. Cameron Oliver has been trying to change this. Since he was

eight years old, Cameron has been telling people that trash is very dangerous for camels. Of all

the young people in Abu Dhabi, Cameron has worked most hard to help the camels. When he was

12, Cameron became the most young person to win an Abu Dhabi award for community service.

10 APPLY.

A Work with a partner. Use the words in parentheses to write superlatives. Then choose the correct answer to complete each fact on the quiz.

General Knowledge Quiz

1. _____ is _the highest mountain_____ (high / mountain) on Earth.

    a. Mount Kilimanjaro   b. Mount Everest   c. K2

2. _____ is _____ (fast / animal) in the world.

    a. the camel   b. the zebra   c. the cheetah

3. _____ is _____ (long / river) in the world.

    a. The Nile River   b. The Amazon River   c. The Yangtze River

4. _____ is _____ (wide / ocean) on Earth.

    a. The Pacific Ocean   b. The Atlantic Ocean   c. The Indian Ocean

5. _____ is _____ (small / continent).

    a. Africa   b. Antarctica   c. Australia

6. _____ is _____ (large / animal) on Earth.

    a. the elephant   b. the blue whale   c. the giraffe

7. _____ is _____ (cold / place) on Earth.

    a. Antarctica   b. Alaska   c. Canada

8. _____ is _____ (close / planet) to the sun.

    a. Mars   b. Venus   c. Mercury

B Check your answers at the bottom of this page. How many of your answers were correct?

C With your partner, write six more general knowledge facts like the ones from the quiz in exercise **A**. Use superlative adjectives and adverbs.

1. The Nile River is the longest river in the world.

D Use the facts from exercise **C** and quiz your classmates.

A: *This is the largest country in South America.*

B: *Is it Argentina?*

A: *No.*

C: *Is it Brazil?*

A: *Yes, it is!*

Charts
8.1, 8.3–8.7

1 READ & WRITE.

A Read the information about the Greendex survey, and look at the chart. Then complete each sentence according to the information in the chart. Use the comparative or superlative form of the adjective or adverb in parentheses. For some sentences, more than one answer is possible.

The Greendex is a survey of 1000 consumers in several countries. It asks consumers how they spend their money. Each consumer receives a score. High scores indicate "green," or environmentally friendly, attitudes. Low scores indicate environmentally unfriendly attitudes.

Greendex: Rankings

	Overall	Housing	Transportation	Food	Goods
Americans	44.7	31.5	54.9	57.0	44.2
Brazilians	55.5	48.9	67.1	57.5	53.8
British	49.4	35.9	62.7	62.2	47.1
Canadians	47.9	35.1	57.8	60.9	45.7
Chinese	57.8	48.2	69.0	63.7	56.8
Germans	51.5	40.3	61.9	61.9	47.1
Indians	58.9	51.4	67.3	71.1	57.3
Japanese	48.5	35.3	65.9	54.7	52.7
Mexicans	53.9	48.0	62.2	53.6	54.5
Russians	53.1	44.1	66.4	60.4	47.9

Transportation

1. The Chinese make _____the greenest_____ (green) choices.

2. Americans are _____ (green) consumers.

3. British consumers make _____ (green) choices than Canadian consumers.

4. Mexican consumers are _____ (green) Japanese consumers.

Food

5. The British are _____ (concerned) the Chinese.

6. Indians are _____ (concerned) consumers.

7. Russians are _____ (concerned) Brazilians.

8. Americans are _____ (concerned) Canadians.

Goods

9. Canadians don't buy goods _____ (responsibly) Mexicans do.

10. Indians buy goods _____ (responsibly).

11. Germans buy goods _____ (responsibly) Brazilians.

12. Americans buy goods _____ (responsibly).

B In your notebook, write four or five sentences based on the housing data from the Greendex chart in exercise **A** on page 227. Use comparative and superlative adjectives and adverbs. Use the sentences from exercise **A** to help you.

Mexicans make greener housing choices than Canadians.

Indian consumers are more concerned about green housing than German consumers are.

Charts 8.1–8.7

2 **EDIT.** Read the article about the results of the Greendex survey. Find and correct eight more errors with comparatives and superlatives.

The Greendex Survey: Some Overall Conclusions

- According to a recent Greendex survey, people in India were the ~~most green~~ ^greenest^ consumers in the world. They scored lower in transportation than the Chinese were, but they scored the highest than the Chinese in three other categories.

- Mexicans were more concerned about green transportation as green food or goods. For them, the low score of all was in the housing category.

- Germans scored highly in the transportation category than they did in the food category. However, they were least concerned about housing than goods.

- The Japanese were one of the least concerned nationality overall. They had one of the most bad scores in the housing category.

- Americans had the lowest overall score of all the nationalities in the survey. Food was the only category in which Americans did not score lower then the other nationalities.

3 LISTEN & SPEAK.

🎧 CD2-33

A Listen to a professor discussing the Greendex survey with her students. Then complete the students' opinions about the survey.

Martin:

1. Most people think that their country is _____ the results show.

2. Many people think they buy goods _____ they really do.

3. We like to think we're trying _____ we can to be green.

Karin:

4. Life in the United States is much _____ without a car.

5. Cars that use less gas are becoming _____ in the United States.

6. Attitudes about the environment aren't changing _____ people think.

Andrew:

7. Most people want to make life _____ for themselves and their families.

8. Everyone wants an _____ life.

🎧 CD2-33

B Look at the sentences from exercise **A**. Then listen again. Do you agree or disagree with the students' ideas and opinions? Why, or why not? Write notes on your own ideas and opinions in your notebook.

C Work with a partner. Share your ideas and opinions from exercise **B**. Use comparatives and superlatives.

I agree with Martin's opinion about goods. People don't shop as carefully as they think they do.

4 WRITE & SPEAK.

A Look at the items in the box. Then rank the items from 1 to 8, with (1 = the least important and 8 = the most important).

_____ a. a big car	_____ d. a smart phone	_____ g. plastic bags
_____ b. stylish clothing	_____ e. meals in restaurants	_____ h. a gold watch
_____ c. a computer	_____ f. a TV	

B In your notebook, write six sentences about the items from exercise **A**. Use comparatives and superlatives and your own ideas and opinions.

I think a computer is less important than a smart phone.

C Work with a partner. Share your rankings from exercise **A** and your opinions from exercise **B**.

Connect the Grammar to Writing

1 READ & NOTICE THE GRAMMAR.

A Before you buy something, do you compare it with similar products? Discuss your shopping habits with a partner. Then read the text.

The Best Sleeping Bag

I needed to buy a new sleeping bag for a winter camping trip. So, I went to a camping store and compared three different brands[1] of sleeping bags: Ultra Comfort, Snowy Down, and Northern Trek. I wanted to look at each sleeping bag very carefully. For winter camping, the Snowy Down had the highest rating. But in some ways, the other two sleeping bags were better. Of the three sleeping bags, the Snowy Down was the warmest, but it was also the most expensive. The Northern Trek cost less than the Snowy Down, but it was just as expensive as the Ultra Comfort. The Ultra Comfort was warmer than the Northern Trek. Finally, the Ultra Comfort was lighter than the other sleeping bags, so it was easier to carry.

I decided not to get the Northern Trek for camping outside. It wasn't as warm as the other sleeping bags. But we were having a mild winter, so I didn't need the warmest kind of sleeping bag. So I looked more closely at the lightest sleeping bag, the Ultra Comfort. That's the one I chose.

[1] **brand:** the commercial name for a product

GRAMMAR FOCUS

In exercise **A**, the writer uses comparatives and superlatives to discuss three sleeping bags.

The Ultra Comfort was **warmer than** the Northern Trek.

. . . it was just **as expensive as** the Ultra Comfort.

Of the three sleeping bags, the Snowy Down was **the warmest** and **most expensive**.

B Read the text in exercise **A** again. Underline the comparatives and circle the superlatives. Then work with a partner and compare your answers.

C Work with a partner. Complete the chart with information from the text in exercise **A**.

Product Details	Ultra Comfort	Snowy Down	Northern Trek
Cost	as expensive as the Northern Trek		
Warmth		the warmest	
Weight			

2 BEFORE YOU WRITE. Think of a product that you plan to buy. Compare three different brands of this product. Complete the chart with information about each brand. Use the chart from exercise **1C** as a model.

Product Details	Product #1	Product #2	Product #3
Cost			

3 WRITE a review comparing the three different brands of the product you chose. Write two paragraphs. Use the information from your chart in exercise **2** and the article in exercise **1A** to help you.

WRITING FOCUS   Correcting Run-on Sentences

A run-on sentence is an error that happens when two independent clauses are connected without a connecting word or correct punctuation.

  ✗ *I enjoyed my winter camping trip next year, I'll invite a few friends to join me.*

To correct a run-on sentence, you can divide the run-on sentence into separate sentences.

  ✓ *I enjoyed my winter camping **trip. Next** year, I'll invite a few friends to join me.*

You can also use a comma and a conjunction (*and, but, or*) between the two independent clauses.

  ✓ *I enjoyed my winter camping **trip, but** next year I'll invite a few friends to join me.*

---

4 SELF ASSESS. Read your review and underline the comparatives and superlatives. Then use the checklist to assess your work.

☐ I used comparative adjectives and adverbs correctly. [8.1, 8.2, 8.3]

☐ I used comparisons with *less* and (*not*) *as . . . as* correctly. [8.4, 8.5]

☐ I used superlative adjectives and adverbs correctly. [8.6, 8.7]

☐ I checked for and corrected run-on sentences. [WRITING FOCUS]

APPENDICES

1   Spelling Rules for Verbs Ending in -*s* and -*es*

1. Add -*s* to most verbs.	like-like**s** sit-sit**s**
2. Add -*es* to verbs that end in -*ch*, -*s*, -*sh*, -*x*, or -*z*.	catch-catch**es** miss-miss**es** wash-wash**es** mix-mix**es** buzz-buzz**es**
3. Change the -*y* to -*i* and add -*es* when the base form ends in a consonant + -*y*.	cry-cr**ies** carry-carr**ies**
4. Do not change the -*y* when the base form ends in a vowel + -*y*.	pay-pay**s** stay-stay**s**
5. Some verbs are irregular in the third-person singular -*s* form of the simple present.	be-**is** go-**goes** do-**does** have-**has**

2   Spelling Rules for Verbs Ending in -*ing*

1. Add -*ing* to the base form of most verbs.	eat-eat**ing** do-do**ing** speak-speak**ing** carry-carry**ing**
2. When the verb ends in a consonant + -*e*, drop the -*e* and add -*ing*.	ride-rid**ing** write-writ**ing**
3. For one-syllable verbs that end in a consonant + a vowel + a consonant (CVC), double the final consonant and add -*ing*. Do not double the final consonant for verbs that end in CVC when the final consonant is -*w*, -*x*, or -*y*.	stop-stop**ping** sit-sit**ting** show-show**ing** fix-fix**ing** stay-stay**ing**
4. For two-syllable verbs that end in CVC and have stress on the first syllable, add -*ing*. Do not double the final consonant. For two-syllable verbs that end in CVC and have stress on the last syllable, double the final consonant and add -*ing*.	ENter-enter**ing** LISTen-listen**ing** beGIN-begin**ning** ocCUR-occur**ring**

3 Spelling Rules for Verbs Ending in -ed

1. Add -ed to the base form of most verbs that end in a consonant.	start-started talk-talked
2. Add -d if the base form of the verb ends in -e.	dance-danced live-lived
3. When the base form of the verb ends in a consonant + -y, change the -y to -i and add -ed.	cry-cried worry-worried
Do not change the -y to -i when the verb ends in a vowel + -y.	stay-stayed
4. For one-syllable verbs that end in a consonant + a vowel + a consonant (CVC), double the final consonant and add -ed.	stop-stopped rob-robbed
Do not double the final consonant of verbs that end in -w, -x, or -y.	follow-followed fix-fixed play-played
5. For two-syllable verbs that end in CVC and have stress on the first syllable, add -ed. Do not double the final consonant.	ORder-ordered HAPpen-HAPpened
For two-syllable verbs that end in CVC and have stress on the last syllable, double the final consonant and add -ed.	ocCUR-occurred preFER-preferred

4 Common Irregular Noun Plurals

Singular	Plural	Explanation
man woman tooth foot goose	men women teeth feet geese	Vowel change
sheep fish deer	sheep fish deer	No change
child person mouse	children people mice	Different word forms
	clothes groceries glasses jeans/pants/shorts scissors	No singular form

5 Spelling Rules for Adverbs Ending in -ly

	Adjective	Adverb
1. Add -ly to the end of most adjectives.	careful quiet serious	carefully quietly seriously
2. Change the -y to -i and add -ly to adjectives that end in a consonant + -y.	easy happy lucky	easily happily luckily
3. Keep the -e and add -ly to some adjectives that end in -e.	nice free	nicely freely
4. Drop the final -e and add -y to adjectives that end with a consonant followed by -le.	simple comfortable	simply comfortably
5. Add -ally to most adjectives that end in -ic.	basic enthusiastic	basically enthusiastically

6 Spelling Rules for Comparative and Superlative Forms

	Adjective/ Adverb	Comparative	Superlative
1. Add -er or -est to one-syllable adjectives and adverbs.	tall fast	taller faster	tallest fastest
2. Add -r or -st to adjectives that end in -e.	nice	nicer	nicest
3. Change the -y to -i and add -er or -est to two-syllable adjectives and adverbs that end in -y.	easy happy	easier happier	easiest the happiest
4. Double the final consonant and add -er or -est to one-syllable adjectives or adverbs that end in a consonant + a vowel + a consonant (CVC).	big hot	bigger hotter	biggest hottest

7   Common Irregular Verbs

Base Form	Simple Past	Past Participle
be	was, were	been
beat	beat	beaten
become	became	become
begin	began	begun
bend	bent	bent
bite	bit	bitten
blow	blew	blown
break	broke	broken
bring	brought	brought
build	built	built
buy	bought	bought
catch	caught	caught
choose	chose	chosen
come	came	come
cost	cost	cost
cut	cut	cut
dig	dug	dug
dive	dived/dove	dived
do	did	done
draw	drew	drawn
drink	drank	drunk
drive	drove	driven
eat	ate	eaten
fall	fell	fallen
feed	fed	fed
feel	felt	felt
fight	fought	fought
find	found	found
fit	fit	fit/fitted
fly	flew	flown
forget	forgot	forgotten
forgive	forgave	forgiven
freeze	froze	frozen
get	got	got/gotten
give	gave	given
go	went	gone
grow	grew	grown
hang	hung	hung
have	had	had
hear	heard	heard
hide	hid	hidden
hit	hit	hit
hold	held	held
hurt	hurt	hurt
keep	kept	kept
know	knew	known

Base Form	Simple Past	Past Participle
lay	laid	laid
lead	led	led
leave	left	left
lend	lent	lent
let	let	let
lie	lay	lain
light	lit/lighted	lit/lighted
lose	lost	lost
make	made	made
mean	meant	meant
meet	met	met
pay	paid	paid
prove	proved	proved/proven
put	put	put
quit	quit	quit
read	read	read
ride	rode	ridden
ring	rang	rung
rise	rose	risen
run	ran	run
say	said	said
sit	sat	sat
sleep	slept	slept
slide	slid	slid
speak	spoke	spoken
spend	spent	spent
spread	spread	spread
stand	stood	stood
steal	stole	stolen
stick	stuck	stuck
strike	struck	struck
swear	swore	sworn
sweep	swept	swept
swim	swam	swum
take	took	taken
teach	taught	taught
tear	tore	torn
tell	told	told
think	thought	thought
throw	threw	thrown
understand	understood	understood
upset	upset	upset
wake	woke	woken
wear	wore	worn
win	won	won
write	wrote	written

8   Patterns with Gerunds

Verb + Gerund

They *enjoy dancing*.
She *delayed going* to the doctor.

admit	detest	mind	regret
advise	discuss	miss	remember
anticipate	dislike	permit	resent
appreciate	enjoy	postpone	resist
avoid	finish	practice	risk
can't help	forbid	put off	stop
complete	imagine	quit	suggest
consider	keep	recall	tolerate
delay	mention	recommend	understand
deny			

Verb + Preposition + Gerund

He *succeeded in winning* the prize.
Are you *thinking about taking* another course?

apologize for	concentrate on	object to	thank (someone) for
argue about	dream about/of	plan on/for	think about
believe in	insist on	succeed in	warn (someone) about
complain about	keep on	talk about	worry about

Noun + Preposition + Gerund

What's the *purpose of doing* this exercise?
I don't know his *reason for being* late.

benefit of	interest in	purpose of
cause of	problem with	reason for

Adjective + Preposition + Gerund

I'm *excited about studying* abroad.
Are you *interested in going*?

accustomed to	excited about	nervous about	tired of
afraid of	famous for	responsible for	upset about/with
bad/good at	(in)capable of	sick of	used to
concerned about	interested in	sorry about/for	worried about

9   Patterns with Infinitives

Verb + Infinitive			
*They **need to leave**.* *I **am learning to speak** English.*			
agree	claim	know how	seem
appear	consent	learn	swear
arrange	decide	manage	tend
ask	demand	need	threaten
attempt	deserve	offer	try
be able	expect	plan	volunteer
beg	fail	prepare	want
can afford	forget	pretend	wish
care	hope	promise	would like
choose	intend	refuse	

Verb + Object + Infinitive			
*I **want you to leave**.* *He **expects me to call** him.*			
advise	convince	hire	require
allow	dare	instruct	select
appoint	enable	invite	teach
ask*	encourage	need*	tell
beg*	expect*	order	urge
cause	forbid	pay*	want*
challenge	force	permit	warn
choose*	get	persuade	would like*
command	help**	remind	

*These verbs can be either with or without an object. (*I **want [you] to go**.*)

After *help*, *to* is often omitted. (*He **helped me move.*)

Verb + Infinitive or Gerund		
*I **love to swim**.* *I **love swimming**.*		
begin	continue	love
(not) bother	hate	prefer
can't stand	like	start

10 Phrasal Verbs and Their Meanings

Transitive Phrasal Verbs (Separable)

*Don't forget to **turn off** the oven before you leave the house.*
*Don't forget to **turn** the oven **off** before you leave the house.*

Phrasal Verb	Meaning	Example Sentence
blow up	cause something to explode	The workers **blew** the bridge **up**.
bring back	return	She **brought** the shirt **back** to the store.
bring up	1. raise from childhood 2. introduce a topic to discuss	1. My grandmother **brought** me **up**. 2. Don't **bring up** that subject.
call back	return a telephone call	I **called** Rajit **back** but there was no answer.
call off	cancel	They **called** the wedding **off** after their fight.
cheer up	make someone feel happier	Her visit to the hospital **cheered** the patients **up**.
clear up	clarify, explain	She **cleared** the problem **up**.
do over	do again	His teacher asked him to **do** the essay **over**.
figure out	solve, understand	The student **figured** the problem **out**.
fill in	complete information	**Fill in** the answers on the test.
fill out	complete an application or form	I had to **fill** many forms **out** at the doctor's office.
find out	learn, uncover	Did you **find** anything **out** about the new plans?
give away	offer something freely	They are **giving** prizes **away** at the store.
give back	return	The boy **gave** the pen **back** to the teacher.
give up	stop doing	I **gave up** sugar last year. Will you **give** it **up**?
help out	aid, support someone	I often **help** my older neighbors **out**.
lay off	dismiss workers from their jobs	My company **laid** 200 workers **off** last year.
leave on	allow a machine to continue working	I **left** the lights **on** all night.
let in	allow someone to enter	She opened a window to **let** some fresh air **in**.
look over	examine	We **looked** the contract **over** before signing it.
make up	say something untrue or fictional (a story, a lie)	The child **made** the story **up**. It wasn't true at all.
pay back	return money, repay a loan	I **paid** my friend **back**. I owed him $10.
pick up	1. get someone or something 2. lift	1. He **picked up** his date at her house. 2. I **picked** the ball **up** and threw it.
put off	delay, postpone	Don't **put** your homework **off** until tomorrow.
put out	1. take outside 2. extinguish	1. He **put** the trash **out**. 2. Firefighters **put out** the fire.
set up	1. arrange 2. start something	1. She **set** the tables **up** for the party. 2. They **set up** the project.
shut off	stop something from working	Can you **shut** the water **off**?
sort out	make sense of something	We have to **sort** this problem **out**.
straighten up	make neat and orderly	I **straightened** the messy living room **up**.
take back	own again	He **took** the tools that he loaned me **back**.
take off	remove	She **took off** her hat and gloves.
take out	remove	I **take** the trash **out** on Mondays.
talk over	discuss a topic until it is understood	Let's **talk** this plan **over** before we do anything.
think over	reflect, ponder	She **thought** the job offer **over** carefully.
throw away/ throw out	get rid of something, discard	He **threw** the old newspapers **away**. I **threw out** the old milk in the fridge.
try on	put on clothing to see if it fits	He **tried** the shoes **on** but didn't buy them.
turn down	refuse	His manager **turned** his proposal **down**.
turn off	stop something from working	Can you **turn** the TV **off**, please?
turn on	switch on, operate	I **turned** the lights **on** in the dark room.
turn up	increase the volume	**Turn** the radio **up**, so we can hear the news.
wake up	make someone stop sleeping	The noise **woke** the baby **up**.
write down	write on paper	I **wrote** the information **down**.

Transitive Phrasal Verbs (Inseparable)

*We'll **look into** the problem.*

Phrasal Verb	Meaning	Example Sentence
come across	find something	*I **came across** this novel in the library.*
come from	be a native or resident of	*She **comes from** London.*
come up with	invent	*Let's **come up with** a new game.*
count on	depend on	*You can always **count on** good friends to help you.*
drop out of	quit	*Jin **dropped out** of the study group.*
follow through with	complete	*You must **follow through with** your promises.*
get off	leave (a bus/a train)	*I forgot to **get off** the bus at my stop.*
get on	board (a car/a train)	*I **got on** the plane last.*
get out of	1. leave (a car/a taxi) 2. avoid	1. *I **got out of** the car.* 2. *She **got out of** doing her chores.*
get together with	meet	*I **got together with** Ana on Saturday.*
get over	return to a normal state	*I just **got over** a bad cold. I feel much better now!*
go over	review	*Let's **go over** our notes before the exam.*
look after	take care of	*He has to **look after** his sister. His parents are out.*
look into	investigate	*The police **looked into** the crime and solved it.*
run into	meet accidentally	*She **ran into** Mai on campus.*

*My car **broke down** again!*

Phrasal Verb	Meaning	Example Sentence
add up	make sense	*What he says does not **add up**.*
break down	stop working	*This machine **breaks down** all the time.*
break up	separate	*Their marriage **broke up** after a year.*
dress up	put on more formal clothes	*He **dressed up** to attend the wedding.*
drop in	visit without an appointment	***Drop in** when you can.*
drop out	leave or stop	*She never liked school, so she decided to **drop out**.*
eat out	eat in a restaurant	*She hates to cook, so she **eats out** frequently.*
fool around	play with	*He **fools around** with old cars for fun.*
get ahead	succeed, improve oneself	*Now that she has a new job, she is **getting ahead**.*
get along	have a friendly relationship	*My coworkers and I **get along** well.*
get up	awaken, arise	*I **got up** late this morning.*
give up	stop trying	*I played the piano for seven years but then **gave up**.*
go ahead	begin or continue to do	*You can **go ahead**. We'll wait for Jane.*
go away	leave, depart	*The rabbits in the garden finally **went away**.*
go down	decrease	*Prices of cars have **gone down** recently.*
go on	continue	*How long do you think this speech will **go on**?*
go out	leave one's home	*Jon has **gone out**. He should return soon.*
go up	rise, go higher	*The price of gasoline has **gone up**.*
grow up	become an adult	*Our daughter has **grown up** now.*
hang on	wait	***Hang on** while I change my shoes.*
hold on	struggle against difficulty	***Hold on** just a little longer. It's almost over.*
look out	be careful	***Look out**! You'll fall!*
make up	agree to be friends again	*They had a fight, but soon **made up**.*
move in	go live in	*We **moved in** last week. We love the area!*
move out	leave a place permanently	*When is your roommate **moving out**?*
run out	use all of something	*Is there more paper for the printer? We ran out.*
sign up	join, agree to do something	*The course looked interesting so I **signed up**.*
sit down	seat oneself	*The restaurant*
speak up	talk louder	*Will you **speak up**? I can't hear you.*
stand up	get on one's feet	*The teacher asked the students to **stand up**.*
stay up	keep awake	*The student **stayed up** all night to study.*
take off	1. go up into the air 2. increase quickly	*1. After a long wait, the airplane finally **took off**.* *2. Sales of the new product have **taken off**.*
watch out	be careful	***Watch out**! There's a lot of ice on this road.*
work out	exercise	*The football player **works out** three times a week.*

11   Guide to Pronunciation Symbols

Vowels		
Symbol	Key Word	Pronunciation
/a/	hot	/hat/
	far	/far/
/æ/	cat	/kæt/
/aɪ/	fine	/faɪn/
/aʊ/	house	/haʊs/
/ɛ/	bed	/bɛd/
/eɪ/	name	/neɪm/
/i/	need	/nid/
/ɪ/	sit	/sɪt/
/oʊ/	go	/goʊ/
/ʊ/	book	/bʊk/
/u/	boot	/but/
/ɔ/	dog	/dɔg/
	four	/fɔr/
/ɔɪ/	toy	/tɔɪ/
/ʌ/	cup	/kʌp/
/ɛr/	bird	/bɛrd/
/ə/	about	/əˈbaʊt/

Consonants		
Symbol	Key Word	Pronunciation
/b/	boy	/bɔɪ/
/d/	day	/deɪ/
/dʒ/	just	/dʒʌst/
/f/	face	/feɪs/
/g/	get	/gɛt/
/h/	hat	/hæt/
/k/	car	/kar/
/l/	light	/laɪt/
/m/	my	/maɪ/
/n/	nine	/naɪn/
/ŋ/	sing	/sɪŋ/
/p/	pen	/pɛn/
/r/	right	/raɪt/
/s/	see	/si/
/t/	tea	/ti/
/tʃ/	cheap	/tʃip/
/v/	vote	/voʊt/
/w/	west	/wɛst/
/y/	yes	/yɛs/
/z/	zoo	/zu/
/ð/	they	/ðeɪ/
/θ/	think	/θɪŋk/
/ʃ/	shoe	/ʃu/
/ʒ/	vision	/ˈvɪʒən/

Source: The *Newbury House Dictionary Plus Grammar Reference, Fifth Edition*, National Geographic Learning/Cengage Learning, 2014

12 Conversion Charts

Length		
When You Know	**Multiply by**	**To Find**
inches (in)	25.44	millimeters (mm)
feet (ft)	30.5	centimeters (cm)
feet (ft)	0.3	meters (m)
yards (yd)	0.91	meters (m)
miles (mi)	1.6	kilometers (km)
Metric:		
millimeters (mm)	0.039	inches (in)
centimeters (cm)	0.03	feet (ft)
meters (m)	3.28	feet (ft)
meters (m)	1.09	yards (yd)
kilometers (km)	0.62	miles (mi)

Weight		
When You Know	**Multiply by**	**To Find**
ounces (oz)	28.35	grams (g)
pounds (lb)	0.45	kilograms (kg)
Metric:		
grams (g)	0.04	ounces (oz)
kilograms (kg)	2.2	pounds (lb)

Volume		
When You Know	**Multiply by**	**To Find**
fluid ounces (fl. oz)	30.0	milliliters (mL)
pints (pt)	0.47	liters (L)
quarts (qt)	0.95	liters (L)
gallons (gal)	3.8	liters (L)
Metric:		
milliliters (mL)	0.03	fluid ounces (fl. oz)
liters (L)	2.11	pints (pt)
liters (L)	1.05	quarts (qt)
liters (L)	0.26	gallons (gal)

Temperature		
When You Know	**Do This**	**To Find**
degrees Fahrenheit (°F)	$(F° - 32) \times \dfrac{5}{9}$	degrees Celsius (°C)
degrees Celsius (°C)	$1.8C° + 32$	degrees Fahrenheit (°F)

Sample Temperatures	
Fahrenheit	**Celsius**
0	–18
10	–12
20	–7
32	0
40	4
50	10
60	16
70	21
80	27
90	32
100	38
212	100

GLOSSARY OF GRAMMAR TERMS

action verb: a verb that shows an action.
  - ➤ He **drives** every day.
  - ➤ They **left** yesterday morning.

active voice: a sentence in which the subject performs the action of the verb. (See *passive voice*.)
  - ➤ Michael *ate the hamburger.*

adjective: a word that describes or modifies a noun or pronoun.
  - ➤ She is **friendly**.
  - ➤ Brazil is a **huge** country.

adjective clause: see *relative clause*.

adverb: a word that describes or modifies a verb, an adjective, or another adverb.
  - ➤ He eats **quickly**.
  - ➤ She drives **carefully**.

adverb clause: a kind of dependent clause. Like single adverbs, they can show time, reason, purpose, and condition.
  - ➤ **When the party was over,** everyone left.

adverb of frequency: (see *frequency adverb*.)

adverb of manner: an adverb that describes the action of the verb. Many adverbs of manner are formed by adding *-ly* to the adjective.
  - ➤ You sing **beautifully**.
  - ➤ He speaks **slowly**.

affirmative statement: a statement that does not have a verb in the negative form.
  - ➤ *My uncle lives in Portland.*

article: a word that is used before a noun: *a, an, the*.
  - ➤ I looked up at **the** moon.
  - ➤ Lucy had **a** sandwich and **an** apple for lunch.

auxiliary verb: (also called *helping verb*.) a verb used with the main verb. *Be, do, have*, and *will* are common auxiliary verbs when they are followed by another verb. Modals are also auxiliary verbs.
  - ➤ I **am** working.
  - ➤ He **won't** be in class tomorrow.
  - ➤ She **can** speak Korean.

base form: the form of the verb without *to* or any endings such as *-ing, -s*, or *-ed*.
  - ➤ *eat, sleep, go, walk*

capital letter: an uppercase letter.
  - ➤ *New York, Mr. Franklin, Japan*

clause: a group of words with a subject and a verb. (See *dependent clause* and *main clause*.)
  - ➤ <u>We watched the game</u>. (one clause)
  - ➤ <u>We watched the game</u> <u>after we ate dinner</u>. (two clauses)

comma: a punctuation mark that separates parts of a sentence
  - ➤ *After he left work, he went to the gym.*
  - ➤ *I can't speak Russian, but my sister can.*

common noun: a noun that does not name a specific person, place, thing, or idea.
  - ➤ *man, country, book, help*

comparative: the form of an adjective used to talk about the difference between two people, places, or things.
  - ➤ I'm **taller** than my mother.
  - ➤ That book is **more interesting** than this one.

conditional: a structure used to express an activity or even that depends on something else.
  - ➤ **If the weather is nice on Sunday,** we'll go to the beach

conjunction: a word used to connect information or ideas. *And, but, or*, and *because* are conjunctions.
  - ➤ He put cheese **and** onions on his sandwich.
  - ➤ I wanted to go, **but** I had too much homework.
  - ➤ We were confused **because** we didn't listen.

consonant: a sound represented by the letters *b, c, d, f, g, h, j, k, l, m, n, p, q, r, s, t, v, w, x, y*, and *z*.

contraction: two words combined into a shorter form.
  - ➤ did not → **didn't**
  - ➤ she is → **she's**
  - ➤ I am → **I'm**
  - ➤ we will → **we'll**

count noun: a noun that names something you can count. Count nouns are singular or plural.
  - ➤ I ate an **egg** for breakfast.
  - ➤ I have **six apples** in my bag.

definite article: the word *the*. It is used before a specific person, place, or thing.
  - ➤ I found it on **the** Internet.
  - ➤ **The** children are sleeping.

demonstrative pronoun: a pronoun that identifies a person or thing.
  - ➤ **This** is my sister, Kate.
  - ➤ **Those** are Jamal's books.

dependent clause: a clause that cannot stand alone as a sentence. It must be used with a main clause.
  - ➤ I went for a walk **before I ate breakfast.**

direct object: a noun or pronoun that receives the action of the verb.

> ➤ Aldo asked a **question**.
> ➤ Karen helped **me**.

direct quote: a statement of a speaker's exact words using quotation marks.

> ➤ Our teacher said, **"Do exercises 5 and 6 for homework."**

exclamation point: a punctuation mark that shows emotion (anger, surprise, excitement, etc.) or emphasis.

> ➤ We won the game**!**
> ➤ Look**!** It's snowing**!**

formal: describes language used in academic writing or speaking, or in polite or official situations rather than in everyday speech or writing.

> ➤ Please do not take photographs inside the museum.
> ➤ May I leave early today?

frequency adverb: an adverb that tells how often something happens. Some common adverbs of frequency are never, rarely, sometimes, often, usually, and always.

> ➤ I **always** drink coffee in the morning.
> ➤ He **usually** leaves work at six.

frequency expression: an expression that tells how often something happens.

> ➤ We go to the grocery store **every Saturday**.
> ➤ He plays tennis **twice a week**.

future: a form of a verb that expresses an action or situation that has not happened yet. Will, be going to, the present progressive, and the simple present are used to express the future.

> ➤ I **will call** you later.
> ➤ We**'re going** to the movies tomorrow.
> ➤ I**'m taking** French next semester.
> ➤ The show **starts** after dinner.

future conditional: expresses something we believe will happen in the future based on certain conditions; the if-clause + simple present gives the condition, and will or be going to + the base form of the verb gives the result.

> ➤ If you don't go to practice, the coach will not let you play in the game.

gerund: an -ing verb form that is used as a noun. It can be the subject of a sentence or the object of a verb or preposition. See page **A7–A8** for lists of common verbs followed by gerunds.

> ➤ **Surfing** is a popular sport.
> ➤ We enjoy **swimming**.
> ➤ The boy is interested in **running**.

gerund phrase: an -ing verb form + an object or a prepositional phrase. It can be the subject of a sentence, or the object of a verb or preposition.

> ➤ **Swimming in the ocean** is fun.
> ➤ I love **eating chocolate.**
> ➤ We are thinking about **watching the new TV show.**

helping verb: (see auxiliary verb.)

if clause: a clause that begins with if and expresses a condition.

> ➤ **If you drive too fast,** you will get a ticket.

imperative: a sentence that gives an instruction or command.

> ➤ **Turn** left at the light.
> ➤ **Don't use** the elevator.

indefinite article: the words a and an. They are used before singular count nouns that are not specific.

> ➤ We have **a** test today.
> ➤ She's **an** engineer.

indefinite pronoun: a pronoun that refers to people or things that are not specific or not known. Someone, something, everyone, everything, no one, nothing, and nowhere are common indefinite pronouns.

> ➤ **Everyone** is here today.
> ➤ **No one** is absent.
> ➤ Would you like **something** to eat?

independent clause: a clause that can stand alone as a complete sentence. It has a subject and a verb.

> ➤ **I went for a walk** before breakfast.

infinitive: to + the base form of a verb.

> ➤ He wants **to see** the new movie.

infinitive of purpose: to + the base form of the verb to express purpose or to answer the question with why. (also in order to)

> ➤ Scientists studied the water **in order to learn** about the disease.
> ➤ We went to the store **to buy** milk.

informal: language that is used in casual, everyday conversation and writing.

> ➤ Who are you talking to?
> ➤ We'll be there at eight.

information question: (see Wh- question.)

inseparable phrasal verb: a phrasal verb that cannot have a noun or a pronoun object between its two parts (verb + particle). The verb and the particle always stay together.

> ➤ I **ran into** a friend in the library.
> ➤ Do you and your coworkers **get along**?

intonation: the rise or fall of a person's voice. For example, rising intonation is often used to ask a question.

intransitive verb: a verb that cannot be followed by a direct object.
- ➤ *We didn't **agree**.*
- ➤ *The students **smiled** and **laughed**.*

irregular adjective: an adjective that does not change form in the usual way .
- ➤ *good → better*
- ➤ *bad → worse*

irregular adverb: an adverb that does not change form in the usual way.
- ➤ *well → better*
- ➤ *badly → worse*

irregular verb: a verb with forms that do not follow the rules for regular verbs.
- ➤ *swim → swam*
- ➤ *have → had*

main clause: a clause that can stand alone as a sentence. It has a subject and a verb. (See *independent clause.*)
- ➤ ***I heard the news** when I was driving home.*

main verb: the verb that is in the main clause.
- ➤ *We **drove** home after we had dinner.*

measurement word: a word that is used to talk about a specific amount or quantity of a non-count noun.
- ➤ *We need to buy a **box** of pasta and a **gallon** of milk.*

modal: an auxiliary verb that adds a degree of certainty, possibility, or time to a verb. *May, might, can, could, will, would,* and *should* are common modals.
- ➤ *You **should** eat more vegetables.*
- ➤ *Julie **can** speak three languages.*

negative statement: a statement that has a verb in the negative form.
- ➤ *I **don't have** any sisters.*
- ➤ *She **doesn't drink** coffee.*

non-action verb: a verb that does not describe an action. Non-action verbs indicate states, sense, feelings, or ownership. They are not common in the progressive.
- ➤ *I **love** my grandparents.*
- ➤ *I **see** Marta. She's across the street.*
- ➤ *They **have** a new car.*

non-count noun: a noun that names something that cannot be counted.
- ➤ *Carlos drinks a lot of **coffee**.*
- ➤ *I need some **salt** for the recipe.*

noun: a word that names a person, place, or thing.
- ➤ *They're **students**.*
- ➤ *He's a **teacher**.*

noun clause: a clause that can be used in place of a noun, a noun phrase, or a pronoun.
- ➤ *I didn't know **that she was here**.*
- ➤ *I'm not sure **if the store is open yet**.*

object: a noun or pronoun that receives the action of the verb.
- ➤ *Mechanics fix **cars**.*

object pronoun: a pronoun that takes the place of a noun as the object of the sentence: *me, you, him, her, it, us, them.*
- ➤ *Rita is my neighbor. I see **her** every day.*
- ➤ *Can you help **us**?*

participial adjective: an adjective that is formed like a present participle (*-ing*) or past participle (*-ed*) form of a verb.
- ➤ *Martin had **tired** eyes.*

particle: a short word that combines with a verb to form a phrasal verb; examples include *on, out, over, into, up, through,* and *back.*
- ➤ *I looked **up** the definition.*
- ➤ *The students ran **into** their teacher at the store.*

passive voice: when the focus of a sentence is on the object of the verb instead of the subject. Active voice focuses on the subject.
- ➤ *My wallet **was stolen**.*

past participle: the form of the verb used in perfect and passive. It usually ends in *-d* or *-ed.*
- ➤ *Jemila has **worked** here for a long time.*

past progressive: a verb form used to talk about an action that was in progress in the past.
- ➤ *He **was watching** TV when the phone rang.*

period: a punctuation mark used at the end of a statement.
- ➤ *She lives in Moscow.*

phrasal verb: a verb and a particle that function as a single verb. See pages **A9–A11** for lists of common phrasal verbs.
- ➤ ***Turn off** the light when you leave.*
- ➤ *She's **figured out** the answer.*

phrase: a group of words that go together but are not a complete sentence (i.e., does not have both a subject and a verb).
- ➤ *He lives **near the train station**.*

plural noun: a noun that names more than one person, place, or thing.
- ➤ *He put three **boxes** on the table.*
- ➤ *Argentina and Mexico are **countries**.*

possessive adjective: an adjective that shows ownership or a relationship: *my, your, his, her, its, our, their*.
- ➢ **My** *car is green.*
- ➢ **Your** *keys are on the table.*

possessive noun: a noun that shows ownership or a relationship. To make most singular nouns possessive, use an apostrophe (') + -s. To make plural nouns possessive, add an apostrophe.
- ➢ **Leo's** *apartment is large.*
- ➢ *The* **girls'** *books are on the table.*

possessive pronoun: a pronoun that shows ownership or a relationship: *mine, yours, his, hers, ours, theirs*. Possessive pronouns are used in place of a possessive adjective + noun.
- ➢ *My sister's eyes are blue.* **Mine** *are brown. What color are* **yours**?

preposition: a word that describes the relationships between nouns. Prepositions show space, time, direction, cause, and effect; often they occur together with certain verbs or adjectives.
- ➢ *I live* **on** *Center Street.*
- ➢ *We left* **at** *noon.*
- ➢ *I'm worried* **about** *the test.*

prepositional phrase: a phrase that has a preposition + a noun or a noun phrase.
- ➢ *I live* **in New York City.**
- ➢ *We saw the movie* **at the new theater.**

present continuous: (see *present progressive*.)

present participle: the form of the verb that ends in *-ing*.
- ➢ *She is* **sleeping.**
- ➢ *They are* **laughing.**

present perfect: a verb form that connects the past to the present.
- ➢ *I* **have washed** *the dishes.*
- ➢ *John* **hasn't called** *today.*

present perfect progressive: a verb form used for a situation or habit that began in the past and continues up to the present or an action in progress that is not yet completed.
- ➢ *I've* **been getting up** *early.*
- ➢ **Have** *you* **been waiting** *for a long time?*

present progressive: (also called *present continuous*.) a verb form used to talk about an action or event that is in progress at the moment of speaking; the form can also refer to a planned event in the future.
- ➢ *That car* **is speeding.**
- ➢ *I* **am taking** *three classes this semester.*
- ➢ *We* **are eating** *at that new restaurant Friday night.*

pronoun: a word that takes the place of a noun or refers to a noun.
- ➢ *The teacher is sick today.* **He** *has a cold.*

proper noun: a noun that names a specific person, place, or thing
- ➢ **Maggie** *lives in a town near* **Dallas.**

punctuation: a mark that makes ideas in writing clear. Common punctuation marks include the comma (,), period (.), exclamation point (!), and question mark (?).
- ➢ *John plays soccer***,** *but I don't.*
- ➢ *She's from Japan***.**
- ➢ *That's amazing***!**
- ➢ *Where are you from***?**

quantifier: a word used to describe the amount of a noun.
- ➢ *We need* **some** *potatoes for the recipe.*
- ➢ *I usually put* **a little** *milk in my coffee.*

question mark: a punctuation mark used at the end of a question.
- ➢ *Are you a student***?**

quoted speech: a statement that includes the exact words someone said. Quotation marks ("/") are used around the exact words.
- ➢ *She said***,** **"I'm not feeling well."**

regular: a noun, verb, adjective, or adverb that changes form according to standard rules.
- ➢ *apple* $\longrightarrow$ *apple***s**
- ➢ *talk* $\longrightarrow$ *talk***ed**/*talk***ing**
- ➢ *small* $\longrightarrow$ *small***er**
- ➢ *slow* $\longrightarrow$ *slow***ly**

relative clause: a clause that describes a noun or indefinite pronoun in a sentence. It comes after the noun or pronoun it describes. It is also called an *adjective clause*.
- ➢ *The student* **that I am sitting next to** *is from Peru.*
- ➢ *I know everyone* **who lives in my building.**

relative pronoun: a pronoun that introduces a relative clause. Common relative pronouns are *who, whom, whose, that,* and *which*.
- ➢ *We met the woman* **who** *owns the shop.*
- ➢ *Here's the book* **that** *you were looking for.*

reported speech: a statement of what someone said that does not have quotation marks.
- ➢ *Adele said* **that she was sick.**

reporting verb: a verb used to report what people say, either in quoted or reported speech (*say, tell, asked*).
- ➢ *Tomo* **said,** *"Hi, how are you?"*
- ➢ *Jennifer* **asked** *if we were busy.*

sentence: a thought that is expressed in words, usually with a subject and verb. A sentence begins with a capital letter and ends with a period, exclamation point, or question mark.
> *The bell rang loudly.*
> *Don't eat that!*

separable phrasal verb: a phrasal verb that can have a noun or a pronoun (object) between its two parts (verb + particle).
> *Turn the light off.*
> *Turn off the light.*

short answer: a common spoken answer to a question that is not always a complete sentence.
> A: *Where are you going?*
> B: *To the store.*

simple past: a verb form used to talk about completed actions.
> *Last night we ate dinner at home.*
> *I visited my parents last weekend.*

simple present: a verb form used to talk about habits or routines, schedules, and facts.
> *He likes apples and oranges.*
> *Toronto gets a lot of snow in the winter.*

singular noun: a noun that names only one person, place, or thing.
> *They have a son and a daughter.*

statement: a sentence that gives information.
> *My house has five rooms.*
> *He doesn't have a car.*

stress: we use stress to say a syllable or a word with more volume or emphasis.

subject: the noun or pronoun that is the topic of the sentence.
> *Patricia is a doctor.*
> *They are from Iceland.*

subject pronoun: a pronoun that is the subject of a sentence: *I, you, he, she, it,* and *they.*
> *I have one brother. He lives in Miami.*

subordinating conjunction: a conjunction that is used to introduce an adverb clause, such as *because, since, even though,* and *although.* (See *conjunction.*)
> *Even though he ate all his dinner, he is still hungry.*
> *She is late because she got lost.*

superlative: the form of an adjective or adverb used to compare three or more people, places, or things.
> *Mount Everest is the highest mountain in the world.*
> *Evgeny is the youngest student in our class.*

syllable: a part of a word that contains a single vowel sound and is pronounced as a unit.
> *The word pen has one syllable.*
> *The word pencil has two syllables (pen-cil).*

tense: the form of the verb that shows the time of the action.
> *They sell apples. (simple present)*
> *They sold cars. (simple past)*

third-person singular: in the simple present, the third-person singular ends in *-s* or *-es.* Singular nouns and the pronouns *he, she,* and *it,* take the third-person singular form.
> *She plays the piano.*
> *Mr. Smith teaches her.*

time clause: a clause that tells when an action or event happened or will happen. Time clauses are introduced by conjunctions, such as *when, after, before, while,* and *since.*
> *I have lived here since I was a child.*
> *While I was walking home, it began to rain.*
> *I'm going to call my parents after I eat dinner.*

time expression: a phrase that tells when something happened or will happen. Time expressions usually go at the end or the beginning of a sentence.
> *Last week I went hiking.*
> *She's moving next month.*

transitive verb: a verb that is followed by a direct object.
> *We took an umbrella.*

verb: a word that shows action, gives a state, or shows possession.
> *Tori skated across the ice.*
> *She is an excellent athlete.*
> *She has many medals.*

voiced: a sound that is spoken with the vibration of the vocal cords. The consonants *b, d, g, j, l, m, n, r, v, w, z,* and all vowels are typically voiced.

vowel: a sound represented in English by the letters *a, e, i, o, u,* and sometimes *y.*

Wh- question: (also called *information question.*) a question that asks for specific information, not *"Yes"* or *"No."*
> *Where do they live?*
> *What do you usually do on weekends?*

Wh- word: a word such as *who, what, where, when, why,* or *how* that is used to begin a *Wh-* question.

Yes/No question: a question that can be answered with *"Yes"* or *"No."*
> *Do you live in Dublin?*
> *Can you ski?*

Note: All page references in blue are in Split Edition B.

Text and Listening

4: Exercise 1. Sources: National Geographic Magazine, November 1999; http://lionguardians.org/the-lion-guardians. **20:** Exercise 2. Source: http://news.nationalgeographic.com/news/2008/08/photogalleries/wip-week96/index.html. **26:** Exercise 1. Source: National Geographic Magazine, June 2010. **33:** Exercise 1. Source: http://www.culturalsurvival.org/current-projects/community-radio-project. **38:** Exercise 10. Source: http://newswatch.nationalgeographic.com/2012/05/21/ng-explorers-help-record-xyzyl-language. **39:** Exercise 1. Source: http://video.nationalgeographic.com/video/specials/nat-geo-live-specials/chin-interview-nglive. **44:** Exercise 9. Source: National Geographic Magazine, November 1998. **51:** Exercise 8. Source: National Geographic Magazine, July 2007. **54:** Exercise 3. http://www.atlasobscura.com/places/ancient-stepwells-india. **54:** Exercise 4. http://www.mandatory.com/2012/05/07/10-guys-who-survived-wild-animal-attacks/4. **60:** Exercise 1. Sources: http://www.sangomaza.co.za; http://www.ancestralwisdom.com/sangoma.html. **68:** Exercise 1. Source: National Geographic Magazine, February 2009; http://www.webmd.com/diet/acai-berries-and-acai-berry-juice-what-are-the-health-benefits; http://environment.nationalgeographic.com/environment/enlarge/chinese-ginseng.html. **73:** Exercise 8. Source: http://education.nationalgeographic.com/education/media/fresh-fruits-vegetables/?ar_a=1. **74:** Exercise 1. Source: http://www.bbc.co.uk/sport/0/football/18887653. **78:** Exercise 7. Source: http://www.news.com.au/breaking-news/eight-glasses-of-water-a-myth-academic/story-e6frfku0-1226385483550. **82:** Exercise 4. Source: http://www.nationalgeographic.com/explorers/bios/jenny-daltry. **88:** Exercise 1. Source: http://www.bbc.co.uk/news/world-radio-and-tv-16833168. **96:** Exercise 1. Sources: http://www.bbc.com/travel/slideshow/20120801-blue-holes-of-the-bahamas; http://www.seadragonbahamas.com/divingseasonsofthebahamas.html. **101:** Exercise 10. Sources: http://www.nationalgeographic.com/explorers/bios/catherine-jaffee. **103:** Exercise 1. Source: National Geographic Magazine, March 2011. **108:** Exercise 9. Sources: http://www.huffingtonpost.com/2012/07/14/kent-couch-lawn-chair-balloonist-tandem-flight-iraqi-fareed-lafta_n_1673162.html; http://www.couchballoons.com. **122:** Exercise 1. Sources: http://news.nationalgeographic.com/news/2010/04/100402-aral-sea-story; http://www.britannica.com/EBchecked/topic/31983/Aral-Sea. **128:** Exercise 11. Sources: http://earthobservatory.nasa.gov/Features/WorldOfChange/decadaltemp.php; http://www.nasa.gov/topics/earth/features/warmingpoles.html. **130:** Exercise 1. Sources: http://ngm.nationalgeographic.com/2011/08/robots/robots-photography#/12-paro-robotic-seal-family-714.jpg; http://online.wsj.com/news/articles/SB10001424052748704463504575301051844937276. **136:** Exercise 1. Source: http://www.theatlantic.com/technology/archive/2012/02/heres-what-humbert-humbert-looks-like-as-a-police-composite-sketch/252866. **140:** Exercise 8. Sources: http://www.census.gov/prod/2013pubs/acs-22.pdf; http://www.laalmanac.com/LA/la10b.htm. **143:** Exercise 11. Source: http://www.reuters.com/video/2012/07/06/ugandan-student-makes-a-billion-through?videoId=236379211&videoChannel=2602. **144:** Exercise 1. Source: http://www.economist.com/node/18277141. **152:** Exercise 3. Source: http://www.dailymail.co.uk/news/article-2135299/Brit-bought-cut-price-island-Seychelles-50-years-ago--lives-blissful-solitude.html. **158:** Exercise 1. Sources: http://www.smh.com.au/articles/2006/03/29/1143441187263.html; http://animals.nationalgeographic.com/animals/mammals/koala. **172:** Exercise 2. Source: http://news.nationalgeographic.com/news/2012/08/120831-venus-two-faced-cat-genetics-animals-science. **173:** Exercise 3. Sources: http://www.pbs.org/wgbh/nova/bowerbirds/trail.html; http://www.theguardian.com/science/neurophilosophy/2012/jan/19/1. **174:** Exercise 1. Sources: http://news.nationalgeographic.com/news/2007/10/photogalleries/primate2-pictures/photo3.html; http://www.livescience.com/10268-surprise-hidden-yellow-tailed-monkey-colony-discovered.html. **178:** Exercise 1. Sources: http://www.bbc.com/future/story/20120622-space-a-travel-guide; http://www.cnn.com/2013/08/15/travel/virgin-galactic-250000-ticket-to-space. **192:** Exercise 1. Sources: http://water.epa.gov/type/oceb/habitat/coral_index.cfm#important; http://www.coris.noaa.gov/about/hazards; http://www.pmel.noaa.gov/pubs/PDF/sutt3748/sutt3748.pdf; http://www.nytimes.com/2012/07/14/opinion/a-world-without-coral-reefs.html. **198:** Exercise 11. Source: http://www.nwf.org/News-and-Magazines/National-Wildlife/Animals/Archives/2010/Kermode-bear.aspx. **200:** Exercise 2. Source: National Geographic Magazine, November 2011. **220:** Exercise 1. Source: http://www.cnn.com/2013/01/15/world/asia/everest-trash-art. **225:** Exercise 11. Source: http://www.cameronscamelcampaign.com. **227:** Exercise 1. Source: http://environment.nationalgeographic.com/environment/greendex.

Photo

Inside Front Cover, left column: Dr. K. David Harrison/Living Tongues Institute for Endangered Language, ©Jim Webb/National Geographic Creative, ©Nav Dayanand, ©Claire Bangser, ©Michael Christopher Brown/National Geographic Creative, **right column:** ©Sandra Lynn Kerr, ©Mark Thiessen/National Geographic Creative, ©Marco Grob/National Geographic Creative, ©Australia Unlimited/National Geographic Creative, ©AFP/Getty Images.

2–3: ©Valdrin Xhemaj/epa/Corbis; **4:** ©Carol Beckwith & Angela Fisher/Photokunst; **5:** ©Chris Johns/National Geographic Creative; **11 left:** ©Robin Smith/Getty Images, **right:** ©Vitalii Nesterchuk/Shutterstock; **12:** ©Jodi Cobb/National Geographic Creative; **13:** ©uniquely india/Getty Images; **17 left:** ©Scott Heppell/AP Images, **right:** ©Robin Smith/Getty Images; **19:** ©Walter Zerla/Cultura Travel/Getty Images; **20:** ©Fernando Vergara/AP Images; **21:** ©Fernando Bustamante/AP Images; **22:** ©AFP/Getty Images; **24–25:** ©Panoramic Images/National Geographic Creative; **26–27:** ©Mark C. Ross/National Geographic Creative; **27:** ©Bill Hatcher/National Geographic Creative; **27 top:** ©Doug Allan/Getty Images, **bottom:** ©Biosphoto/SuperStock; **32:** ©iStockphoto/Thinkstock; **33:** ©GILLARDI Jacques/Getty Images; **34:** ©Pete McBride/National Geographic Creative; **38:** ©Dr. K. David Harrison/Living Tongues Institute for Endangered Language; **39 top:** ©Jim Webb/National Geographic Creative, **bottom:** © StockShot/Alamy; **40:** ©Mikey Schafer/National Geographic Creative; **44:** ©Royal Geographical Society (with IBG); **45:** ©pkchai /Shutterstock; **46:** ©CM Dixon/Glow Images; **47:** ©Art Media/Glow Images; **51:** ©Kazuhiko Sano/National Geographic Creative; **54:** ©Ajit Solanki/AP Images; **55 top left:** ©TexPhoto/iStockphoto, **top right:** ©Reinhold Leitner/Shutterstock, **bottom left:** ©Pieter De Pauw/fotolia, **bottom right:** ©iStockphoto/Thinkstock; **56:** ©Charlie Edward/Shutterstock; **58–59:** ©Keren Su/Getty Images; **60–61:** © Chris Johns/National Geographic Creative; **67:** ©Michael Christopher Brown/National Geographic Creative; **68 left:** ©Nikki Bidgood/Getty Images, **middle:** ©Rogerio Assis/SambaPhoto/Getty Images, **left:** ©picture alliance/Frank May/Newscom; **69:** ©AFP/Getty Images; **73:** ©rachel dewis/iStockphoto; **74–75:** ©Peter Powell/EPA/Newscom; **79:** ©Simon Woodcock/Alamy; **82:** ©suttisukmek/iStockphoto; **83:** ©GlobalStock/iStockphoto; **84:** ©Russell Sadur/Getty Images; **86–87:** ©Justin Guariglia/National Geographic Creative; **88:** ©David Bank/Getty Images; **89:** © Rafael Ben–Ari/Chameleons Eye/Newscom; **95:** ©Lledo/Shutterstock; **96–97:** © Wes C. Skiles/National Geographic Creative;

(continued on page C 2)